A PLACE QUITE NORTHWARD

Visitors to Northumberland 1500 - 1850

Tim Griffiths

Published in 2015 by FeedARead.com Publishing

Copyright © The author as named on the book cover.

First Edition

A CIP catalogue record for this title is available from the British
Library.

CONTENTS

to Marie, for her love and patience

They are gone down to Newcastle, a place quite northward, it seems, and there they are to stay.

Jane Austen, *Pride and Prejudice*

I have relied heavily on the excellent collection of old books in the collection of the Literary & Philosophical Society of Newcastle upon Tyne. I wish to place on record my acknowledgement of the assistance and support given to me by the librarian Kay Easson, by Caroline Grove, and by the other staff of this excellent institution.

CHAPTER 1

A LABORIOUS JOURNEY – THE SIXTEENTH CENTURY

Wherefore after that I had pondered the honest and profitable studies of these historiographs, I was totally inflamed with a love to see thoroughly all those parts of this your opulent and ample realm, that I had read of in the aforesaid writers: in so much that, all my other occupations intermitted, I have so travelled in your dominions both by the sea coasts and the middle parts, sparing neither labour nor costs, by the space of these six yeares past, that there is almost neither cape, nor bay, haven, creek or pier, river or confluence of rivers, breches, washes, lakes, meres, fenny waters, mountains, valleys, moors, heaths, forests, woods, cities, boroughs, castles, principal manor places, monasteries, and colleges, but I have seen them; and noted in so doing a whole world of things very memorable.

John Leland

A Royal Progress to Scotland

To see everything, and to describe a whole world of things very memorable – this prospectus for an ideal travel writer comes from a letter sent by the antiquary John Leland in January 1546 as a New Year's gift to his patron Henry VIII. Leland's friend John Bale published it in 1549, with the title of *The Laborious Journey and Serche of John Leland*. Travelling around England in the 16th century certainly involved many laborious journeys, and by 1549 Leland's sanity had given way under the self-imposed stress of his ambition to explore the entire country and to describe it in encyclopaedic detail. His collection of notes and documents did however survive him, and became a treasure trove for later antiquaries. Among those documents we can find an eye-witness account by the Somerset herald John Young of the journey undertaken by Margaret Tudor in 1503 as she travelled north to Edinburgh to assume her position as wife of James IV of Scotland.

Born on 29th November 1489, Margaret was the eldest daughter of Henry VII, and therefore Princess Royal of England. From her infancy Henry had entered into negotiations with the Scottish court for her to become the wife of James IV. When Margaret's elder brother

5

Arthur died on 2nd April 1501, leaving Margaret second in line to the English throne, this dynastic marriage rose to the top of the agenda for both the English and Scottish courts. In words that resonate down the centuries Henry brushed aside reservations expressed in his Council:

> Some of the table…..did put the case; that if God should take the king's two sons without issue, that then the kingdom of England would fall to the king of Scotland, which might prejudice the monarchy of England. Whereunto the king himself replied; that if that should be, Scotland would be but an accession to England, and not England to Scotland, for the greater would draw the less; and that it was a safer match for England than that of France. This passed as an oracle, and silenced those that moved the question.

The marriage was celebrated at the royal manor of Richmond on 24th January 1503, with the Earl of Bothwell acting as proxy for James IV. On 16th June Henry and Margaret travelled together to Collyweston, a castle belonging to her grandmother Margaret, Countess of Richmond. After staying there for some while she bade farewell to her father and rode on north, making a grand entry into York and continuing to Durham.

As befitted a queen of Scotland (and potential queen of England) Margaret's royal progress was an affair of pomp and pageantry. Margaret herself, resplendent in a rich riding-dress, rode a white palfrey attended by 3 footmen and with a bishop riding on either side. Her master of horse Sir Thomas Wortley followed behind, leading another palfrey for her use. There was also an elaborate litter carried between 2 coursers. Margaret used this litter on the approach to large towns and at other times when she tired of riding. Other participants in the progress included 24 ladies in waiting with attendant squires, a troupe of minstrels and trumpeters, the Somerset herald whose account of the progress is preserved by Leland, and 4 ladies of the bed-chamber travelling in a car or charrette. The progress was swelled at the entrance to each county by the local lord and his considerable escort, ready to accompany the queen on her journey through his territory. Agnes Strickland summarises the queen's arrival at Newcastle:

> Queen Margaret lodged in the castle at Durham under the immediate protection of the Bishop; and she reposed there until the 24th of July,

when she commenced her journey to Newcastle. She made her toilet afresh a mile before she entered that town, in which her reception was unusually brilliant; for, besides the religious processions, with their banners and crosses upon the bridge-end gate, were many children vested in white surplices, who sang melodious hymns, and played on instruments of divers sorts. The streets were hung with tapestry, and all the 'window-loops and ship tops were full of people;" and "there were gentlemen and gentlewomen in such great numbers it was a pleasure to see. However, no artillery or ordnance was shot off' – a remarkable omission as our Herald thought. "But in state and fair array was the Queen brought to her lodging at the Friars Austin; and when she had entered, every man departed to his own dwelling."

Since the physical conditions of travel remain important throughout the period of this survey we should note the comment of a local historian:

The first wheeled carriage which ever crossed the Tyne adapted for the conveyance of passengers, was probably that in which the ladies of Princess Margaret, daughter of Henry VII, accompanied their mistress on her nuptial journey into Scotland. It is described as "a chare richly dressed, with six fair horses, led and conveyed by three men, in which were four ladies, lasting the voyage". Considering the state of the roads and the absence of springs, which were then unknown, it seems marvellous that the ladies did *last the voyage*.

On 25th July Margaret joined in the celebrations for the feast of St James, the patron and name-saint of her husband, and attended mass. In the evening she was the guest of honour at a banquet given by the Earl of Northumberland. She then left Newcastle on the following day and travelled as far as Morpeth, before continuing on 27th July to Alnwick where she spent 2 nights at the castle. From Alnwick she rode north to the border town of Berwick, where she enjoyed an appropriately elaborate reception:

Much sweet minstrelsy, and excellent good cheer, were provided for her Grace's reception by the Governor or Captain of Berwick. She was entertained with "courses of chase in the enclosure of the walls, and recreated with the sports of great dogs and bears tugging each other, and loud shooting of artillery," – amusements more suitable to the warriors who kept securely the fiercely-contested stronghold of Berwick-upon-Tweed, than to a young lady in her fourteenth year.

After resting at Berwick for 2 days Margaret rode out of the north gate of the town to make a triumphal entry into her new realm. Progress remained laborious, and at times the accompanying soldiers carried out emergency roadworks to allow the cavalcade and accompanying wheeled car to proceed. Progress towards the union of the two kingdoms was equally slow. The survival of Margaret's younger brother as Henry VIII meant that Margaret did not become queen of England and, while relations between the kingdoms remained on a reasonably friendly footing during her father's lifetime, the accession of her brother led to England becoming embroiled in continental adventures and eventually into a war with France. This prompted the revival of the 'auld alliance' and the disastrous Scottish invasion of northern England. On the evening of 9th September 1513 Margaret's husband James lay dead on Flodden Field, achieving the dubious distinction of becoming the last British sovereign to be killed in battle. Many of the Scottish nobility, including his own son by an earlier marriage, were also killed. The battle of Flodden did not however bring peace, and throughout the remainder of the 16th century the borders reverted to the state of intermittent lawlessness that had been more or less customary over the long period since the campaigns of Edward I more than two centuries earlier. How far this affected travel to the region is difficult to judge, but the records of a journey made by one of the bursars of Merton College, Oxford, in the late summer and autumn of 1464 are a useful corrective to the view that visitors to the region travelled in constant fear for their lives and property. 1464 was a troubled year; the Wars of the Roses added significantly to the level of conflict and disturbance, and the Yorkists had won a decisive victory at the battle of Hexham in May. Nevertheless the bursar of Merton set out calmly on his horse in mid August, arriving in Newcastle around the middle of the day on 23rd August and enjoying dinner with wine before continuing to Ponteland, where he spent the night. On the following 2 days he rode via Rothbury and Alnwick Moor to Alnwick, hiring a guide to lead him over the moor. After 2 nights in Alnwick he proceeded to Embleton, a living of Merton College, where he spent a month supervising the gathering of the harvest and ensuring that the proper tithes were set aside for the benefit of his college. He then returned to Newcastle by way of Newminster and Bedlington, before riding south to Durham at the beginning of October. The expense records preserved by the college suggest a routine business journey, with the bursar taking the opportunity to meet clerical friends en route and enjoying good food and wine when the opportunity arose.

A Strategic Defence Review

The Tudor monarchs and their chief advisers worked hard on strengthening the role of the state and on improving the bureaucracy which made such control possible. It is therefore no surprise that 16th century Northumberland was the subject of various surveys. As we have seen the temporary lull in hostilities between England and Scotland did not survive the death of Henry VII, and in 1541 Henry VIII commissioned 2 knights to undertake a military inspection of the frontier. Sir Robert Bowes (c.1493-1555) was no stranger to Northumberland; the head of a prominent Durham family he was experienced in border warfare and a member of the council of the north. Sir Ralph Elleker (c.1489-1546), a Yorkshire notable, was equally familiar with the area, having been knighted on Flodden field for his part in that battle. The knights arrived in Berwick on 8th October 1541, rode the full length of the border between Northumberland and Scotland, and submitted their written report on 2nd December 1541, a rate of progress that modern commissions of enquiry would do well to emulate. The scope of the survey is best set out in their own words:

> A view and survey as well of all the waste grounds endlong the borders or frontier of the East and middle marches of England foranenst Scotland as a description of the present state of all castles, towers, barmkins and fortresses situate and being near unto the said frontier or borders, together with certain devices thought by us most expedient for the repairing, strengthening, replenishing and peopling of the said frontier or borders for the best continual defence of the state.

The written report takes the form of a gazetteer of places along and behind the border, clearly based on a checklist of items to be covered and questions to be asked. This methodical checklist approach foreshadows the method adopted by Arthur Young in his agricultural tour of 1769 (see Chapter 6 below). The authors recommend the repair and reconstruction of many border castles and forts, but recognise some logistical problems:

9

Also we think that there is in these parts convenient store of limestone, freestone and rough stone sufficient for the building and reparations of the said towers and barmkins; but there is no store of timber wood in those parts so that, if it shall be the king's majesty's pleasure that such works and buildings should set forward in those parts, there must needs be a great provision of timber made in places upon the sea coast or upon rivers navigable, and the same to be conveyed by ship to Holy Island and Tweedmouth and there to be wrought and broken in pieces after such lengths and sorts as shall be requisite in the said buildings, for sparing of much carriage which surely is very needful, the carriage of beasts be so small and weak in these parts.

There would certainly have been no carts or waggons to transport timber and other materials. Crofts characterises northern England in the 16th and 17th centures as packhorse country, as opposed to the waggon and cart areas of most of southern and central England, and adds the interesting suggestion that the development of waggon transport stemmed from the need to transport significant agricultural surpluses. Such surpluses were not a feature of northern agriculture and, outside the coal-mining areas, there was little bulk produce that would call for waggon transport and justify the major investment required to upgrade the road system. The timber required for the reconstruction work therefore needed to be shipped to the nearest practicable landing place, and then cut into lengths that could be loaded onto packhorses for the final stage of its journey.

The survey by Bowes and Elleker is particularly valuable for its description of those remoter parts of the county which were least visited during the whole of the period covered by this study. 18th century antiquaries were to follow the line of the Roman wall, but the 1541 survey gives a graphic picture of a country ravaged by centuries of border warfare. Riding west from Hexham to Walton they remark on the many waste grounds north and south of the Picts Wall, as it was then commonly known. West of Walwick, for instance, "there be diverse townships and hamlets, that were in past times inhabited, now lying desolate and waste". A fortified house at Carrawburgh, built only 40 years previously, now lies unoccupied, and the area around is uncultivated and used only for summer pasture. The same story holds good for the older, now dilapidated, castle at Sewingshields. The authors consider a proposal to garrison these 2 strongpoints, but doubt whether even this would give poor farmers sufficient security against the raiders from Liddesdale, Gilsland and Bewcastle. Their downbeat conclusion is that the situation is likely to go on deteriorating until such time as the government can establish its control in the bandit countries of the border. They find that the common people, constantly threatened and intimidated by the reivers, get little support and encouragement from their own lords and masters

The authors pay particular attention to the bandit country of Tynedale, where they emphasise the extreme difficulties experienced by travellers unfamiliar with the area as a result of the number of rivers, streams and marshes, not to mention deliberate obstacles set up by the locals so that "unless it be by such as know and have experience of those said strait and evil ways and passages, it will be hard for strangers having no knowledge thereof to pass thereby in any order, and especially upon horseback".

The neglect of agriculture in what the authors regarded as a potentially rich and fertile region encouraged the growth of banditry and prompted them to recommend the transfer of the surplus working population to other parts of the country:

> There is within that country of Tynedale a great number of good grounds both fertile and commodious for tillage, hay and pasture, the which truly occupied and laboured for the most profit would sustain and bear a good number of people in truth, even as many as so much ground in any part of that country is able to do. Albeit at this present the said country of Tynedale is overcharged with so great a number of people more than such profits as may be got and won out of the ground within the said country are able to sustain and keep.
> Whereby the young and active people for lack of living be constrained to steal or spoil continually either in England or Scotland for the maintenance of their living. And so determine themselves to continue there in such sort all their lives rather than they will leave that country and search to get their living in other countries and places by true labour or any other lawful policies. The which surely as we think is one of the greatest disorders there, that would be speedily reformed to have the superfluous number of people (more than be sufficient to labour and manure the said country of Tynedale) to be set and dispeopled in other countries far distant from Tynedale, there to get their livings by their handy labours.

The authors assume that it will be necessary to implement this policy by force. In the meantime they recommend vigorous policing and exemplary punishments to maintain law and order. Where poverty is the root cause of crime policing and punishment are often of limited effect. But James I may have had their recommendations in mind in the following century when he ordered the exile of the most recalcitrant reiver family, initially to the Low Countries and subsequently to Roscommon in Ireland, with no right of return across the water.

In a second report, written in 1550, Bowes remains critical of the youth of Northumberland, but displays a canny appreciation of the frequent unreliability of witnesses:

> The whole country of Northumberland is much given to riot, especially the young gentlemen or headsmen, and diverse of them also to thefts and other greater offences which…..would be justly corrected for the example of other[s], for the whole country is much given to wildness. Albeit the complainants for the most part will allege more in their complaint than the truth and seek much to have credence without hearing the answer of the other party, which is very dangerous in the administration of justice amongst them, for either party do much covet to be heard alone. And when his adversary is absent [he] will give many evil informations of him oftentimes more than truth and be very loth to come face to face with their adversary. And in absence of the party adverse they be full of evil reports which they covet to….speak under silence rather than openly, but it is perilous to give credence thereunto until the other party is heard to answer for himself.

Bowes could have added that judges who heard parties in private not only encouraged perjured evidence but also gave those parties the opportunity to offer bribes. The plea for open justice is also a plea for justice free of corruption.

Later in the century Elizabeth's council considered and rejected a proposal to fortify the frontier with a wall similar to that constructed on Hadrian's orders more than 1400 years earlier. Building and garrisoning such a wall would have been a huge drain on the public purse and it is perhaps fortunate that Elizabeth's well-known parsimony scuppered a project that would have been obsolete by the time of its completion. Within a few years the border ceased to be a major preoccupation of either government. The decline in its importance is evidenced by William Camden's decision to treat the British Isles as a single subject of study, and it is to Camden and his predecessor John Leland that we now turn.

The Early Antiquaries

John Leland (c.1503-1552), the antiquary who preserved the eye-witness account of Margaret Tudor's progress to Scotland, was one of the most brilliant men of his age. Educated at St Paul's school and Christ's College Cambridge he spent some years in Paris in the 1520s, getting to know Guillaume Budé and other scholars of the French renaissance and acquiring a lifelong love of old manuscripts. He became a more than competent Latin poet and studied classical Greek as well as several modern languages. On his return to England he became a royal chaplain and in 1533 Henry VIII commissioned him to carry out a full survey of the libraries in the monasteries and colleges of England. It was at this time that he began his travels, which he continued until his sudden descent into insanity in the spring of 1547.

In the early years of his work Leland's task was primarily that of cataloguing. He developed a particular interest in British authors, in the history of Britain, and in books on the lives of famous men. With the implementation in 1536 of Henry's policy of dissolving the monasteries Leland turned to the rescue of what he could from sale and destruction. Some works went to the royal libraries, many more perhaps to his private collection. As he explains in the passage quoted as the epigraph to this chapter this prompted him to explore the England of which he had read so much in his books. The objective he set himself was no less than to anticipate the work of the Victoria County Histories; he proposed, among other projects, a 50 volume work entitled *De Antiquitate Britannica*, with 1 volume for each county in England and Wales, and an additional 6 volumes on the islands around the coast. He never completed the volume on Northumberland, nor indeed any of the other volumes of this massive work.

Despite Leland's pivotal position in the story of the discovery of Britain we can rarely be certain of the dates of his travels or of his exact routes. We know that one journey took him as far as the Tyne, since a brief note records a journey north from Chester-le-Street:

Thence to Gateshead 7 miles by mountainous ground with pasture, heath, moor and furze. And a little this side Gateshead is a great coal pit.

In 25 words he touches briefly but precisely on topography, agriculture and industry, thus affording us a preliminary indication of the range of his interests, but on this occasion Leland turned west at Gateshead, heading up into Weardale rather than crossing the Tyne to visit Newcastle. Extracts from Latin texts on the regal and ecclesiastical history of Anglo Saxon Northumbria, included in the fourth volume of Lucy Toulmin Smith's edition of the *Itinerary*, clearly represent the fruits of library research rather than personal observation, and the same may well be true of much of the historical information about Newcastle included in the fifth and final volume of that edition.

We can however be confident that Leland visited Newcastle, of which he says:

The strength and magnificence of the walling of this town far passeth all the walls of the cities of England and of most of the towns of Europa.

In a series of jotted notes he gives us a rapid tour of the town:

Tyne bridge hath 10 arches and a strong ward and tower on it. A gate at the bridge end. Then turning on the right hand to the quay a chapel of the town with a Maison Dieu. Then a certain house with a water gate and a square hall place for the town, and a chapel there, as I remember.
Then a main strong wall on the haven side to Sandgate to Tynemouth way. Then 5 towers to Pandon gate. There hard by doth ..... Dean water drive a mile and passeth through the ......, on this water there is a little arched bridge. And about this quarter stood the house of the Friars *ordinis Sancti Trinitatis*.

And so on for a further 4 paragraphs. No doubt Leland would have worked up these notes into a continuous narrative if he had lived to complete his proposed county history. We can however note his fascination with fortifications and religious establishments, both of which were very important to people in the 16th century. It is probable that from Newcastle Leland travelled north at least as far as Alnwick. His description of Morpeth has the ring of an eye-witness account:

Morpeth, a market town, is 12 long miles from Newcastle. Wansbeck a pretty river runneth through the side of the town. On the hither side of the river is the principal church of the town. On the same side is the fair castle standing upon a hill, belonging with the town to the Lord Dacres of Gilsland.

The town is long and meetly well builded with low houses, the streets paved. It is far fairer town than Alnwick.

A quarter mile out of the town on the hither side of Wansbeck was Newminster Abbey of White Monks, pleasant with water and very fair wood about it.

For other parts of the county Leland relied heavily on local informants. His account of Corbridge, a town "full meanly builded", is based on information received from the vicar, probably Anthony Musgrave (or Musgrove), vicar of Hexham Abbey until its dissolution in 1537 and then of St Andrew's Church until his death in 1544. Much of his information about Newcastle and Northumberland is derived from Dr Richard Davell, a rich pluralist "who had been at one time or another vicar of Bedlington, archdeacon of Northumberland, master of the Virgin Mary Hospital, Newcastle, canon of Exeter, and a prebendary of York" This latter debt is clearly acknowledged by Leland in his account of the coast of Northumberland:

As I learned of Doctor Davell the mouths of Blyth and Wansbeck be little above 3 miles distant one from the other, and the ground betwixt them is of some called Bedlingtonshire, for Bedlington is the the parish church there and some hamlets or villages belong unto it.

The isle of Coquet standeth upon a very good vein of sea coals, and at the ebb men dig in the shore by the cliffs, and find very good.

There lie certain islands adjoining to Farne Island bigger than Farne itself. But in them is no habitation. Certain big fowls, called St Cuthbert's birds, breed in them, and puffins, birds less than ducks having grey feathers like ducks but without painted feathers, and a ring about the neck, be found breeding there in the cliffy rocks.

St Cuthbert's birds, known more colloquially as cuddy ducks, are the eider ducks which breed on the islands. As we shall see later Thomas Pennant gave an excellent description of them in the account of his tour of 1769 (see Chapter 6 below). It is difficult to believe however that anyone who had actually seen puffins on the Farne islands could have failed to observe their habit of breeding in burrows, or indeed their distinctively shaped and multi-coloured bills. One suspects that

15

Dr Davell was himself relying on information from others and that some of the details have been lost in transmission. William Harrison in his great *Description of England* (1586), which makes up much of the opening volume of Holinshed's *Chronicles*, obviously had Leland's notes to hand since he transcribed the passage on puffins almost word for word. The frequent transmission of inaccurate information from one antiquary to another stems from an abiding trust in the authority of the written word. As a result it can sometimes be difficult to establish whether a writer's comments are based on personal observation, on second or third hand nformation from local informants, or from research undertaken in a library perhaps several hundred miles distant from the region.

It was Dr Davell who provided Leland with his information about the Roman wall, noting the better state of preservation in those areas less subject to stone-robbing:

> Doctor Davell told me that St Nicholas church in Newcastle standeth on the Picts wall. Betwixt Thirlwall and North Tyne in the waste ground standeth yet notable pieces of the wall, which was made *ex lapide quadrato* [of squared stone], as it there appears yet. Look whereas the ground is best inhabited through the wall, so there it least appeareth by reason of buildings made of the stones of the wall. The wall on the farther side towards the Picts was strongly ditched. Beside the stone wall, there appear yet in very many places *vestigia muri caespitii* [traces of the turf wall], that was an arrow shot this side of the stone wall, but that it was thoroughly made as the stone wall was it does not well appear there.

This comment is particularly revealing. Leland's ambition was that his county volumes should cover everything of importance: topography, agriculture, history, the genealogy of prominent families, market towns and cities, bridges, churches, castles, country houses and important municipal buildings. It is fully in line with this ambition that the description of the Roman wall is technically far more accurate than that given by Bowes and Elleker in their contemporary survey. What is missing from the survey, and from Leland's vision, is the insight given by Bowes and Elleker into the living conditions of the ordinary people of Northumberland. Leland's failure to see 98% of the population is hardly unique to him or to his age – many tours nowadays focus on antiquities, such as the Pyramids of Egypt, while totally ignoring the people who live under their shadow – but is perhaps worth noting in the context of his stated aim to include everything of importance in his massive work.

William Camden (1551-1623) visited Northumberland in 1600 in the company of his fellow antiquary Robert Cotton. Although this is more than half a century later than Leland's travels it makes sense to look at Camden now since he was, in more ways than one, Leland's natural successor. Also a pupil at St Paul's school Camden continued his education at Oxford, with which he maintained a somewhat troubled relationship throughout his life. He joined the circle around William Cecil (Lord Burghley) and it was probably in that environment that he acquired a taste for British history and for all things antiquarian. His appointment to Westminster school as second master in 1575 gave him time to develop those interests and to follow Leland's example of travelling to carry out research on the ground. In 1586 he published, in Latin, the first edition of his *Britannia*; 5 further Latin editions followed in his lifetime, in addition to the first English translation in 1610 on which he collaborated with the translator Philemon Holland. *Britannia* is every bit as ambitious as Leland's great project. The title itself indicates that Camden set out to encompass not only England and Wales, but also Scotland and Ireland, an instance of presumptuous intellectual empire-building at a time when the idea of a United Kingdom had yet to be invented. Britannia was also the Roman name for the whole island of Great Britain, and the title thus emphasises the focus on history as the main theme of his work. Camden was fortunate in being able to acquire a complete manuscript copy of Leland's notes, and carried out considerable research on his own account, not only into Roman and Anglo Saxon history but also into the history of the island before the Romans, a subject up to then largely shrouded in myth. He is however far less interested than Leland in the contemporary world, although his chapters on Northumberland and Lindisfarne do include some interesting comments.

Camden's journey to Carlisle and the north in 1600 was his last major journey and enabled him to include much additional information in the later editions of his *Britannia*. As befits an antiquary he starts with the Roman wall, of which he gives an evocative and rightly famous description:

Here are still such strong traces of the wall that one may follow its track and, in the wastes as they are called, I myself have seen large pieces of it running a great way, wanting only the battlements.

I have seen its track running in high hills in an extraordinary manner, and then coming down to levels, where the country is more open, having a broad deep ditch in front without, now filled up in many places, and within an agger or military way, but greatly interrupted. It had a number of towers or castles, called *Castle Steads*, and within small fortified towns, now called *Chesters*, whose foundations are visible, of a square form, and towers between them in which the soldiers were stationed to awe the barbarians.

Camden's account of the wall, particularly his meticulous transcription of stone inscriptions, remains important to modern archaeologists since substantial parts of the wall, and some of the inscriptions, have disappeared in the last four centuries. In two matters where he self-confessedly relied on local information his research is now generally discounted. The first of these statements was dismissed by his 18th century translator Richard Gough as 'fanciful and fictitious':

The inhabitants say a brass pipe artificially set in the wall ran all along between each tower and castle (of which they have occasionally found pieces), that whatever was spoken through it at one tower was conveyed immediately to the next, to the third, and so on to all without interruption, to give notice where the enemy's attack was to be apprehended.

What the Romans did for us did not extend to the invention of a telephone system, but it is possible that the inhabitants had misinterpreted the remains of aqueducts and water conduits as channels for the supposed pipes. More tantalising is the report Camden quotes about the plants growing along the line of the wall:

I purposely omit the vulgar reports about this wall, but cannot conceal from the reader this circumstance, which I had from persons of credit. A fixed tradition remains in the neighbourhood, that the Roman garrisons on the borders planted here up and down for their own use many plants good for curing wounds. Hence some pretenders to surgery in Scotland resort here every summer to collect plants, whose virtues they have learned by some practice, and extol them as of sovereign efficacy.

It is likely that Camden was relying on notes written in 1574 by an unknown author on the basis of information given by Archbishop Threkeld of Hereford, a native of Burgh-by-Sands:

> The Scots leeches or surgeons do yearly repair to the said Roman wall next to this [Caervoran] to gather sundry herbs for surgery, for that it is thought the Romans thereby had planted most needful herbs for sundry purposes but, howsoever it was, these herbs are found very wholesome.

There seems no good reason to doubt this contemporary report that Scottish apothecaries visited the Wall area to gather medicinal plants. What those plants might have been is unclear, and the phrase 'howsoever it was' betrays a judicious scepticism by the anonymous author about their supposed Roman origin. Field garlic, wild onion, chives and upright chickweed grow on the Whin Sill along the line of the Roman Wall and we know that the Romans used herbs, both for medicinal purposes and in their cooking. Archaeologists have often identified certain buildings in the main forts along the wall as hospitals. Whether or not these buildings are correctly identified it is likely that some provision was made in the forts for the treatment of sick and injured soldiers, and that those responsible for their care did what they could to ensure a supply of suitable plants. Camden's report does therefore have a certain plausibility lacking in his report of the brass telephone system but, so far as I am aware, there is no archaeological evidence linking the Roman herb gardens (assuming they existed) with the plants collected by the Scottish apothecaries. The continued existence of native species proves nothing either way and, despite the rampant growth of plants such as rhododendron and Japanese knotweed, the survival rate of introduced species in the wild is rather low. The tradition recorded by Camden finds its final, much romanticised, echo two centuries later in a poem by Walter Scott:

> Take these flowers, which, purple waving,
>   On the ruin'd ramparts grew,
> Where, the sons of freedom braving,
>   Rome's imperial standard flew.
>
> Warriors from the breach of danger
>   Pluck no longer laurels there;
> They but yield the passing stranger
>   Wild-flower wreaths for beauty's hair.

Camden saw much of the Wall, but felt unable to visit part of the central section because of the danger of bandits, locally known as moss troopers. Such caution was probably well justified, certainly more so than that of the timorous Dr Eedes who travelled in 1583 from Oxford to Durham and then preferred to remain in the security of the cathedral close:

> An expedition to Newcastle was proposed, and Blencowe urged it, but Deedes was afraid. The Borders at that time were in a state of restlessness, and travelling was not too safe. In particular a certain outlaw called 'Jocky' was then a terror to the wayfarer, and stories were afloat of travellers murdered in their beds. At all events the excursion was never undertaken in the four weeks that the visitors were in Durham.

Despite their concerns about security Camden and Cotton were able to penetrate the wild and remote area of Redesdale, traditional bandit country also traversed by Bowes and Elleker in their survey of 1541. Camden records the pattern of pastoral life based on seasonal transhumance:

> All hereabouts in the *wastes*, as they call them, as also in Gilsland, ones sees a set of people like the ancient Nomads, of a warlike disposition, who watch here with their flocks from April to August in scattered huts called *Sheales* and *Shealings*.

In a more general survey of the county he notes the enduring distinction between life in the hills and life on the coastal plain:

> The country is in great measure rough, unfit for cultivation, and seems to have communicated its hardness to its inhabitants, who are made more fierce by their Scottish neighbours either harassing them with war or mixing with them in peace, making them most warlike, and excellent light horsemen. Being as it were devoted to war, there is no person among them of any consequence but has his fort or castle…..
> A little cultivation makes the country on the coast and Tyne agreeable to live in. In other places it is much more disagreeable and horrid. In many parts those minerals called *Linthantraces*, by us *sea-coal*, are dug in great plenty to the great benefit of the inhabitants.

Descending from the hills Camden visited Corbridge where he examined the vicar's pele and the ruins of the Roman town, and Newcastle, of which he offers us a concise and accurate account:

> Where the wall and the Tyne almost meet stands Newcastle, the chief town in these parts, famous for its harbour formed by the Tyne, which is deep enough to receive very large ships and shelters them so well that they are not exposed to wind or shoals. The town stands on a very unequal declivity on the north side of the river, over which is a most beautiful bridge, on the left of which, as you enter, stands the castle. On a steep hill to the right are the market place and the best built part of the town, from whence you have a troublesome ascent to the higher part, which is much larger.

It is likely also that Camden visited Lindisfarne where he noted the proliferation of rabbits and viewed the "tolerably commodious harbour defended by a fort on the hill to the south-east". However he devotes most of his note on Lindisfarne and the Farne Islands to their place in monastic history rather than to their contemporary appearance.

A Royal Progress to London

A couple of years before Camden another visitor came north to Berwick:

> Myself upon occasion of business in the month of April, and the year 1598, took a journey to these said confines, namely to Barwick, a town then very strongly fortified by the English to restrain the sudden incursions of the Scots, and abounding with all things necessary for food, yea with many dainties as salmons and all kinds of shellfish, so plentifully as they were sold for very small prices. And here I found that for the lending of sixty pound there wanted not good citizens who would give the lender a fair chamber and good diet as long as he would lend them the money.

The writer is Fynes Moryson (1566-1629), an experienced traveller who made a four year long tour of the Continent between 1591 and 1595 and then, almost without drawing breath, set off a return trip to Jerusalem, leaving on 29th November 1595 and returning on 10th July 1597. In the course of this journey he lost his brother, who died of dysentery at Antioch.

Moryson's comments on the quality of the food at Berwick, particularly on its salmon, are echoed in later writers. To this day the Tweed is generally considered the finest salmon-fishing river in Britain and the fish that used to be sent down on horseback to London and sold as Newcastle salmon were usually brought down from Berwick. His report of merchants accepting the use of capital as adequate reward for providing board and lodging is supported by the account given of Scotland by the French traveller Stephen Perlin in 1558:

> In this country (as I have seen it practised) a man who is possessed of an hundred golden, or sun crowns, will lend them to a merchant, for which the merchant will maintain him a whole year in his house, and at his own table, and at the end of the year will return him his money.

Perlin's visit to Scotland draws our attention to the lack of any foreign visitors to Northumberland during the 16th century, and indeed also during the following century. One obvious reason is the difficulty of travel; another is succinctly expressed by the Swiss traveller Thomas Platter:

> London is the capital of England and so superior to other English towns that London is not said to be in England, but rather England to be in London, for England's most resplendent objects may be seen in and around London; so that he who sightsees London and the royal courts in its immediate vicinity may assert without impertinence that he is properly acquainted with England.

Moryson's other observation is that Berwick was "*then* very strongly fortified". This is precisely accurate, as Moryson was engaged on writing his *Itinerary* in the years from 1606 to 1617, by which time Berwick's position had radically changed. Elizabeth I died at 2.00am on Thursday 25th March 1603 and one of her courtiers, Sir Robert Carey, galloped north from London with the determination to be the first to bring the news to her nominated successor, James VI of Scotland and now James I of England. Carey was a member of Elizabeth's inner circle and a Warden of the Northern Marches, but his career had depended on Elizabeth's personal favour and was thus threatened by her impending death. It is not therefore surprising that Carey determined to look after number one:

I did assure myself it was neither unjust nor dishonest for me to do for myself, if God at that time should call her to his mercy.

Carey arrived at the court in Edinburgh on the late evening of Saturday 27th March, having covered 400 miles in less than 70 hours. Even granted his foresight in setting up a relay of fresh horses this was an almost incredible ride with Carey achieving an average daily distance of 220 kilometres. It is not surprising that he presented himself before James "be-blooded with great falls and bruises". In his *Memoirs* Carey gives us his own account of this ride, indicating that he set out after escaping from the efforts of members of the Privy Council to prevent his journey:

> I....took horse between nine and ten o'clock, and that night rode to Doncaster. The Friday night I came to my own house at Witherington [Widdrington], and presently took orders with my deputies to see the borders kept in quiet, which they had much to do: and gave order the next morning the King of Scotland should be proclaimed King of England, and at Morpeth and Alnwick. Very early on Saturday I took horse for Edinburgh, and came to Norham about twelve at noon, so that I might well have been with the King at supper time: but I got a great fall by the way, and my horse with one of his heels gave me a great blow on the head that made me shed much blood. It made me so weak that I was forced to ride a soft pace after, so that the King was newly gone to bed by the time that I knocked at the gate.

James gave him immediate reassurance for his initiative and promised to be as good a master to him as Elizabeth had been. Carey subsequently enjoyed a solid if unspectacular career at James's court and his wife was appointed to take care of the young and sickly Prince Charles, who was to become James's heir as the result of the death of his elder brother Henry. Charles created for him the new title of Earl of Monmouth three days after his own coronation in February 1626.

James set out from Edinburgh on Wednesday 5th April. The royal party included the French ambassador:

> ......whose wife was carried betwixt Edinburgh and London by eight pioneers or porters, one four to relieve the other four by turns, carrying her in a chair with slings.

The ambassador's wife may have enjoyed a journey marginally more comfortable than that endured by Margaret Tudor's ladies in waiting, but one feels pity for the porters. The royal party came to Berwick where the reception party, described in Millington's overblown prose, echoes that provided a century earlier:

> And when his Highness came within some half mile of the town and began to take view thereof it suddenly seemed like an enchanted Castle. For from the mouths of dreadful engines.....came such a tempest as dreadful, and sometimes more deathful, than thunder; that all the ground thereabout trembled as in an earthquake, the houses and towers staggering; wrapping the whole town in a mantle of smoke, wherein the same was a while haid from the sight of his royal owner.

James went out of his route to visit Robert Carey at Widdrington, thus giving him a further mark of his favour. James was enjoying himself; after riding 37 miles non-stop from Berwick he indulged in a spot of impromptu hunting:

> His Majesty, having a little while reposed himself after his great journey, found new occasion to travel further. For, as he was delighting himself with the pleasure of the park, he suddenly beheld a number of deer near the place. The game being so fair before him, he could not forbear, but according to his wonted manner forth he went and slew two of them. Which done, he returned with a good appetite to the house where he was most royally feasted and banqueted that night.

The royal party arrived in Newcastle on Saturday 9th April:

> Upon Sunday, being the 10th April, His Majesty went to the church, before whom the Bishop of Durham preached. And that day, as it is most Christianlike custom, being spent in devotion, he rested till Monday, which he bestowed in viewing the town, the manner and beauty of the bridge and quay, being one of the fairest in all the north parts. Besides, he released all prisoners; except those that lay for treason, murder and Papistry; giving great sums of money for the release of many that were imprisoned for debt, who heartily praised God, and blessed His Majesty, for their unexpected liberty.
> So joyful were the townsmen of Newcastle of His Majesty there being, that they thankfully bare all the charge of his household during the time of his abode with them, being from Saturday till Wednesday morning. All things were in such plenty and so delicate for variety that it gave great contentment to His Majesty; and on the townsmen's part there was was

nothing but willingness appeared, save only at His Majesty's departure, but of that there was no remedy.

Exactly a century therefore after Margaret Tudor's dynastic marriage her great-grandson brought about the union of the English and Scottish crowns and journeyed back down the Great North Road, retracing Margaret's journey in the opposite direction. For Northumberland this was indeed the end of one era and the start of another. On his accession to the throne of England James I set out his vision of a United Kingdom in which Northumberland and Cumberland would be transformed from Border counties into the new Middle Shires. On his arrival at Newcastle in April 1603 he abolished March Law by proclamation, and in December 1603 ordered the decommissioning of the fortress at Berwick. By July 1604 the garrison had been reduced to 100 men, some of them pensioners, and the ordnance was shipped south to the Tower of London.

The next century would see the beginnings of a new kind of travel to the north.

CHAPTER 2

BEFORE AND AFTER THE CIVIL WARS – 1604-1675

> This degraded piece of land, this scene of butchery, gave rise to that celebrated joke upon King James's favourite *Cow*, which he brought from Scotland when he acceded to the crown. She having no taste for English manners, silently retreated without even a farewell to the monarch; and was the only person in his whole train that ever returned to Scotland. When the courtiers expressed their surprise, how she could find the way, as she could speak neither Scotch nor English, the King replied, *that* did not excite his wonder so much as how she could travel over the Debatable Ground without being stolen.
>
> William Hutton

Walkers and Riders

Our account of the sixteenth century was framed by the royal progresses of Margaret Tudor and James I. Henry VII's prophecy that the union of the crowns would concentrate power in England was fully borne out by events. The apocryphal saga of the royal cow journeying north over the Debatable Ground north of Gilsland reflected the reality that London had become the centre of power for the Stuart monarchs. James established his capital there and made only one return visit to Scotland, in 1617; Charles did not travel north until 1633 when he decided that it would be politic to be crowned in Edinburgh as well as in London. He came north again in 1639, this time with an army prepared to do battle with the Scots, and then in 1641 for an unsuccessful charm offensive in Edinburgh. His final involuntary visit commenced in May 1646 when he was brought to Newcastle as a prisoner of the Scots and was kept under guard until January 1647 when he was delivered to the English Parliament which would finally condemn him to death. Two centuries elapsed before the next visit by a reigning monarch. In September 1849 Queen Victoria travelled to Newcastle to inaugurate Robert Stephenson's High Level Bridge, returning in the following year to Berwick to inaugurate the Royal Border Bridge, also Stephenson's work, and Newcastle Central Station. The failure of the German Hanoverian kings to travel north may reflect Thomas Platter's view that to see London was to see

England, or possibly a desire to shun a city so closely associated with the downfall and death of a previous monarch.

Others did of course take the road north. In 1618, the year after James's return visit, the poet and playwright Ben Jonson (1572-1637), formerly a pupil of William Camden at Westminster school but by now in middle age and weighing between 18 and 20 stone, walked all the way from London to Edinburgh and, after spending some time in Scotland, back again. Why Jonson undertook this journey remains unclear, and until recently it was believed that he had walked alone. However a recently discovered document in a Cheshire family archive provides an account of the journey written by a previously unsuspected travelling companion. From this we learn that Jonson and his companion left London on Wednesday 8th July and, following a somewhat leisurely and zigzag route to take in visits to friends and patrons, arrived in Durham on Saturday 22nd August. After 3 nights in Durham they continued to Newcastle where they spent another 5 nights. Leaving Newcastle on Sunday 30th August they took 9 days to walk the coastal route to Berwick, where they arrived on Monday 7th September. Jonson's visit to Newcastle prompted him to write some riddling lines on the tower of St Nicholas church:

My Altitude high, my Body foure square,
My Foot in the Grave, my Head in the Ayre,
My Eyes in my sides, five Tongues in my Wombe,
Thirteen Heads upon my Body, four Images alone;
I can direct you where the Winde doth stay,
And I tune Gods Precepts thrice a Day.
I am seen where I am not, I am heard where I is not,
Tell me now what I am, and see that you misse not.

While these lines hardly qualify as serious literature they are significant in marking the early development of a new approach to travel in which visitors appreciate buildings for their own sake rather than as relics of antiquity, and take a lively interest in people and contemporary social life. Loxley notes, for instance, that on 26th August Jonson visited the Royal Grammar School, then located opposite St Nicholas's church, and presented "the Master a piece to buy a book with".

Meanwhile on Tuesday 14th July, only 6 days after Jonson's own departure, another poet set out on foot on the long journey from London to Scotland and back. This was John Taylor (1578-1673), a Thames bargeman whose skill in writing popular doggerel earned him the title of the Water Poet. Although leading a horse to carry his baggage and provisions he made and kept a resolution to complete the journey without using any money and without begging. Fortunately he had friends and patrons along the route, while his reputation and the novelty of his undertaking ensured that he was usually well lodged and fed, with a plentiful supply of ale. *The Pennyles Pilgrimage*, his own account of the journey, is written in a mixture of verse and prose, and an early passage describing his departure from London is a good specimen of his lively style:

> This foresaid Tuesday night 'twixt eight and nine,
> Well rigged and ballast'd, both with beer and wine,
> I stumbling forward, thus my jaunt begun,
> And went that night as far as Islington.
> There did I find (I dare affirm it bold)
> A maidenhead of twenty five years old,
> But surely it was painted, like a whore,
> And for a sign, or wonder, hang'd at t'door,
> Which shows a maidenhead, that's kept so long,
> May be hanged up, and yet sustain no wrong.

Taylor took a different road to Scotland, going via Carlisle. Like Jonson however he spent some weeks in Scotland and at one point the two men met, probably on Taylor's initiative since there is some suggestion that Jonson was rather peeved at what he saw as a copycat expedition. Towards the end of September Taylor walked back south to Newcastle by way of Berwick. This part of his account is written in prose, which we may regret, but his reporting of a topical news item is another example of the new approach to travel evidenced in these two journeys. The passage also supports Fynes Moryson's testimony on Berwick's reputation for abundant fishing:

> In the river of Tweed, which runs by Berwick, are taken by fishermen that dwell there infinite numbers of fresh salmons, so that many households and families are relieved by the profit of that fishing. But (how long since I know not) there was an order that no man or boy whatsoever should fish upon a Sunday. This order continued long amongst them, till some eight or nine weeks before Michaelmas last, on a Sunday, the salmons played in

such great abundance in the river, that some of the fishermen (contrary to God's laws and their own order) took boats and nets and fished, and caught three hundred salmons; but from that time until Michaelmas day that I was there, which was nine weeks, and heard the report of it, and saw the poor peoples lamentations, they had not seen one salmon in the river; and some of them were in despair that they should never see any more there, affirming it to be God's judgment upon them for the profanation of the Sabbath.

Which may be read as a 17th century parable on the perils of over-fishing..

From Berwick Taylor took the main road south via Belford and Alnwick to reach Newcastle, where he met an old acquaintance:

I found the noble Knight, Sir Henry Witherington, who, because I would have no gold or silver, gave me a bay mare, in requital of a loaf of bread that I had given him two and twenty years before at the island of Flores.

This spectacular piece of generosity has its origin in the ill-fated Azores expedition of 1597 when some of the troops spent 5 days on Flores and ran short of food while waiting for re-embarkation. Penniless Taylor may have been, but not friendless.

In choosing to travel on foot Jonson and Taylor displayed an eccentric streak, though they can hardly compete for eccentricity with Count Schaumborg Lippe, an 18th century German prince, who made a bet that he could ride a horse backward from London to Edinburgh. A wager may also lie behind the decision of three soldiers from Norwich to undertake a tour in the late summer of 1634. One of the group, Lieutenant Hammond, wrote an account which opens with a paragraph typical of his rather pompous style:

Three Southern Commanders, in their places, and of themselves and their purses, a Captain, a Lieutenant, and an Ancient, all voluntary members of the noble Military Company in Norwich, agreed at an opportune and vacant leisure to take a view of the cities, castles, and chief situations in the Northern, and other Counties of England. To that end and purpose, all business and excuses set apart, they had a parley and met on Monday the 11th of August 1634 and, mustering up their triple force from Norwich, with soldiers' journeying ammunition, they marched forth that night to the maritime town of Lynn.

The fact that they served as voluntary members and had command of their own purses indicates that they were all gentlemen of good social standing. Nevertheless, in an age when few people travelled for pleasure, it is remarkable enough that these 3 soldiers should have set out on such a journey. The intention to cover so much of England in a 7 week tour makes this journey unique. Possibly a hard military drinking session in the mess-room provoked the challenge of covering 26 counties during the 7 weeks of their summer leave, a challenge that anticipates by more than 2 centuries Phileas Fogg's similarly rash bet that he could travel around the world in 80 days. In the following year Lieutenant Hammond was to undertake a further tour, this time on his own, which took in the southern and western counties (excluding Cornwall) not visited in 1634.

The first leg of their journey took them north through Lincolnshire and Yorkshire, and they arrived at Durham late on a dark evening. They were fortunate to find an "honest Gentleman" who guided them "to our Inn, the Lion, where our Host, an honest Trout, caused us to be carefully attended by his She-attendants". On the following morning, Thursday 21st August, they made a brief tour of the town and a detailed inspection of the cathedral, and then accepted an invitation from the Dean to lunch with the clergy. A lavish and protracted meal meant that they did not leave till late in the afternoon, arriving at Newcastle in the evening, where they stumbled down the steep and stony slopes to the river by the faint lights they could see below. They found lodgings in Pilgrim Street "where our host, a good fellow, and his daughter, and an indifferent Virginal player, somewhat refreshed our weary limbs".

After a day in Durham they had even less time to spare for Newcastle, spending only a morning in a survey of the town:

> We found the people and streets much alike, neither sweet nor clean, yet seated in a vale between two mighty hills, in two Counties parted by that famous River, which we passed by a fair stone bridge of 10 Arches with some towers, to which comes the ships.
> The Key is fair and long, and a strong wall there is between it and the Town, on which we marched all abreast. On the top of the old Castle built by Robert Duke of Normandy we saw all the way downe to Shields, some 7 miles distance, where the Sea's entrance is, in which channel lay

not that number of ships, vessels and barks that sometimes doth, for we were informed that the river is capable of receiving 2.3.4. or 500 sail at a time, and to ride therein safely at anchor, without damnifying one another.

Having perhaps surfeited on the ecclesiastical splendours of Durham the Norwich Three missed out on the Newcastle churches, a standard item on the itinerary of most travellers. However their circuit of castle, walls, bridge, quayside and river anticipates the sights viewed by later travellers, while also reflecting their professional interest as soldiers. The old quayside and the quantity of shipping on the river provoked almost universal admiration among travellers.

Leaving Newcastle in the afternoon of the same day the soldiers declined to ride north "having no stomachs for Tweed, nor those inhabitants". Instead they rode to Hexham, again arriving after nightfall and not without danger. The road along the Tyne to Hexham was notoriously difficult and our travellers describe it as rocky and steep, narrow and intricate. Approaching the town they had to cross the river:

> And now when we had thought that all dangers were passed we met a gulf too, at the entrance into Hexham, over the rapid River Tyne, where for want of boat or bridge we were enforced in the vale of night to pass a swift deep stream, over high great tumbling stones, in such danger both to our horse and to our selves, as had we not fortunately happened on a guide, that knew the fording-place well, we had there ended our travels.

Hexham however proved a fortunate resting-place. They found an inn where they were "as well accommodated with cheap and good fare, sweet lodging, and kind usage, as travellers would desire". And on the following morning they found a guide with good local knowledge who led them along the line of the Roman wall towards Carlisle. So ends their brief transit of Northumberland, a matter of less than 48 hours from start to finish. Yet, brief though it was, this visit is significant. It is the earliest example of a tour to the region undertaken solely for pleasure, and the travellers were not aristocrats or gentlemen of leisure, but regular soldiers taking a holiday from their everyday work. They travelled independently, staying in public inns, but were also ready to socialise when opportunities arose.

Captain Rugg's Great Bottle Nose

Sir William Brereton (1604–1661) visited Northumberland only a year after the Norwich Three. A baronet from the county of Cheshire, he is representative of the wealthy and leisured travellers of the age. His travels took him to France and the Netherlands as well as to various parts of England, Scotland and Ireland. In the following decade he served as a general in the Parliamentary army, commanding the forces in the Chester area and making his name at the battle of Nantwich in January 1644 and in the subsequent siege of Chester itself.

Brereton was able to spend more time in Northumberland than the Norwich soldiers. He arrived in Newcastle on 22nd June 1635 and was immediately impressed:

> This is beyond compare the finest and richest town in England, inferior for wealth and building to no city save London and Bristol, and whether it may not deserve to be accounted as wealthy as Bristol, I make some doubt…….
> There is every day a market kept here, and in a dainty market-place. Tuesday and Saturday, a mighty market, and much provision comes out of Northumberland; infinite store of poultry. This town (a great part of it) placed upon the highest and steepest hills that I have found in any great town; these so steep as horses cannot stand upon the pavements, - therefore the daintiest flagged channels are in every street that I have seen: hereupon may horse or man go without danger of sliding.

He describes the local government of Newcastle, recording that the town was run by a mayor, a recorder, a sheriff and 12 aldermen. He notes that the town had substantial income of between £5000 and £6000 a year "besides great collieries employed for the use and supply of the commons and poor of the town". The town had been assessed in the sum of £3570 for the notorious ship tax, compared to £1800 for York. Such an interest in local government may seem strange to us, but in Cheshire Brereton was both a magistrate and a leading member of local society. His comments on how things were done in Newcastle are typical of the comments made by other travellers of the time. Early road-books, such as Emanuel Bowen's *Britannia Depicta* (1720), summarised the local governance of each significant town, no doubt on the assumption that these details would be of interest to travellers. William Gray's *Chorographia* (1649), a nearly contemporary survey of Newcastle, confirms Brereton's account of the structure of local government and goes into more detail on the market:

> On the east side of it [Middle Street] is the Flesh Market, I think the greatest market in England, for all sorts of flesh and poultry that is sold there every Saturday; the reason is not the populousness of the town that makes it, it is the people in the country (within twelve miles of the town), who makes their provision there, as likewise all that lives by the coal trade, for working and conveying coals to the water; as also the shipping which comes into this river for coals, there being sometimes four hundred sails of ships in the river at one time. There is such a concourse of people out of the country in the streets every Saturday to sell all sorts of corn and flesh, buy all sorts of provision for house and family, receive money of masters of coal for coal-work, that every Saturday's market is like a fair, for all sorts of wares provisions and manufactures.

On the next day Brereton took a boat from the quayside to Tynemouth and the Shields in order to view the salt works. Visitors frequently mention these and Brereton had a particular interest as his brother owned similar works in Cheshire. There had been salt pans at Shields since the ninth century, with coal furnaces being used to boil the sea-water. Brereton gives a lengthy technical description of the process, noting that there were 24 pans fired by 12 furnaces. He adds an equally lengthy, and somewhat confused, analysis of the income, expenditure, and profits of the enterprise. A reference to "Dobson's letter" indicates that he was sufficiently interested in the economics of the business to ask the agent or manager to send him these details in writing, possibly so that he could share these with his brother. As later travellers will confirm the works were highly polluting; Brereton says "here is such a cloud of smoke as amongst these works you cannot see to walk". In the early years of the following century Daniel Defoe commented on the view from the top of the Cheviot:

> We saw plainly here the smoke of the salt-pans at Shields, at the mouth of the Tyne, seven miles below Newcastle; and which was south about forty miles.

The pollution caused by the salt-works, by glass manufacture, and by the mining and carriage of coal, must have been a major factor in ensuring that the people and streets were, in the words of the Norwich Three, "neither sweet nor clean".

33

Brereton's other special interest was duck decoys. He describes Mr Swan, his landlord in Newcastle, as "a very forward man" to have erected a decoy and finds another at Ponteland on his way north from Newcastle. The ODNB entry on Brereton throws light on this by noting that Brereton had himself constructed a duck decoy near Chester, adding that this was a source of much litigation with his neighbours. Other visitors are silent on this subject, a reminder that accounts of travel tell us as much about the visitors as about the places that they visit.

Over the next 2 days Brereton rode north from Newcastle to Berwick, making an excursion from Belford to visit Lindisfarne. Here he took the opportunity, again typical of travellers of the period, to pay a social visit and to observe local wildlife:

> In this island, in a dainty little fort, there lives Captain Rugg, governor of this fort, who is as famous for his generous and free entertainment of strangers, as for his great bottle nose, which is the largest I have seen. This is a dainty little fort, built tower-wise upon the top of a little round hill, which is a rock; this planted with ordinance; below, on very top of the hill, a neat flagged and walled court before the door, where two brass ordinances, the one brought from Cales, and three iron ordinance, one of them came also thence. There are neat, warm, and convenient rooms in this little fort.
> Here in this island was brought unto us a young seal, or, as some call it, a sea-calf, which was this morning left upon the sands dry; they nourish it with milk. It hath an head and eyes like a calf, and hath two fins before like feet, and two behind, which it cannot draw up like fins, whereby also it is enabled to move in a creeping manner, and that slowly, yet constantly and restless; it hath a navel, and cries.

After this somewhat plaintive digression Brereton spent one night at Berwick before continuing north into Scotland on 26th June. Visiting Edinburgh and Glasgow he spent 9 days in Scotland before sailing from Port Patrick to Ireland on 4th July.

If Brereton was a Parliamentary Roundhead then John Aston (1602-1650), who came to Northumberland in 1639, was definitely a Cavalier. Aston, who attended Charles I as 'Chamber-man Extraordinary', came north from his home in Yorkshire as a member of the army which Charles had raised to fight the Scots in what became known as the first bishops' war. The Scots having rejected bishops, Charles decided that he needed to establish by the exercise of military might the point of principle enunciated by his father James in the words 'No bishop, No King', a phrase later immortalised for generations of schoolchildren in *1066 and All That* by Sellars & Yeatman. A totally inconclusive expedition came to an end on 18th June as a result of the treaty of Berwick, without a shot being fired on either side.

Aston had arrived in Newcastle on 4th May. He took lodgings in the Side at the house of William Bonner, a linen draper, and was in town to witness the formal entry and welcome of the king on 6th June. The king himself took lodgings in Pilgrim Street at the house of Mr Lydall, one of the aldermen. On 12th June the army moved north, with Aston lodging overnight at Stannington and making acquaintance with the local fleas:

> This was a very mean town, and with much difficulty I got such a lodging at one widow Gayles as was there to be expected, so mean and uncleanly as it made me first feel the smart of backbiters in this journey.

Aston's military duties kept him with Charles's army in the north of the county for nearly 6 weeks. During this period he and some fellow officers visited Lindisfarne where they observed 2 regiments of foot marching over the causeway on their way to Berwick. He learned from the locals that more ships and soldiers had landed on the Farne Islands on their way to join the army. Before leaving Lindisfarne Aston and his companions followed the example of Brereton in paying a call on Captain Rugg, "known commonly for his great nose", who gave them "such courteous welcome as his poor habitation would afford". The governor himself had clearly not changed in the intervening 4 years, but the quality of entertainment on offer appears to have declined, perhaps as a result of the financial constraints on royal expenditure arising from Charles's dispute with his Parliament.

Such social calls were an important part of the travels of wealthy gentlemen of the period. Those going on the Grand Tour of the Continent would be furnished with letters of introduction to ensure that they had an entrée to society in each important town. For travellers in England the arrangements were less formal. I have seen no mention of letters of introduction for visitors to Northumberland. It seems to have been understood that visitors to a town would make their presence known to local dignitaries, and that some entertainment would be offered. There was significant class solidarity which sounds, and was, exclusive, but the practice of offering and receiving private hospitality, in however limited a circle, probably gave visitors more contact with local people than that typically experienced by modern tourists.

We should note in passing that another member of Charles I's entourage was the royal physician William Harvey, best known for his discovery of the circulation of the blood. He accompanied Charles on each of his visits in 1633, 1639 and 1641, and in November 1646 made a successful petition to the House of Lords to be allowed to attend the king during his period of imprisonment. The wording of the petition is evidence of the style in which he was accustomed to travel:

> He humbly prayeth your honours' pass for himself with three servants and four horses, or in coach with other necessaries, to go to Newcastle or elsewhere to repair to the King's Majesty and attend and return as his services shall require and he shall pray for your honours' health and happiness.

A Frenchman's View of Northumberland

Most foreign travellers to England stayed in the south, visiting London and the royal palaces, enjoying boat trips along the Thames to Richmond, and visiting Oxford, Cambridge and Stratford. Few came north. An exception was Monsieur Jorevin de Rocheford who left an account of his journey through Northumberland in 1666. Like John Taylor, but unlike most of our other visitors he entered Northumberland from Scotland:

> Barrwick is the first town by which I re-entered England, and, being a frontier to Scotland, has been fortified in different manners. There is in it at present a large garrison, as in a place of importance to this kingdom. It is bounded by the river Tweed, which empties itself into the sea, and has a great reflux, capable, but for sands at the entrance into its port, of bringing up large vessels. I arrived here about ten of the clock on a Sunday; the gates were then shut, it being church time, but were opened at eleven, as is the custom in all fortified places.

He continues with a lengthy description of the upper and lower town areas of Berwick, finding it "to be one of the greatest and most beautiful towns in England". He particularly admired the large houses of the wealthy citizens of the lower town, and the open areas with their great fountains. Unsurprisingly he exhibits special enthusiasm for Berwick's great bridge:

> The greatest part of the streets in the lower town are either up or down hill; but they are filled with many rich merchants, on account of the convenience and vicinity of its port, bordered by a large quay, along which the ships are ranged. There is not a stone bridge, in all England, longer or better built than that of Berwick, which has sixteen large and wonderfully well-wrought arches; it is considered as one of the most remarkable curiosities of the kingdom.

Grose, who printed this translation in his *Antiquarian Repertory*, rather grudgingly concedes that Jorevin was a "tolerable topographer". This does scant justice to the observational acumen that Jorevin displays in his description of Northumberland. He notes that wolves, allegedly still common in Scotland, were no longer to be found in Northumberland. As a result "the flocks of sheep are left out all night in the fields, without any shepherd to guard them". And in this context he mentions the great sheep pens which are such a distinctive feature of the Northumbrian hills, yet are consistently overlooked by other visitors. On his visit to the River Tyne he notes how exports of coal, lead and tin have made Newcastle "one of the most mercantile places in the kingdom". This observation is parallelled in the writings of other visitors, but his description of the upper market area is unusually detailed:

> To see Newcastle properly, one must begin at the place where I entered, which is a broad street distinguished by a large market-place in the middle, gently descending, where the houses are built with great stones, such as are used for grindstones for cutlers, and are brought from hence to Paris, being so remarkable for their size. This street, after passing over against the butchery, comes to the fish-market, a great covered building, ornamented with a fine fountain, with a handsome bason receiving the water. I must just observe, that butchers meat is no where to be seen finer than in England. The sheep are so large and so fat as to surpass little cows in height; besides this, their wool is extremely fine, of which we see in Paris, cloth called English cloth, as beautiful as if made of silk. The great street also joins this fish-market. In going up it, you see a rivulet made by several fountains, and which cleans it in its descent. There is in the middle of this street a meeting of two others, and a fine fountain, that

disperses its waters into different parts of the town. From hence you may go and see the great church, not far from the old market-place, which is a great space of a round figure, surrounded by the houses of diverse workmen. Here a market is held once a week.

The inclusion of grindstones as another important export is supported by the contemporary evidence of William Gray in his *Chorographia*. After a description of the castle Jorevin picks up the theme of local industry in his accounts of Gateshead and of the boat trip down to the mouth of the Tyne:

The lesser part of the town, called Gatesend, to go into which you must pass over a large stone bridge, covered with houses and shops, is inhabited by divers manufacturers, employed in making cloth and worsted stockings in great quantity, which are here very cheap; wherefore they are sent all over Europe, even to Paris. They are esteemed for the fineness of their wool and the excellence of their workmanship. I was told they used in England machines, whereby stockings were made in a small time; but here they are knit, in the same manner as in France, somewhat different from the manner used in Turkey and Spain, as I have remarked in those countries. One may go down the river at every ebb, by means of little boats, to see its mouth, the great port where vessels are loaded with coal; where also one may see a quantity of salt made from sea-water, which is boiled with fire made of this coal.

An Official Visitor and the Earliest Railways

With the upheavals of civil war finally over people felt able to travel more freely. London lawyers, benefiting from long vacations, were among those with sufficient time and money to make the long trip northward. An early example was John Stainsby of Clement's Inn who visited Northumberland in the Hilary vacation of 1666. While his main interest lay in tombs and other funerary monuments he shared the antiquarian habit of recording local traditions:

A custom in the town of Morpeth (but since the wars omitted) to choose one out of the young men in the town to be St George, and all the rest of the young men to attend him, and upon St George day all to come to church and at the rehearsing of the creed the St George to stand up and draw his sword. Another custom in the said town to have a Lord of Misrule chosen against Easter, and to continue till Whitsunday, and he to keep a barrel of ale upon the bridge and make all passengers drink thereof, and to collect money of them for repair of the highways, and give a just account at Whitsunday.

Another lawyer, the Right Honourable Francis North (1637-1685), Baron of Guilford, came to Newcastle on the official business of the northern circuit in around 1675. As a lawyer North took a particular interest in the problems posed by the border reivers. While making it clear that these problems were to a considerable extent past history, with a consequent substantial increase in the value of landed estates in the county, North suggests that banditry was not entirely a thing of the past and that it remained necessary for judges and the Border commission to pass frequent death sentences on those convicted.

The annual assizes provided the opportunity for much municipal banqueting and for showing important visitors the highlights of the city and the surrounding area. It is therefore interesting to note the programme arranged for North by the local magistrates:

> His lordship's entertainment at Newcastle was very agreeable, because it went most upon the trades of the place, as coal-mines, salt-works and the like, with the wonders that belonged to them; and the magistrates were solicitous to give him all the diversion they could: and one was the going down to Tynemouth castle in the town barge. The equipment of the vessel was very stately; for, a-head, there sat a four or five drone bagpipe, the North-country organ, and a trumpeter astern; and so we rowed merrily along. The making salt I thought the best sight we had there. The other entertainment was a supper in the open air upon an island in the Tyne somewhat above the town; and all by the way of ligg [lie] and sit upon the ground: but provisions for a camp and wine of all sorts very fine. In short, all circumstances taken together, the cool of the evening, the verdant flat of the island with wood dispersed upon it and water curling about us, view of the hills on both sides of the river, the good appetites, best provisions, and a world of merry stories of the Scots (which by the way makes a great part of the wit in those parts), made this place very agreeable, where every one walked after his fancy and all were pleased.

The island, known as King's Meadows, lay opposite Elswick and has since disappeared as a result of dredging work on the Tyne. North saw further salt-pans at Seaton Sluice when he dined with Sir Ralph Delaval at Seaton Delaval and had a guided tour of the port and sluice-gates, an impressive example of the 17th century engineering. More significantly he was the first visitor to give an account of the early waggonways, or Newcastle roads as they became known, alluding both to the legal arrangements for their construction and to the flanged wheels that were crucial to the development of this new technology:

> Another thing that is remarkable is their way-leaves; for when men have pieces of ground between the colliery and the river, they sell leave to lead coals over their ground; and so dear that the owner of a rood of ground will expect £20 per annum for this leave. The manner of the carriage is by laying rails of timber from the colliery down to the river, exactly straight and parallel; and bulky carts are made with four rowlets fitting these rails; whereby the carriage is so easy that one horse will draw down four or five chaldron of coals, and is an immense benefit to the coal merchants.

What is remarkable in the programme of this official visit, and no doubt of others of which we have no record, is both the determination of the magistrates and of Sir Ralph Delaval to show off local industry and the latest developments in industrial technology, and the assumption that this programme would be of interest to visitors whose expertise lay in the field of the law. Mention of the Newcastle waggonways also takes us back 70 years to an earlier visitor whom we have not so far considered. For, while the Roman emperor Hadrian is popularly considered the individual to have made the greatest personal mark on the landscape of Northumberland, Huntingdon Beaumont (1561-1624) might reasonably challenge that claim. As early as 1649 William Gray noted his contribution to the development of mining technology:

> Master Beaumont, a gentleman of great ingenuity and rare parts, adventured into our mines with his 20,000 pounds; who brought with him many rare engines, not known then in these parts; as the art to bore with, iron rods to try the deepness and thickness of the coal; rare engines to draw water out of the pits; waggons with one horse to carry down coals from the pits to the staiths.

Beaumont, a Midlands industrialist, had built the first waggonway shortly after 1600 to convey coal from pits at Strelley, west of Nottingham, to the Trent. He hoped to establish a route to the London market and thereby challenge the dominance of Newcastle. The waggonway was a technical success, but navigational problems in the river Trent meant that the transportational logjam was simply shifted from the pithead to the riverside staithes. Beaumont found that his partners withdrew their support and he then decided to bring his new technology to the north east. Here again he was frustrated as the Newcastle hostmen, with their exclusive rights to mine coal along the banks of the Tyne, refused to make room for him. Instead, in 1606 or 1608, he leased collieries in the area inland from Blyth and, among other technological innovations, built the earliest local waggonways to carry coals from Bebside and Plessey to the port at Blyth. Unfortunately for Beaumont he was competing with an entrenched monopoly at a time when coal prices were falling. The venture came to an end in 1614 and the subsequent foreclosure by his creditors on the Strelley assets led to Beaumont being committed to prison for debt in 1618, remaining incarcerated until his death in 1624. It is a sad irony that the Tyneside coal-owners, who had spurned his technological innovations, very soon found themselves in need of them. The exhaustion of the riverside mines, and the consequent need to transport coal over greater distances to the staiths, led to the construction of the Whickham Grand Lease Way in 1621, at a time when Beaumont was still alive and languishing in prison. A recent detailed study has identified 7 further waggonways built before the date of Lord North's visit in 1675, all except one situated on the south bank of the river. The exception was the Benwell way which, with an unusually steep gradient, would not have required horses to drag the loaded wagons to the river. It is reasonable to conclude that North and his fellow judges were taken to one of the waggonways constructed on the south side of the river.

CHAPTER 3

A QUARTET OF PLEASURE TRIPS – 1677-1705

The imposition in travelling is abominable; the innkeepers are insolent, the hostlers are sulky, the chambermaids are pert, and the waiters are impertinent; the meat is tough, the wine is foul, the beer is hard, the sheets are wet, the linnen is dirty, and the knives are never clean'd!! Every home is better than this?

John Byng

In this chapter we will look at a quartet of pleasure trips undertaken in the three decades straddling the turn of the 18th century. After the dark years of religious upheaval and civil war these tours bring a welcome sense of light and fresh air. They inaugurate a new age of travel to the region. The second member of the quartet, Celia Fiennes, is also unusual in being one of the very few independent woman travellers to visit Northumberland and to leave an account of her experiences. We start however with Thomas Kirk, a bibulous Yorkshireman and, in contrast to Lord North, a decidedly unofficial visitor.

Birds and Bottles – The Journeyings of Thomas Kirk

Kirk came to Northunberland with one or more companions in June 1677, arriving in Newcastle on Thursday 17th June and departing from Berwick on Monday 28th June.

They saw little enough of Newcastle. Having arrived at around 10pm on the Thursday they visited St Nicholas Church on the Friday morning and indulged in a drinking session with their landlord, a wine merchant who treated them with "excellent good wine" in his cellar. They then hired the wind-musicians and fiddlers known as the town waits and took the boat down to Tynemouth to view Cliffords Fort and to call in on Captain Love, the Deputy Governor. His wine, being "neither white nor Rhenish", was not up to standard so they treated him with some of their own that they had taken with them on the boat. By now they were clearly in excellent spirits, and not to be downcast by the weather:

In our return we had abundance of rain, and were wet through the tilt; the fiddles were almost drowned, yet we made them play before us through the streets.

In passing I note that the order of preference for connoisseurs was Rhenish, then other white wine, and finally red wine. In *The Merchant of Venice* Salarino contrasts Shylock with his daughter Jessica, much to the former's disadvantage:"There is more difference between thy flesh and hers than between jet and ivory, more between your bloods than there is between red wine and Rhenish". And in 1785 John Byng found in Oxford a price list from 1667, in which Rhenish wines cost over 50% more than French wines.

From Newcastle Kirk rode north with overnight stops at Morpeth ("but a little town, situated very low upon the river Wansbeck" – an accurate observation as those who suffered from the 2008 floods will confirm) - and at Alnwick, where they drank wine with a Mr Brandling who lived at the Abbey. From Bamburgh Kirk and his companions crossed to the Farne Islands and engaged in practical ornithology of a kind that would nowadays render them subject to prosecution by the RSPB:

Here we took boat for the Farne Islands; there are about seven in all, but three more remarkable, the Farne, the South Wideopen, and the Staple, etc. The Farne is next the shore, whereon is a kind of castle and a light-house upon it; there are sheep and rabbits, and about the rocks several sorts of fowl make their nests. In the Wideopen grows a certain sort of weed with a white flower: amongst this grass are such infinite numbers of nests of several sorts of sea fowl, that one can scarce walk for treading on them. The Staple is still further from the shore, and the sea here is very rough; the watermen were unwilling to go thither with us, yet we came there we were very well satisfied. On this island is grass, and none of the former weed: we found holes there like coney holes, wherein one of the wherrymen put in his hand, and pulled out a sea-fowl off her nest, called a coulterneb [puffin], a bird as large as a partridge, with a strong beak. The wild pigeons do likewise build in these holes. When the men put in their arms, they know not whether they shall pull out a coulterneb or a pigeon. On one corner of this isle stand several rocks out in the sea all in a row, about half-a-yard, or a quarter or half-a-quarter of a yard distance one from another; they are about four or five yards square a-piece, and as high as any ordinary steeple; they are within two or three yards of the shore, which is as high as the rocks; upon the tops of these rocks are as many birds as can stand one by another, most of willimants and scouts; they have black backs and white bellies; they are not so large as a crow; they have but one egg a-piece, which they hold sometimes under one foot and sometimes under both feet; if they go easily off them, the eggs will stick in the places where they leave them upon the shelving side of the hard rock, but if they be frighted from them hastily, the eggs will roll from the place. We threw stones at them, and felled many of them into the sea; but few of them would stir but those we hit with stones. All the sides of the rocks are as full as they can hold of several birds; here are some scarps, a bird as black as a crow, but much larger. We stoned one a great while, but till she was hurt, she would not get off her nest, but made a great noise and gaped at us.

The incident, reprehensible as it may now seem, is evidence of their obvious desire to enjoy life to the full during this summer holiday. While many visitors came to Northumberland on business of one sort or another, it is good to know that there were also those who came simply for pleasure.

A Lady of Quality

Celia Fiennes (1662-1741) belonged to an aristocratic family with a strong noncomformist tradition. Her father, the second son of the 1st Viscount Saye and Sele, had been one of Cromwell's colonels. Fiennes, who never married, made a series of tours around England and probably succeeded in visiting all of the English counties at least once. In 1702 she wrote up her journals of these tours, but did not publish these in her lifetime. Her longest tour was the Great Journey of 1698, the title consciously modelled on the Grand Tour of the continent and emphasising Fiennes's belief that touring one's own country was in every way as beneficial as travelling abroad, a point made in her general introduction to the journals:

> Now this much without vanity may be asserted of the subject, that if all persons, both Ladies, much more Gentlemen, would spend some of their time in journeys to visit their native land, and be curious to inform themselves and make observations of the pleasant prospects, good buildings, different produces and manufactures of each place, with the variety of sports and recreations they are adapt to, would be a sovereign remedy to cure or preserve from these epidemic diseases of vapours, should I add laziness? It would also form such an idea of England, add much to its glory and esteem in our minds and cure the evil itch of overvaluing foreign parts…………But much more requisite is it for

Gentlemen in general service of their country at home or abroad, in town or country, especially those that serve in parliament, to know and inform themselves the nature of land, the genius of the inhabitants, so as to promote and encourage all projects tending thereto........but to their shame it must be owned many if not most are ignorant of anything but the name of the place for which they serve in parliament; how then can they speak for or promote their good or redress their grievances?

This passage tells us a lot about Fiennes: her conviction that touring to broaden the mind should be open to all, not simply to men; above all, her fascination with manufacture and with the celebration of all things new. A brave woman, she toured on horseback, travelling alone with 2 or more servants. This may sound like a contradiction in terms, but servants are virtually invisible in travel diaries, sometimes to the extent that we do not know whether they were present or not. This invisibility persisted into the 19th century, as is evidenced by an incident in *Sense and Sensibility* when Elinor and Marianne Dashwood take a walk from their cottage in Barton:

Amongst the objects in the scene, they soon discovered an animated one; it was a man on horseback riding towards them. In a few minutes they could distinguish him to be a gentleman.

It is clear that the sisters 'see' only 1 rider, even when that rider is too far off to be identified as a gentleman. Yet, when Edmund finally reaches them, we learn that he was not alone since "he dismounted, and giving his horse to his servant, walked back with them to Barton." This invisibility is also inaudibility, in that the travel diaries which we read are written by the masters and not by their servants. We miss much by not having a parallel narrative of their experiences of travel in a strange land.

On her Great Journey of 1698 Fiennes left London in late March and toured for some weeks in East Anglia and the Midlands before stopping for a long month at her aunt's house near Rugeley. Continuing in early June she travelled north via Chester and Holywell, took the Mersey ferry to Liverpool, and rode through the Lakes to Carlisle. From there she made a brief and unsatisfactory excursion into Scotland, getting no further than the village of Aitchison Bank 2 miles beyond the border. As with her earlier excursion into Wales at Holywell ("they speak Welsh, the inhabitants go barefoot and barelegged – a nasty sort of people") this very brief taste of Scotland served only to reinforce her prejudices about English superiority and she beat a hasty retreat, refusing even to touch the food offered to her in a cottage that had been swept specially for her on her arrival. She did however buy the salmon, an excellent bargain, to have it cooked for her later the same day when she reached Brampton, and enjoyed some "exceeding good claret". Her only positive words about both Wales and Scotland are in commendation of the fish and wine, both the result of proximity to the sea and, in the case of the wine, no doubt of smuggling.

Safely back on English soil Fiennes rode to Brampton and then entered Northumberland along the line of the Roman wall, known to her as the Picts wall. This was not a comfortable journey:

> It's a sort of black moorish ground and so wet I observed as my man rode up that sort of precipice or steep his horse's heels cast up water every step and their feet cut deep in, even quite up to the top. Such up and down hills and sort of boggy ground it was, and that night drawing fast on, the miles so long, that I took a guide to direct me to avoid those ill places.
> This Haltwhistle is a little town; there was one inn but they had no hay nor would get none, and when my servants had got some elsewhere they were angry and would not entertain me, so I was forced to take up in a poor cottage which was open to the thatch and no partitions but hurdles plastered; indeed the loft as they called it which was over the other room was sheltered but with a hurdle. Here I was forced to take up my abode, and the landlady brought out her best sheets which served to secure my own sheets from her dirty blankets, and indeed I had her fine sheet with hook seams to spread over the top of the clothes, but no sleep could I get, they burning turf and their chimneys are sort of flues or open tunnels that the smoke does annoy the rooms.

After a long and difficult day and a sleepless night one might have expected Fiennes to take things easy, especially as the following day was the hottest day of her whole 6 month tour. This would be to underestimate her toughness, since she rode from Haltwhistle to Newcastle, visited various sites in the city, and in the evening continued on her way to Durham. En route she was impressed by Hexham:

> This is one of the best towns in Northumberland except Newcastle.....it's built of stone and looks very well; there are 2 gates to it, many streets,

some are pretty broad, all well pitched with a spacious market place with a town hall on the market cross.

From Hexham Fiennes took the road along the Tyne which both the Norwich Three and Lord North had found so difficult and dangerous. It is entirely characteristic of her to downplay the difficulties and to make it sound much more like a ride through a Constable landscape:

> Thence I went 4 mile along by the Tyne, the road was good hard gravelly way for the most part but very steep up hills and down; on one of these I rode a pretty while with a great precipice on the right hand down to the river. It looked hazardous but the way was very broad; the river looked very refreshing and the cattle coming to its sides and into it where shallow to cool themselves in the heat.

On her approach to Newcastle she observed pairs of horses yoked with pairs of oxen pulling chaldrons of coal from the pits to the river. This was a standard method of old style haulage. As noted in the previous chapter there were at this time no horse drawn waggonways on the north bank of the Tyne so that Fiennes did not have the opportunity to observe this new technology, which would no doubt have fascinated her. With her interest in industry and manufacture she does however comment on the specific properties of the local sea-coal:

> This is the sea-coal which is pretty much small coal though some is round coals, yet none like the cleft coals. This is what the smiths use and it cakes in the fire and makes a great heat, but it burns not up light unless you put most round coals, which will burn light, but then it's soon gone and that part of the coal never cakes. Therefore the small sort is as good as any; if it's black and shining that shows its goodness. This country all about is full of this coal, the sulphur of it taints the air and it smells strongly to strangers. Upon a high hill 2 mile from Newcastle I could see all about the country which was full of coal pits.

She was much impressed by Newcastle itself, where her comments on the water supply focus on the practicalities of the daily life of ordinary people in a way that marks out her observations from those of other travellers:

> It is a noble town though in a bottom. It most resembles London of any place in England, its buildings lofty and large of brick mostly or stone. The streets are very broad and handsome and very well pitched, and many

of them with fine conduits of water in each, always running into a large stone cistern for everybody's use. There is one great street where in the market cross there was one great conduit with two spouts which falls into a large fountain paved with stone which held at least 2 or 3 hogsheads for the inhabitants.

She was impressed also by the Saturday market, where she noted the price of meat and commented favourably on both the range and price of other goods. It was clearly much more than a food market, even if she was less than impressed by the local cheeses:

Here is leather, woollen and linen, and all sorts of stands for baubles. They have a very different sort of cheese, little things looks black on the outside and soft sour things.

Fiennes also noted, as male visitors did not, that "their shops are good and are of distinct trades, not selling many things in one shop as is the custom in most country towns and cities".

Her observation of contemporary life took her also to the bowling-green on the Forth. Ralph Thoresby was to visit this in May 1703, describing it as "the very curious bowling-green, built at the public charge, and where are the best orders kept, as well as made, that ever I observed". Fiennes's description is fuller, with more emphasis on social life in the Forth, suggesting a 17th century northern parallel to the Mediterranean *passeggiata*:

There is a very pleasant bowling-green a little walk out of the town with a large gravel walk round it with two rows of trees on each side making it very shady. There is a fine entertaining house that makes up the fourth side before which is a paved walk under pyasoes [piazzas] of brick; there is a pretty garden by the side shady walk, it's a sort of Spring Garden where the gentlemen and ladies walk in the evening; there is a green house in the garden.

Although Fiennes spent no more than half a day in Newcastle, and probably no more than 30 hours in Northumberland as a whole, her precise and detailed observations provide us with valuable glimpses of day to day life at the time. Although impressed by St Nicholas's church her description of it is relatively cursory, and she was clearly far more interested in her visits to 2 modern institutions, the Barber Surgeons' Hall and the Hospital of Holy Jesus. Her account of the first calls to mind the famous anatomy demonstrations depicted by Rembrandt:

> I went to see the Barber Surgeons' Hall which was within a pretty garden walled in, full of flowers and greens in pots and in the borders. It's a good neat building of brick; there I saw the room with a round table in it, railed round with seats or benches for the conveniency in their dissecting and anatomising a body and reading lectures on all parts. There were two bodies that had been anatomised: one the bones had been fastened with wire, the other had had the flesh boiled off and some of the ligaments remained and dried with it, and so the parts were held together by its own muscles and sinews that were dried with it. Over this was another room in which was the skin of a man that was taken off after he was dead and dressed, and so was stuffed the body and limbs; it looked and felt like a sort of parchment. In this room I could take a view of the whole town, it standing on high ground and a pretty lofty building.

But, when set beside Rembrandt's *chiaroscuro*, Fiennes's picture is bathed in light, from the flowers in the entrance garden to the aerial view of the town from the lecture theatre. For Fiennes this is a gleaming example of modernity, which she values far more highly than the ruins of castles and Roman walls. Her final visit in the town is another celebration of the new:

> Just by is a very good Hospital [Hospital of Holy Jesus] for 14 widows of tradesmen of the town, 2 good rooms a piece; a walk under a pyasoe with pillars of brickwork as is the whole building. There is a large fountain or conduit of water for their use and an open green before their house all walled in.

As with the bowling green and the Barber Surgeons' Hall Fiennes remarks on the gardens and modern amenities of this new municipal foundation. From the hospital she made her way over the old Tyne bridge and rode south to Durham.

A Lawyer's Progress

In 1818 William Blackwood of Edinburgh published an anonymous journal entitled *North of England and Scotland in 1704*. The author remains unidentified but internal evidence suggests that he was a London-based lawyer with a professional interest in ecclesiastical law. While Fiennes had traced in reverse the route taken by the Norwich

Three both the 1704 traveller, and Joseph Taylor a year later, followed the Great North Road from London to Edinburgh, passing through Newcastle and Northumberland on their way.

Our traveller left London on 30th March 1704 with a month's vacation ahead of him. He rode his own horse and travelled alone without a servant. His difficulties began early, as the southern section of the Great North Road was always in poor repair as a result of the volume of local traffic (including herds of animals and heavy waggons drawn by up to 10 or 12 horses or oxen):

> I set out from Royston, and with a great deal of toil, travelling about 2 miles an hour at most, through the worst and deepest ways I ever rode and (I believe) is in England......
> From Huntingdon I travelled nine miles, through a bad road to Stilton; and in this passage my horse tumbled down with me in the dirt, which I took very unkindly of him.

The road was long and difficult. In his early novel *Rob Roy* Walter Scott found it boring:

> I should have been glad to have journeyed upon a line of road better calculated to afford reasonable objects of curiosity, or a more interesting country, to the traveller. But the north road was then, and perhaps still is, singularly deficient in these respects; nor do I believe you can travel so far through Britain in any other direction without meeting more of what is worthy to engage the attention.

On 8th April, 10 days after setting out from London, this traveller finally approaches Newcastle along "a very dirty road" from Durham. His breathless and garbled account betrays his wish to "do" Newcastle as quickly as possible so as not to allow any slippage in the very tight schedule he has set himself.

> A little before I came to Newcastle I passed so near some of the coal pits that I had a curiosity to go see them. At the mouth they like large wells not streamed, and over them are wooden engines to draw up the coals in baskets; but I did not much care to go down any of them, so I went on for Newcastle and came through a long poor street, on which are some straggling houses, over the river Tyne.

His reluctance to risk the descent into the old-style bell pits in a basket suspended from a rope is fully understandable. More than a century later 2 VIPs exhibited a similar reluctance when visiting Wallsend:

> Two interesting visitors came to Wallsend on 9th December, 1815; these were their Imperial Highnesses the Archdukes John and Louis of Austria. They were shown round by Mr Buddle, and took great interest in the work above ground, but no persuasion could induce them to venture down the shaft.

We do not know whether Mr Buddle informed the Archdukes that 35 miners had lost their lives in the Wallsend mine in a series of explosions between 1782 and 1803, or indeed whether he made them aware of the fact that 75 miners had been trapped by the flooding of the nearby Heaton colliery in May 1815, the search for their bodies still being underway at the time of the royal visit.

Once in the town our traveller takes particular interest in the court-house "where the judges, in their circuits, sit on *nisi prius* causes and criminal matters for this city", and also in the castle "where the judges, in their circuits, sit to try criminals and civil causes". He knew precisely where Lord North and the other circuit judges carried out their judicial functions on their visits to the city. With only a month for his vacation our 1704 traveller made this a long day, riding from Durham to Alnwick and stopping for brief inspections of Newcastle and Morpeth en route. In Newcastle he no doubt found a guide in the Sandgate area since his tour covered only the buildings that lay on his direct route from the old bridge to the north road out of the town. There is indeed nothing to suggest that he did more than note the buildings as he rode past them; the only buildings that he definitely entered were 2 churches, principally St Nicholas' Church, which "has in it a good organ, and the top of the font is prettily carved and painted, and most of the pews have some carved work about them".

The emphasis on roads, churches and legal matters continues as he travelled northwards:

> All the way the road was very bad from Newcastle to Morpeth, being 9 miles. On the south side of the town, about half a mile from it, is the church where the divine service is of mornings, if fair weather, and the remains of an old castle; and nearer, just by the town, on the same side of

51

it, is a small river they call the Wansbeck, over which is a bridge; but here is no tide, though this place is but 6 miles from the sea. Just by the end of the bridge, of the north side of the river, is a pretty chapel, where service is in the afternoons of course, and in wet weather both mornings and afternoons, and so is properly a chapel of ease to the town, it saving them from going half a mile to their church. This town is a borough and sends 2 members of parliament. It consists of 2 long streets, and is governed by 2 bailiffs and 7 aldermen. In this town is a gaol belonging to the county, out of which some prisoners had lately escaped by making burrows through the ground which is loose and sandy.

This passage also evidences the interest of our traveller, like Sir William Brereton 70 years earlier, in the details of municipal government. Continuing north from Morpeth he lodged overnight at Alnwick ("a poor straggling town, chiefly thatched, it has a decayed wall round it") and on the following day continued his ride:

….to Belford, another small thatched village, and so struck out of the road to the sea-side, to Bele-on-the-Hill [Beal], also a small village, where the people trade much in cockles, and here I hired a guide to show me a safe passage 2 miles over the sands (the sea being out) to the Holy Island. This island, the people told me, is 7 miles about. In it, of the south side or end of the island, is a small thatched ragged town, the people whereof subsist by catching fish, which they carry over the sands, on their bare feet, to Berwick, and sell there; but they seem very poor, and the whole town consists of a few scattered houses. Of the east side of the town is a large old church, partly broken down.

Our traveller has no time for the ruins of the old priory, nor indeed for the castles of Lindisfarne and Bamburgh ("I don't see of what great use either are"). Had he come towards the end of the 18th century he might have viewed ruins and castles as prime examples of the picturesque rather than as useless piles of old stonework, but he might also have seen the poor fishermen as figures in a landscape rather than as objects of compassion. It is perhaps worth noting that he displays no interest at all in people in Newcastle, the town appearing strangely depopulated, but then comments on the convenient arrangements for church-goers in Morpeth and finally notices the poor when he comes to Beal and Berwick. In the next chapter we will catch up with him in a memorable encounter with a group of washerwomen north of the border. His final stopping place in England was, inevitably, Berwick, where his normal preoccupations are once more evident:

Just above the river Tweed, coming towards Berwick, there is so steep a hill that I could hardly get down it; and just under this hill, by the river side, are many houses inhabited by people that seem to be very poor; and almost at every door is fish hanging out................

Berwick is but small, and has but one church, being but one parish, and is not very populous. It has a strong wall round it, and a large dry ditch without that, which was wet till an engineer of King James the 2nd drained it; and this is a garrisoned town.

The town is governed by a mayor, one alderman, and 4 bailiffs, and tries causes of nisi prius and criminals within itself, the recorder being judge; and this town is in England, though has particular privileges and customs to itself. The chief street is a good wide street, but there are some thatched houses in it. Of the east end of this street is a large handsome stone market-place; and on the east end of the town is the Queen's house, which is but an indifferent house for a prince; and in this house the governors live.

Northward of this town, and about a quarter of a mile from the inner gate, are the ruins of a strong wall and castle, and a large ditch, now dry.

About 4 miles from hence, northward, is a small ditch that parts England from Scotland; and all hitherto is within the liberty of Berwick.

From Berwick his route took him north into Scotland and on to Edinburgh. On his return he took the alternative road by way of Carlisle and back along the Tyne to Newcastle, but his comments here are extremely brief. His note on Hexham however neatly encapsulates both his legal pedantry and his contempt for old buildings:

I came to Hexham, a good north country market town with a wide space in the middle for the market. Hexhamshire was a county by itself till it was laid (by stat.14.Eliz.cap 13) into Northumberland. The church here seems to have been of note in its time, but is now ruinous and old, and seems to be the remains of a cathedral; but this, as well as most of the churches near Scotland, have suffered in the Scotch wars. This was an old bishopric, by the name of Episcopus Hagustaldensis (vide Mon.Angl.2 par.fol.91)

Leaving Newcastle again on 21st April our traveller took a week to ride back to London, arriving home on 27th April and thanking God for his safe deliverance from this journey.

Another Lawyer (and friends)

Joseph Taylor, a barrister of the Inner Temple, rode north from London with his friends Mr Harrison and Mr Sloman on 2nd August 1705 and arrived in Newcastle on 23rd August where they lodged in the market place with a Scotchman Mr Kennedy, the landlord of the Bull Inn. An advertisement in the Scots Courant on 25th July 1715 shows that Mr Kennedy was still in business in Newcastle:

> Whereas it was given out that Andrew Kennedy in Newcastle had given over trade and public business. These are to certify, that the same is malicious and false, he only having removed to the new great Inn called The Black Bull and Crown at the foot of the Side, where is good accommodation for men and horses.

The day on which they travelled from Durham to Newcastle was a day of public thanksgiving for one of Marlborough's victories, and on their arrival in Newcastle they saw a large bonfire in front of the town hall and witnessed the procession of the mayor and aldermen after their official thanksgiving dinner. In Newcastle they visited the churches of St Nicholas and St Andrew, the official residence of the mayor, Sir William Blackett's house, the Custom House and the Town Hall. On this round of visits they also viewed the bowling-green and noted the "fine shady walks all round it, in which the ladies often divert themselves". They also made a more general tour of the town, with particular comments on charitable and public provision for poorer members of society:

> We walked afterwards on the key, along the banks of the Tyne, which is very pleasant, and came back upon the terrace made on the wall, which runs from one end of the key to the other, we saw also the new hospital, called the Keelman's Hospital. It maintains [*figure omitted*] persons and every keelman pays 1d a tide to support it. A gentlewoman has settled £20 per annum here for the education of 34 poor children of St John parish, they are taught to read write and cast accounts, and every child that is discharged has a Bible, Common Prayer Book and Whole Duty of Man given him. Another gentlewoman has settled £60 per annum after her decease for 2 other charity schools in the parishes of St John and St Nicholas, the one for boys, the other for girls, and the 3rd part of £1000 lately bequeathed to charitable use is to be applied to the erecting a school in St Andrew's parish. The trade of this town consists most in coals, iron, cinders for malt, and salt. Corn and victuals are very cheap, and on a

market day there is almost as great a show as in Leadenhall. We were told the revenue of the town, which arises chiefly out of coals and ballast, amounts to near £10000 per annum, which makes it the most flourishing town in the north of England; They have a very advantageous proverb amongst them, which is, that they pay nothing, for the way, the word, nor the water, for the Ministers are maintained, the streets paved, and the conduits kept up, at the public charge of the town.

They stayed in Newcastle for several nights, drawing down money from a merchant Mr Crambleton, and taking advantage of his recommendation of a Gentleman of the Custom House to be their guide to Tynemouth where they saw the castle and a wreck in the channel at the entrance to the river. It is worth hearing Taylor's own account of the remainder of that eventful day and night:

We came back by Shields, a small port, where we stayed to drink a bowl of punch and see the salt-works: We inquired into the nature of making it out of sea water and were informed they do it by boiling it in leaden pans, wherein the water evaporating, the salt remains behind, and they make of ox's blood to clarify the brine, by raising the scum, which they take off: The people that work in the salt-works are very brutish and seem to have no notion of religion or decency, they trouble not the Minister to join them together but the women are got with child behind the furnaces, and there they also lie in: When we went into these works we were obliged to keep our heads under the pans or else the steam which comes from them would have stifled us, though the smell is very sweet: 'Twas late before we returned, but we had the pleasure to see the fires by the coal pits, which are everywhere round Newcastle, burning all night to make cinders. Having a particular recommendation to Mr Green, who lives in the Bigg Market, we waited on him. He showed us all the civility imaginable, and invited us on Sunday to dinner with him, and gave us a handsome Entertainment. We waited on his lady and daughter to St Nicholas Church in the afternoon, where there was a very great congregation: he afterwards engaged us to go to Mr Bewick's at Close House, within 7 miles of Newcastle, to dine there, we were entertained very genteely, and danced with the ladies after dinner. Here we first learned the Northumberland Volunteer, to the tune of Sike a Wife as Willy had, which we afterwards practised very frequently. Mrs Bewick, the young lady, sung and played a thorough bass upon the spinet very well, and with these diversions, and country dances, we spent the day very merrily. In the evening we returned to Newcastle with Mr Green, who to add to our pleasure in this place, made another entertainment at his own house, and there invoked all the pretty Goddesses of the town, of whom the most beautiful were Mrs White, who deserved the title of the fair Enamoretta, her Sister the sweet Violetta, and Mrs Writle, that of the charming Astraea. After a handsome collation, and dancing, we waited on the ladies home, and afterwards Mr Bewick came to our lodgings, where drinking a glass of wine, we proposed to send for the Music, and serenade all the ladies of the town; we had 2 Hautboys [oboes] and 2 Violins, with which we marched round the town, from 3 in the morning, till towards 6: we caused 3 serenading tunes to be particularly played at Sir William Blacket's, Enamoretta's and Astraea's houses, which soon called up the pretty creatures to their windows. About 8 in the morning 29th August we left Newcastle, without sleeping in it that night, and rode to Morpeth.

In calling for musicians and, no doubt link boys to hold torches, Taylor and his friends were following the example of Thomas Kirk and his companions 30 years earlier. After the solitary outsider of 1704, observing but keeping his distance, Taylor and his friends are joyful extroverts whose adventures recall those of Thomas Kirk in 1677. Like Kirk their social and bibulous life continued in Berwick, where they made the acquaintance of the Captain of the Guard as a result of a misunderstanding over the private firearms that they were carrying. But all's well that ends well:

We soon satisfied the Captain, and rectified all mistakes over 2 bowls of punch, there being no wine in the town, which we admired at, having found plenty all along in Yorkshire, Durham and Northumberland. We dined on salmon which is here very cheap, and may well be so if the story be true they told us, that they caught this year 17 score at one haul, but the cook dressed them so intolerably that it put us in mind of the old proverb 'that God sends meat, but the Devil sends the cooks'.............We drunk so late with the Captain, and the officers of the garrison, that the time was come for those in duty to go the grand rounds and, the ceremony being a novelty to us, they invited us to along with them. We were attended by a file of musketeers and, as we went round the town, every sentry demanded the word, which was given in the usual form. As soon as we arrived at the main guard the officers entertained us with brandy, the best liquor they could give us after a cold walk by the seaside in a northern climate, after which we went home to bed with a promise that the gates should be opened for us in the morning as soon as we pleased.

On the following day they crossed the border into Scotland, but I leave Taylor's account of that to the following chapter.

CHAPTER 4

THE NARROW ROAD TO THE DEEP NORTH
Diversions on Travel and on the Scots

> Ask where's the North? at York, 'tis on the Tweed;
> In Scotland, at the Orcades; and there,
> At Greenland, Zembla, or the Lord knows where:
> No creature owns it in the first degree,
> But thinks his neighbour farther gone than he.
> Ev'n those who dwell beneath its very zone,
> Or never feel the rage, or never own;
> What happier natures shrink at with affright,
> The hard inhabitant contends is right.

Alexander Pope, *Essay on Man*

The Long Road North

On the morning of 27th March 1689 Matsuo Basho, most famous of all Japanese poets, left Edo (Tokyo) and, with a few possessions on his back, set off on foot and horseback towards the north of Honshu, the main island of Japan. Only 45 years old he felt prematurely aged and, not expecting to return, had sold his house before his departure. In the event he spent six months on the road, travelling first to the sacred mountains of the north and then back south along the west coast to the neighbourhood of Kyoto, where he spent two years before returning to Edo in 1691. Although he survived this journey his sense of his own mortality was well founded since he was to die in 1694 in the course of a new journey to the south of the country. Basho's journey to the north was a pilgrimage, part religious, part poetic. The way-stations were places celebrated by earlier poets, and Basho usually managed to write a poem of his own at each such station to confirm his place in this very Japanese literary tradition.

For Basho travel to the unknown regions of the north was a metaphor for the journey of life itself. Such existential angst was not the stock-in-trade of those down-to-earth travellers who visited Northumberland in the 16th and 17th centuries but it is interesting to note, in two quite separate cultures, the almost simultaneous birth of the urge to explore the remoter parts of one's own country. English and European travellers may not have viewed their journeys as religious or literary pilgrimages, but would have shared Basho's experience of the *longueurs* of the road as well as his moments of delight in the discovery of new places and new people. As far as we know none of the travellers to the English north went so far as to sell their houses and possessions before taking to the road. However it was common for merchants undertaking a long journey in this country to make a will before their departure. The journey from London to Newcastle was indeed long and difficult. How much further and how much longer was a question that travellers would often have asked. A preliminary, far from adequate, response to that question is that the Great North Road stretched for 274½ miles from London to Newcastle, with a further 118½ miles from Newcastle to Edinburgh, making a total of 393 miles if a traveller wished to cover the whole distance from London to Edinburgh. The rate at which this distance might be covered depended, then as now, upon road conditions and during this period travel was often arduous and sometimes impossible. The diarist John Evelyn, who had travelled widely on the Continent, praised the cobbled roads of France:

> The way from Paris to this city [Orleans], as indeed most of the roads in France, is paved with a small square freestone, so that the country does not much molest the traveller with dirt and ill way, as ours in England does, only 'tis somewhat hard to the poor horses' feet, which causes them to ride more temperately, seldom going out of the trot, or *grand pas*, as they call it.

Ten years later, in 1654, Evelyn made his most extensive English tour, travelling as far north as York where he climbed the tower of the Minster and look north towards Durham. In 1656 he commenced, but quickly abandoned, a more ambitious tour:

> I began my journey to see some parts of the north-east of England; but the weather was so excessive hot and dusty, I shortened my progress.

In fact he travelled only as far as Ipswich and was back home by 11th July, a mere 4 days after his grand departure, thus depriving us of the benefit of his observations of the north-east. Evelyn had good grounds for his opinion that the major roads in France provided a more reliable all-weather travelling surface than those of England where the heavy traffic of waggons, horses and other animals quickly churned up the roads, creating quagmires in wet weather and dust storms when the sun shone and dried the roads. Such roads, and there were many of them, were known as 'deep'. Responsibility for maintenance fell on parish councils, who did not have the technology, the expertise or the financial resource to lay and repair proper road surfaces. We have already heard the complaint of the anonymous 1704 lawyer who on riding north from Royston could manage no more then "about 2 miles an hour at most, through the the worst and deepest ways I ever rode". Where the road was particularly bad riders would use the adjoining fields, making forced diversions that added to the length of their journeys and sometimes took them right away from the road that they thought themselves to be following. Parliament was slow to act; the earliest Turnpike Act, passed in 1663, covered the Great North Road in the counties of Hertford, Cambridge and Huntingdon. It was not until the 1690s, after the 1688 revolution, that Parliament returned to this subject, passing 4 new Turnpike Acts and 3 general Highways Acts. These included the Act of 1697 requiring the setting up of signposts at major junctions.

But then as now the enactment of legislation did not necessarily mean that people took any notice of it. The standard mile of 1,760 yards had been defined in a statute of 1593. It is perhaps unsurprising that Fynes Moryson found that this standardisation had not reached northern England by the time of his journey to Berwick in 1598, but the 17th century saw little change. In 1639 the Water Poet John Taylor combined his observation on long miles with a typical commentary on the comparative strength of northern ale:

> The further I travelled northward the more the miles were lengthened, and the pots shrunk and curtailed; but indeed what the liquor wanted in measure it had in strength, the power of it being of such a potency that it would fox a dry traveller before he had half-quenched his thirst.

Christopher Morris, who quotes John Taylor on this topic, notes that even in 1698, more than a century after the passage of legislation to establish the statute mile, the old British mile of 2,428 yards was still the standard measure in many parts of England, including the northern counties. Such variations would have confused the traveller from London and, at worst, could leave him benighted on a lonely moor as a consequence of misunderstanding the true distance to the next town.

The publication of road-books, beginning with John Ogilby's *Britannia* of 1675 probably did as much as anything else to compel general acceptance of the statute mile as a standard measure of distance, rather as the introduction of a regular time-tabled train service between Newcastle and Carlisle in the 1830s led, rather more quickly, to the abolition in 1841 of Carlisle time, previously 12 minutes behind Greenwich and Newcastle time.

Ogilby's *Britannia* gave the independent traveller a guide to the main roads and a summary of towns and other places of interest, primarily country houses or gentlemen's 'seats'. It was however a door-stopper of a book and the only practical way to use it as a travelling companion was to cut out the pages relevant to one's proposed itinerary. In format it consisted of a series of strip maps, similar to those now available for route planning from the internet, with the disadvantage that taking a wrong turn at a junction took one right off the map with no indication of how to find one's way back to the planned route. As noted above signposts were required at major junctions under an Act of 1697 but, failing these, the only recourse was to ask for directions from the locals. Celia Fiennes and others were only too well aware that this was rarely a reliable source of information. In an age when few people had the need or opportunity to travel many lived all their lives without going more than 4 or 5 miles from their homes. Some will have been genuinely ignorant of how to get to a town 10 miles away; others may have enjoyed giving false directions to an upper-class stranger whose appearance and manner aroused distrust and suspicion. In more remote areas it was sensible to hire a guide. The Norwich soldiers were fortunate to find such a guide when they were in difficulty at the ford on the approach to Hexham, and benefited from that experience in hiring another guide on the following day to take them along the Roman wall to Carlisle. Celia Fiennes also employed a guide when making her excursion from Carlisle into the Scottish borders, and it is probable that the same guide accompanied her on her ride out of Scotland via Longtown to Brampton. That this was a notoriously dangerous area is attested by Walter Scott in his account of Guy Mannering's walk across the Waste of Bewcastle, just to the north of the route taken by Celia Fiennes.

It is worth noting that all the travellers whose accounts we have considered in the previous 2 chapters followed either the Great North

Road from Durham to Berwick or the cross-road from Tynemouth to Carlisle. This becomes less surprising if we consider that these are the only roads in Northumberland to be mapped in Ogilby's *Britannia* and in Emanuel Bowen's *Britannia Depicta*, published in 1720 as a more portable version of Ogilby's massive tome. Bowen's descriptions of places in Northumberland give the traveller some idea of what to expect on a visit:

> Newcastle in Northumberland before the Conquest was called Monkchester as belonging to the Monks, but since Newcastle from the castle built there by Robert eldest son of William the Conqueror. It is situated upon the river Tyne, a town and county large, populous. Well built and with respect to trade is the chief emporium of the north.....It hath 4 parish churches and 1 in Gateshead a suburb, from hence are sent 6000m chaldron of coals yearly, fairs are Lammas and St Luke each holding 10 days.
>
> Morpeth in Northumberland is a borough by prescription and of great antiquity.....It has 2 markets weekly Wednesday and Saturday, Wednesday is reckoned the greatest in England for live cattle except Smithfield, with a fair yearly Holy Thursday.
>
> Berwick is a town of great strength having the sea on east and south and the river Tweed on the south west, being encompassed with a wall and fortified with a strong castle.....the town being a thoroughfare between England and Scotland it hath a large and sumptuous bridge consisting of 15 arches and is in length 300 yards; the river abounds with fine salmon in rocks & in shipping off of corn consists their chief trade. 2 markets weekly viz Wednesday and Saturday and 1 fair yearly held in Trinity Week.

I suspect however that Celia Fiennes would have cavilled at the description of Haltwhistle as "a town furnished with good accommodation for travellers".

There was little alternative to travelling by road, however bad the roads might be. In later life John Taylor expanded his range of publication with *The Carrier's Cosmography*, listing the London carriers in alphabetical order of the towns served. He also mentions that "at Galley Quay passage for men and carriage for goods may be had from London to Berwick", presumably with a stop en route at Newcastle. While none of the travellers whom we have considered came north by sea some of them did avoid the difficult road between Newcastle and Tynemouth by taking a boat along the Tyne. This was certainly the route taken by Thomas Kirk and it is likely that Joseph Taylor, guided by "a gentleman of the Custom House", also went by river. Even this route was not without its dangers, as Ralph Thoresby makes clear in the diary entry for 8th September 1681:

> Morning, visited some drapers, in order to their accounts; then went with E.H. down to Shields by water, but it proved a most terrible stormy day; visited Tinmouth Castle, now almost ruined, and maintained by a slender garrison; and the new fort called Clifford's, fortified with thirty culverins, and ten demi-culverins, under the government of the Earl of Newcastle; in the evening not daring, without imminent hazard, as the ship-master said, to return by water, were forced to hire horses and return by land to Newcastle.

To return to the question posed towards the start of this chapter, how long did it take travellers from London to reach Northumberland? There is no single answer, but a useful starting point is the stage-coach service which began in the latter years of the Protectorate:

> The earliest definite evidence of stage-coaches in the north is contained in a 1658 advertisement in *Mercurius Politicus*, where the route from York to Newcastle and Edinburgh is one of those advertised. In the early days coaches left London for York each Monday, Wednesday and Friday, with the Monday coach continuing weekly to Newcastle and fortnightly to Edinburgh. The journey from London to York took 4 days, with probably a further 2 days to Newcastle and a day's rest at Newcastle on the Sunday. The Edinburgh coach took a further 6 days to travel from Newcastle to Edinburgh. The fare was £3 from London to Newcastle, £4 from London to Edinburgh.

In 1712, half a century later, the fortnightly service from London to Edinburgh still took 13 days. The 6 days required for the final 118 miles from Newcastle is evidence that the fitness of the roads for wheeled traffic had improved little since Margaret Tudor's nuptial progress in 1502. The travellers whose accounts we have considered did not however make use of the stage-coach nor, with the exception of Sir Robert Carey in 1603, did they take the fastest and most expensive option of travelling post, hiring a fresh horse at each stage. We get our best indication of what was reasonably feasible for a single rider from the account left by the anonymous lawyer who rode north in 1704. With a day's break at Lincoln he took 9 days to travel from London to Durham, and a further 5 days to complete the journey to

Edinburgh. In all he took 29 days to complete the round trip, and this probably represents the limit of what was achievable in a month's tour if any time were to be set aside for sight-seeing. Obviously these timings were flexible. Joseph Taylor and his friends, travelling in the following year, made a leisurely progress north, taking 22 days to reach Newcastle and, after a break of 5 days there, a further 2 days to arrive at Berwick. They then decided to ride from Berwick to Edinburgh, a distance of 55 miles, in a single day, starting at 6.00am and, with only 2 rest stops, arriving at their destination at 7.00pm.

Those travellers who could afford the luxury of a private carriage probably travelled even more slowly than those on horseback, although what was achievable would again depend partly on whether they used their own team of horses throughout or changed hired horses at each stage. Lord North brought his carriage north to Newcastle but:

> ....because the hideous road along by the Tyne, for the many and sharp turnings, and perpetual precipices, was for a coach, not sustained by main force, impassable, his lordship was forced to take horse and to ride most part of the way to Hexham.

The Great North Road itself was notoriously deep in certain stretches, including the passage over the moors north of Durham and the quagmire on the stretch through what is now Gosforth. As the above extract reveals the road to Carlisle was even worse. As an eminent judge Lord North was clearly accustomed to riding in his own carriage, and this passage is evidence that the only road in Northumberland passable by carriages at this time was the Great North Road itself, and that probably only with difficulty. Celia Fiennes had done her research well. In some earlier tours of southern England she had taken her private carriage but, on her great tour to the north in 1698, she left the carriage at home and travelled on horseback. Coaches were in any case not always the safer option since they could easily be overturned, sometimes trapping the occupants. The search for improved vehicle safety was clearly a contemporary preoccupation since John Evelyn records in his *Diary* a proposal put to the Royal Society on 30th October 1685:

> Sir Richard Bulkeley described to us a model of a chariot he had invented, which it was not possible to overthrow in whatsoever uneven way it was drawn, giving us a stupendous relation of what it had performed in that

kind, for ease, expedition, and safety; there was only inconveniences yet to be remedied – that it would not contain above one person; that it was ready to [catch] fire every 10 miles; and that being placed and playing on no fewer that 10 rollers, made so prodigious noise as was almost intolerable. These particulars the virtuosi were desired to excogitate the remedies, to render the engine of extraordinary use.

If this recalls the experiments carried out in the grand academy of Lagado, visited by Samuel Gulliver in the course of his voyage to Laputa, then this is because Swift was deliberately satirising some of the more bizarre proposals put to the Royal Society and deliberated there with great earnestness. Swift's language nearly mirrors that of Evelyn, as in his description of one projector "who had found a device of ploughing the ground with hogs", but sadly:

It is true upon experiment they found the charge and trouble very great, and they had little or no crop. However, it is not doubted that this invention may be capable of great improvement.

Journey's End

At the end of each day travellers required accommodation and food. Almost invariably this necessitated reaching a town provided with one or more inns. Failure to do could prove uncomfortable. On his return south through the Scottish lowlands the anonymous 1704 lawyer lost his way in a Scotch mist and was forced to sit out the night on a desolate moor, afraid to move lest either he or his horse were swallowed up in the bog. Less dramatically Celia Fiennes's spat with the innkeeper at Haltwhistle resulted in a sleepless night in a smoke-filled private cottage. It is therefore unsurprising that travellers valued the comforts and amenities of the larger towns and perceived the long intervening stretches of road as treks to be endured rather than as landscapes to be appreciated. A traveller recording his first, and probably only, experience of riding from Durham to Newcastle will often do no more than note the number of miles travelled on a 'dirty' road, and possibly add a comment on the desolate aspect of the moors which he has traversed. Celia Fiennes's enthusiastic appreciation of the riverside scenery between Hexham and Newcastle is a rare exception to the rule that travellers reserve their positive comments for the towns and cities.

While travellers usually succeeded in finding accommodation at an inn, what they found when they got there was wholly unpredictable; beds could be wet and filthy, and inn food could be excellent, poor, or sometimes simply not on offer. General practice was that the innkeeper would charge for food, for both traveller and horse, but not for accommodation. We are fortunate that William Brereton made a note of the expenses that he incurred during his tour in 1635:

Place	Inn	Comments
Newcastle	The Postmaster, Mr Swan – at the Sign of the Swan	8d ordinary – mean entertainment
Alnwick	The Postmaster	Good victuals and lodging – 6d ordinary and 4d breakfast
Berwick	Crown	An excellent inn – good lodging – 8d ordinary – good victuals – 6d per man – this is an honest inn

70 years later, in 1705, Joseph Taylor recorded the expenses incurred on his tour:

Place	Nights Spent	Cost
Newcastle	6	£9 6s 8d
Morpeth	1	£0 17s 6d
Alnwick	1	£0 19s 2d
Berwick	1	£1 1s 6d

Although Taylor and his companions were notably extravagant the amounts quoted are so much in excess of those given by Brereton that they probably represent the total costs for all 3 travellers rather than simply Taylor's personal share.

As noted above the beds at inns could be unsatisfactory or worse. Celia Fiennes's account of her night at Haltwhistle where "the landlady brought me out her best sheets which served to protect my own sheets from her dirty blankets" is evidence of a widespread practice among wealthier travellers of including a pair of sheets in the luggage carried by one of their servants, a luxury not available to those riding unaccompanied. Fiennes was not amused when night-clothes, probably including the sheets, went missing after she had entrusted them to the guide who accompanied her on her way back south from Durham to Darlington. That this custom of carrying one's own sheets persisted for at least another 100 years is evidenced by the travel diaries of John Byng who traversed much of England and Wales in his holiday rides in the final 2 decades of the 18th century. That the custom was eminently sensible is undoubted. Thomas Tryon painted a graphic and wholly unappealing picture of beds which absorbed a cocktail of 'pernicious excrements' from human bodies and were infested by lice, fleas, moths and small worms. Bed sharing, a common practice in inns, added to the dangers, 'the most injurious to the Health and Preservation of Mankind'. It is perhaps fortunate for Thomas Tryon's peace of mind that he did not have access to modern microscope technology. Even without this the combination of damp beds, fleas, bed bugs and lice resulted in many a sleepless night for travellers, and was no doubt a source of disease as well.

Whatever the state of the accommodation those arriving at an inn on a Saturday evening would normally expect to stay for 2 nights before resuming their journey on the Monday morning. The fortnightly stage-coach from London to Edinburgh broke its journey at Newcastle for this day of rest, both to give the passengers a much needed respite from the continual jolting and to comply with the statutory prohibition of commercial traffic on Sundays. As Joan Parkes has noted private travellers were able to move freely provided that they obtained a warrant signed by a Justice, perhaps not the easiest procedure to comply with if one arrived at a town late on a Saturday afternoon. A contemporary witness is the Dutchman William Schellink (1623-1678) who travelled widely in England in the years 1661 to 1663:

> In the whole of England it is not permitted to travel on the Sabbath by water or on land or in any vehicle, or to hire horses, carriages, or coaches. As we did not want to have to pay a fine of 10 shillings per head we applied to the Lord Mayor of Gravesend for a free pass, which we obtained by pretending that we had some dispatches or secret letters for their Excellencies the Dutch ambassadors.

As with the practice of taking one's own sheets on a tour the prejudice against travelling on a Sunday had a long innings. We should acknowledge however that in the seventeenth century the custom of the Sabbath break was not just a matter of convenience, or of legal or social compulsion. For many people it was central to their understanding of how to live a good life. The Norwich Three, travelling fast around 26 counties in 1634, nevertheless rested on successive Sundays at York and Carlisle, attending church in the morning and sight-seeing and visiting in the afternoon. A devout believer would feel serious qualms of conscience if forced to travel on a Sunday, as is shown by Ralph Thoresby's diary entry for 23rd February 1678:

> Die Dom. Constrained utterly against my mind to travel from Royston to Stamford, though the Lord's Day; but either do so, or be left upon the road about a hundred miles from home and not knowing a foot of the way.

Even as late as the end of the Napoleonic wars Jane Austen, writing her last completed novel *Persuasion*, could cite the moral disapproval of Sunday travelling as a factor in Anne Elliott's assessment of her cousin Mr Elliott:

> He certainly knew what was right, nor could she fix on any one article of moral duty evidently transgressed; but yet she would have been afraid to answer for his conduct. She distrusted the past, if not the present. The names which occasionally dropt of former associates, the allusions to former practices and pursuits, suggested suspicions not favourable of what he had been. She saw that there had been bad habits; that Sunday-travelling had been a common thing; that there had been a period of his life (and probably not a short one) when he had been, at least, careless on all serious matters.

Anne Elliott's gut feeling that her cousin is unsuitable as a suitor does of course prove fully justified, although the assessment as a whole, and not solely the reference to Sunday-travelling, is surely meant to suggest an outdated punctiliousness deriving from her isolated provincial upbringing. Walter Scott probably better reflects the general opinion of the early eighteenth century when he casts a nostalgic glance back at the old customs of the road:

> There was, in the days of which I write, an old-fashioned custom on the English road, which I suspect is now obsolete, or practised only by the vulgar. Journeys of length being made on horseback, and of course by brief stages, it was usual always to make a halt on the Sunday in some town where the traveller might attend divine service, and his horse have the benefit of the day of rest, the institution of which is as humane to our brute labourers as profitable to ourselves. A counterpart to this decent practice, and a remnant of old English hospitality, was that the landlord of a principal inn laid aside his character of publican on the seventh day, and

invited the guests who chanced to be within his walls to take a part of his family beef and pudding. This invitation was usually complied with all whose distinguished rank did not induce them to think compliance a derogation; and the proposal of a bottle of wine after dinner, to drink the landlord's health, was the only recompense ever offered or accepted.

With this further mention of Walter Scott it is time to consider the attitudes of English travellers as they approached, and in some cases, crossed, the Scottish border.

Crossing the Border

As is the case in many other parts of the world the border between England and Scotland is an accidental historical construct. During most of the Roman occupation the effective frontier of the province of Britannia ran along the line of Hadrian's Wall which, in Northumberland, follows the Tyne from Wallsend to Newcastle and then the northern rim of the Tyne valley as far as the Portgate where it crossed Dere Street (now the A68) running north from Corbridge to the forward bases at High Rochester (Otterburn) and Newstead. While the Romans exercised military, political and economic influence in the region north of the wall the available evidence suggests that this was mainly concentrated along the northern line of Dere Street itself and in the area north of the Solway at the west end of Hadrian's Wall. There is little archaeological or documentary evidence of significant Roman influence in the greater part of Northumberland, that area which lies north of the wall but between Dere Street and the coast. A road, popularly known as the Devil's Causeway, branched off Dere Street 4 miles north of Corbridge and ran from there to Berwick, being connected to the fort at High Rochester by a cross-road from Whittingham. These are however the only Roman roads identified in the whole region bounded by Hadrian's Wall on the south, Dere Street on the west and the Firth of Forth on the north. This substantial area was the home of the Votadini or Otadini, a people with their main settlement at Traprain Law north of the Tweed. Probably a community of subsistence livestock farmers they appear to have co-existed peaceably with the Romans, neither posing a military threat nor offering any economic incentive for annexation of their territory.

Around the year 600, 2 centuries after the withdrawal of the Roman army, the Votadini reappear in Aneirin's great heroic poem *Y*

Gododdin. Although one of the founding texts of the Welsh literary tradition the poem celebrates the group of 300 brave warriors (echoes of Thermopylae) who marched south from Edinburgh and met their deaths fighting against enormous odds with the Anglo Saxon invaders. Catraeth, the site of the battle commemorated in the poem, is better known to English speakers as Catterick, a town which (like Otterburn) has been associated with the military for nearly 2,000 years. The Roman governor Agricola had established this base during his advance into the north in 79 AD, and there is evidence of its importance as a supply base in the letters written two decades later from Vindolanda, the pre-Hadrianic fort lying on the Stanegate to the north of Haltwhistle.

In the centuries after the battle of Catraeth the old territory of the Votadini/Gododdin was incorporated into the Anglo Saxon kingdom of Northumbria which at least for a period extended from the Humber to the Firth of Forth. The collapse of that kingdom and the subsequent centralisation of power in both England and Scotland led over a long period to the establishment of the present border, though not before Berwick had changed hands at least a dozen times. This did not however bring peace between the two kingdoms. State warfare continued regularly, if intermittently, into the sixteenth century and the crushing defeat of the Scottish army at Flodden Field in September 1513. And, whether or not the kingdoms were officially at war, the armed cattle raiders known as reivers ensured that the border zone remained a dangerous and uncertain region. It is therefore no coincidence that Northumberland has the highest concentration of castles and other fortified buildings of any English county.

Had this been merely historical baggage then it is reasonable to suppose that the old antagonisms might have substantially evaporated by the time of the Act of Union of 1707. Unfortunately the military threat remained so that for our travellers the antagonisms were a matter of contemporary politics. In September 1640, only 6 years after the visit of the Norwich Three, a Scottish army invaded Northumberland at the invitation of the English Parliament, defeated a royalist army at Newburn Ford and marched unopposed into Newcastle. The Treaty of Ripon left the Scots in occupation of Northumberland and Durham, and with an allowance of £850 per day to cover the costs of their occupation. Though this sum appears modest to modern ears it should be set against Brereton's estimate of Newcastle's annual revenue of between £5000 and £6000. Once here the Scots stayed until they were finally induced to leave in January 1647, handing over King Charles to the Parliamentary government and receiving the first £100,000 of a £400,000 compensation payment. In the meantime the Scots had ensured that the occupation paid for itself, a policy that does much to explain the legacy of bitterness among the people of Northumberland. In *Chorographia*, published in 1649, William Gray quotes the local proverb, "A Scot, a rat, and a Newcastle grindstone, you may find all the world over". The last Scottish army to invade England came south a century later in 1745, though this time by way of Carlisle. This invasion, the defeat of the Jacobites at Culloden, and the subsequent reprisals against the Scots created a further legacy of mistrust and bitterness on both sides of the border.

The Norwich Three, the earliest of our leisure travellers, turned westward from Newcastle towards Hexham, "having no stomachs for Tweed, nor those inhabitants". Three decades after the union of the Crowns they still considered Scotland to be hostile territory. 64 years later, as we have seen, Celia Fiennes made her brief unhappy excursion across the border, demonstrating that her customary broad-mindedness did not extend to those whom she regarded as foreigners. Joseph Taylor, writing of the tour made by him and his companions in 1705, gives a more detailed account of the approach to the border:

August the 31st about 6 in the morning we left Berwick and took a post boy with us: about 2 miles distance we came to a small dike which is the boundary between England and Scotland. Upon our first entrance into Scotland we embraced one another with all the friendship imaginable. We were now got into a very desolate country, and could see nothing about us but barren mountains and the black northern seas; we often cast our eyes back at dear England, and were pleased so long as we could but see the top of the mountain Cheviot, but at length that also withdrew from our eyes. We had a great deal of cause to leave our country with regret, upon account of the discouragements we received from every body, even upon the borders of Scotland, and by what I could gather from the discourse of all persons I conversed with, I concluded I was going into the most barbarous country in the world. Every one reckoned our journey extremely dangerous, and told us 'twould be difficult to escape with our lives, much less without the distemper of the country, Yet notwithstanding all these sad representations we resolved to proceed, and stand by one another to the last. The first County we came into in

Scotland was Meres or Merch formerly called Berwickshire, because it belonged to that place, the Tweed for 8 miles divides Northumberland and this country. The first place we came to was called Eyton, a little village on the right hand side of the road; there were but a few little cottages together, surrounded with a small row of trees, without any place of entertainment.

If we set aside the somewhat stagey self-dramatisation this passage encapsulates many of the attitudes displayed by English travellers on their approach to the border. It is an accident of history that Berwick lies in England rather than in Scotland but, that being so, the Scottish traveller arriving in England came immediately to a substantial town with a lively garrison population whereas the English traveller going north was faced with miles of bleak wilderness and no centre of civilisation south of Edinburgh. As Celia Fiennes discovered the same was true for those travellers who cross the border further west. From Aitchison Bank she would have had to travel 18 miles to the next town with no guarantee of finding accommodation. Those travellers who reached Edinburgh were impressed, but south of Edinburgh the concept of Scottish culture was a contradiction in terms. That this was not wholly an English perception is confirmed by James Boswell when as a young man he set out from Edinburgh on his road to the fleshpots of London and found himself stranded for several hours at Eyton as a result of an accident to his carriage:

Never did I pass three hours more unhappily. We were set down in a cold ale-house in a little dirty village. We had a beefsteak ill-dressed and had nothing to drink but thick muddy beer. We were both out of humour so that we could not speak. We tried to sleep but in vain. We only got a drowsy headache. We were scorched by the fire on the one hand and shivering with frost on the other. At last our chaise came, and we got to Berwick about twelve at night. We had a slice of hard dry toast, a bowl of warm negus, and went comfortable to bed.

It is fair to make the point that some travellers, for instance William Brereton and Daniel Defoe, registered no disquiet in visiting Scotland, but for many crossing the border was a venture into the unknown. The combination of poor agricultural land and centuries of insecurity made the prospect even more dismal for seventeenth and eighteenth century travellers, and no doubt Celia Fiennes was not the only one to turn back at the first village. It is a pleasing coincidence that our 1704 lawyer returned to England through that same village, expressing heartfelt thanks for finding himself once again on English soil:

> I set out early in the morning the next day [18th April] and came through Ackle ffecken [Ecclefechan], a small village, and so to Allison Bank, another small village, and the last I was at in Scotland, and here I dined. And soon after, setting out for Carlisle, I passed a small stream and was, to my joy, on English ground, and hope I shall never go into such a country again. I had heard much talk of it, and had a mind to see it for variety; and indeed it was so to me, for I thank my God, I never saw such another, and must conclude with the poet, Cleveland, that:
>> Had Cain been Scot, God sure had changed his doom,
>> Not made him wander, but confined him home.

The reference is to *The Rebel Scot* by John Cleveland (1613-1658), a poem written in response to the Scottish occupation of the northern counties in the 1640s. Extensive extracts from this lively and libellous poem can be found in the *New Oxford Book of Seventeenth Century Verse* edited by Alastair Fowler (OUP 1991). More than a century later Charles Churchill, a friend of John Wilkes and a savage critic of Scottish and allegedly Jacobite influence at the court of King George III, picks up the theme of Cain in a satirical curse on himself:

> Of those evils which, to stamp men curst,
> Hell keeps in store for vengeance, may the worst
> Light on my head; and in my day of woe,
> To make the cup of bitterness o'erflow,
> May I be scorned by every man of worth,
> Wander, like Cain, a vagabond on earth,
> Bearing about a hell in my own mind,
> Or be to Scotland for my life confined.

By 1763 however, when Churchill wrote these lines in his poem *The Conference*, travel to and from Scotland had become a matter of undramatic routine, leaving it to London-based politicians and pamphleteers to fan the flames of old disputes.

For as long as the speed of travel was restricted to the speed of the horse the crossing of the border, and the long transit of the Merse, symbolised the passage from English civilisation to a bleaker and more backward culture. To the classically educated gentlemen who passed this way there would undoubtedly have been echoes of the attitude of the Greeks to the barbarian societies on their frontiers. Charles Harper reminds us that such attitudes persisted throughout the period covered by this study:

> "Seeing Scotland, Madam," said Dr Johnson, in answer to Mrs Thrale's expressed wish to visit that country, "is only seeing a worse England. It is seeing the flower gradually fade away to the naked stalk". This bitter saying of the Doctor's comes vividly to mind when leaving Berwick on the way to Edinburgh. Passing the outskirts of the town at a point marked on the Ordance map with unexplained name of "Conundrum", the country grows bare and treeless on approaching the sea, and at Lamberton Toll, three miles north, where "Berwick Bounds" are reached and Scotland entered, the scene is desolate in the extreme. The cottage to the left of the road at this point, formerly the toll-house of the turnpike-gate that stood here, is a famous place, rivalling Gretna Green for the runaway matches, legalised at the gate until 1856, when changes in the law rendered a part of the once-familiar notice in the window out-of-date. It ran, "Ginger-beer sold here, and marriages performed on the most reasonable terms"; an announcement which for combination of the trivial and the tremendous it would be difficult to beat.

Those who crossed the border from Berwick might be treated to the sight of the washerwomen of the Merse. For a tailpiece to this chapter we turn therefore to the virtuoso description offered by our anonymous lawyer on his journey in 1704:

> This was a fine sunshiny day, and a very hot one, perhaps, as ever was known for the time of year; and as I passed along over several brooks, were women washing their linen after the manner of their country, which I was altogether unacquainted with. Their way was, they put their linen in a tub about knee-high, and got into the tub without shoes or stockings, and holding up their clothes to their middles, to save them from soap, trod round and round upon the linen till the water was foul, and then poured it out and put in clean, till the linen was so white as they thought fit. At first I wondered at the sight, and thought they would have been ashamed, as I was, and have let down their clothes till I was by; but though some would let them down half way their thighs, others went round and round, and sometimes with another, without letting down their clothes at all, or taking any notice of me; and particularly a pair of young wenches that were washing together, at my coming by, pulled up their clothes the higher and, when I was by, stood still and fell a-laughing. I was surprised at this and was resolved to say somewhat to the next I came to that showed no more modesty than these had done. It happened the next was a

sturdy old woman and the water spattering up, and the sun shining hot on her skin, I told her she would spoil her breeches. 'And look, your honour,' says she' 'these are but old ones; they have 2 great holes in them already,' and, seeing I had not assurance enough to stand it, cried after me, 'and do but see how shagged they are'. And still, when I was at a further distance, said she, 'When you go to England I must get you to buy me a new pair'. So being out of reach of her thumb and nails I ventured to look back, and saw her holding up one leg as if she meant to show me what a dismal condition those breeches of hers were in, and still she had something to say, 'Spoil my breeches, brother' quoth she. I never durst to say anything to any of them afterwards.

CHAPTER 5

NORTH ON BUSINESS

Someone mentioned to Socrates that a certain person hadn't changed his ways as a result of travelling. "I can well believe it," replied Socrates, "He took himself along on the journey".

Michel de Montaigne, *On Solitude*

In the first three chapters we followed a chronological sequence in considering visits to the region between 1502 and 1705. As we move into the eighteenth and nineteenth centuries we shall adopt a more thematic arrangement. In this chapter therefore we look at four individuals who came north on business, and will follow this with a chapter on industrial and agricultural surveys of the region.

The tours undertaken in the seventeenth century all followed either the Great North Road or the main cross-road from Tynemouth to Carlisle. A common feature of these 17th century tours is that Northumberland was a stage on the journey rather than its destination. In both these aspects they differ from the survey tours undertaken in the sixteenth century by Bowes and Elleker, Leland and Camden. For a variety of reasons the eighteenth century visitors whom we shall consider in this chapter and in subsequent chapters often made Northumberland their destination and travelled around it more widely than those who came north in the previous century. From Daniel Defoe onwards we will also find several visitors who introduce a clear political or cultural agenda into the accounts of their tours, a development which is interesting in itself and which also leads to the observation and recording of matters that might otherwise have escaped notice. While, like Socrates and Montaigne, we may doubt whether they learned much from their travels, we can find much to interest us in their perceptions of the region and of its people.

On Her Majesty's Secret Service

Daniel Defoe (1660-1731) first came to Newcastle on 30th September 1706. Travelling under the assumed name of Alexander Goldsmith he was on his way to Edinburgh as an agent for Robert Harley, Minister of the North in Queen Anne's government. His mission was to foster support for the proposed Act of Union and to rubbish the opposition. As with other travellers he found the roads difficult:

> I have had a severe journey hither but it begins to mend now and the two last have been the only days without rain since I left London, which has made me longer getting here than I expected.

He was delayed in Newcastle for an extra day by the failure of one of his horses "worn out with the fatigue of the journey" and had to claim an extra £12 to reimburse the cost of a replacement to enable him to continue his journey to Morpeth and Edinburgh. This was the first of several visits that Defoe paid to Scotland and, although Defoe is often desperately unreliable, I see no reason to doubt the accuracy of the statement in his preface to *A Tour through the Whole Island*, at least in so far as it relates to his acquaintance with Northumberland:

> Besides these several journeys in England he has also lived some time in Scotland, and has travelled critically over great part of it; he has viewed the north part of England and the south part of Scotland five several times over; all of which is hinted here, to let the readers know what reason they will have to be satisfied with the authority of the relation, and that the accounts here given are not the produce of a cursory view, or raised upon the borrowed lights of other observers.

There is a local tradition that Defoe took up residence in Newcastle for a couple of years between 1710 and 1712, sometimes with the embellishment that he wrote *Robinson Crusoe* while living in a house in Gateshead near the Tyne Bridge, the supposed site of the house being marked with the traditional blue plaque. None of his recent biographers give any credence to this tradition and, of the 64 letters from 1710-1712 included in the collected edition, only 2 were written from Newcastle. The first of these is dated 3rd October 1712, when Defoe was once again en route to Edinburgh, travelling this time under the name of Claude Guilot and reporting to Harley on Jacobite agitation in Newcastle:

> I'll trouble your Lordship no more with these follies. My stay among them is so small as cannot go far in turning such a stream, but I endeavour to undeceive the most reasonable and moderate and leave them to work upon the rest.

The great floods have hindered my travelling for some time. The like rains, especially on the border, having not been known for a long time.

Another letter dated in the same month is endorsed by Harley's office as having been posted from Newcastle but in it Defoe simply reports on the current state of affairs in Edinburgh. We do know that Defoe had an interest in the *Newcastle Gazette* published by Joseph Button, a bookseller with a shop on the old Tyne Bridge, but this is not so significant as it may sound since it was part of his job as a government agent to exercise clandestine influence on newspapers in many towns.

What Defoe has to say about Newcastle is found in his *Tour* where he describes the town as "a spacious, extended, infinitely populous place" with "the longest and largest key for landing and lading goods that is to be seen in England". After commenting on impressive public buildings such as the Mayor's house, the Exchange, the Keelmen's Hospital and the Barber Surgeons' Hall, Defoe gives his overall assessment of the town and its industry:

> The situation of the town to the landward is exceeding unpleasant, and the buildings very close and old, standing on the declivity of two exceeding high hills which, together with the smoke of the coals, makes it not the pleasantest place in the world to live in; but it is made amends abundantly by the goodness of the river, which runs between the two hills and which, as I said, bringing ships up to the very keys and fetching the coals down from the country, makes it a place of very great business. Here are also two articles of trade which are particularly occasioned by the coals, and these are glass-houses and salt pans; the first are at the town itself, the last are at Shields, seven miles below the town; but their coals are brought chiefly from the town. It is a prodigious quantity of coals which those salt works consume; and the fires make such a smoke, that we saw it ascend in clouds over the hills, four miles before we came to Durham, which is at least sixteen miles from the place...........
>
> It is not only enriched by the coal trade, but there are also very considerable merchants in it who carry on foreign trade to diverse parts of the world, especially to Holland, Hamburg, Norway, and the Baltic.
>
> They build ships here to perfection, I mean as to strength and firmness and to bear the sea; and as the coal trade occasions a demand for such strong ships, a great many are built here. This gives an addition to the merchants' business in requiring a supply of all sorts of naval stores to fit out those ships. Here is also a considerable manufacture of hardware, or wrought iron, lately erected after the manner of Sheffield, which is very

helpful for employing the poor of which this town has always a prodigious number.

Like Celia Fiennes Defoe was brought up in a strong noncomformist tradition but differed from her in that his family background was in trade. Defoe himself was a persistent, if unsuccessful, entrepreneur. This commercial experience is reflected in his recognition of the variety of industry and business based in the north east and, crucially, of the way in which these various industries depended on each other for their existence and growth. For Defoe work and trade, rather than ownership of land, were the foundations of a prosperous society and he took every opportunity in his *Tour* and in his other writings to emphasise the critical importance of manufacture. Work is also a key theme in his novels where his heroes and heroines all work hard, if often disreputably, to earn their living and, in most cases, their ultimate fortune. In this Defoe differs sharply from most other novelists writing in the eighteenth century. He was to use his knowledge of Newcastle industry in his 1722 novel *Colonel Jack* when the hero and his friends, having deserted from the army, seek refuge in Newcastle in the hope of securing a sea-passage to London:

> We contrived to come into Newcastle in the dusk of the evening; and even we durst not venture into the public part of the town, but made down towards the river, something below the town where some glass-houses stand. Here we knew not what to do with ourselves but, guided by our fate, we put a good face upon the matter and went into an ale-house, sat down and called for a pint of beer.

The setting here is the quayside below Byker where the old industry is remembered in the street names of Glasshouse Street and Bottlehouse Street. Colonel Jack obtains a sea-passage, but not to London. He and his friends are made drunk and then kidnapped by a rogue dealer who puts them on board a ship bound for Virginia where they must serve a term of years as white slave-workers. Like Robinson Crusoe and Moll Flanders Colonel Jack displays all Defoe's customary virtues of hard work, thrift and ingenuity to make his fortune out of this seeming disaster.

Defoe however put his local knowledge to more immediate and practical use. I have mentioned above his reference to the Keelmens'

Hospital, an institution visited by Joseph Taylor and his friends on their journey in 1705. In the *Tour* Defoe gives his own brief comment:

> Here is a large hospital built by contribution of the keelmen, by way of Friendly Society, for the maintenance of the poor of their fraternity, and which, had it not met with discouragements from those who ought rather to have assisted so good a work, might have been a noble provision for that numerous and laborious people. The keel men are those who manage the lighters, which they call keels, by which the coals are taken from the staithes or wharfs and carried on board the ships, to load them for London.

The background to this "discouragement" was the attempt in 1711 by the mine owners to gain control of the hospital financed by the contributions of the keelmen. After much pampleteering and lobbying by Defoe the House of Commons ruled in favour of the keelmen.

Defoe's pamphlets on the issue make clear that the 1d per tide levy (Defoe and Joseph Taylor agree on the amount) was deducted from the keelmen's wages under a voluntary form of PAYE. The sums involved may have been substantial since Defoe estimates the total number of keelmen as 1600, 400 of whom spent the winters in Scotland with their families. Defoe's complaint is that the employers were failing to apply the deductions to the proper purpose of financing the hospital. While Defoe was perhaps all too willing to piggy-back on multifarious causes to make political points I feel that, for whatever reason, he was genuinely committed to the cause of the keelmen. Whether this supports the tradition of his residence in Newcastle I leave for others to judge. He was certainly in the area enough to note the Northumberland accent:

> I must not quit Northumberland without taking notice that the natives of the country, of the ancient original race or families, are distinguished by a shibboleth upon their tongues, namely a difficulty in pronouncing the letter *R*, which they cannot deliver from their tongues without a hollow jarring in their throat, by which they are plainly known, as a foreigner is in pronouncing the *Th*. This they call the Northumbrian *R*, and the natives value themselves upon that imperfection because, forsooth, it shews the antiquity of their blood.

He also picks up the Scottish theme, in the novel and interesting context of Scottish influence on local buildings:

79

......you have in England abundance of Scotsmen, Scots customs, words, habits, and usages, even more than becomes them; nay, even the buildings in the towns and in the villages imitate the Scots almost all over Northumberland; witness their building the houses with the stairs (to the second floor) going up on the outside of the house, so that one family may live below and another above, without going in at the same door, which is the Scots way of living and which we see in Alnwick and Warkworth and several other towns. Witness also their setting their corn up in great numbers of small stacks without doors, not making use of any barns, only a particular building which they call a barn but which is itself no more than a threshing-floor, into which they take one of those small stacks at a time and thresh it out, and then take in another.

Perhaps his most notable and original contribution is his famous description of the ascent of the Cheviot. Reading the preface to Volume 1 of the *Tour* Defoe promises a full and true description of the northern counties, but "without loading our work with fragments of antiquity, and dressing up the wilds of the borders as a paradise, which are indeed but a wilderness". This comment mirrors the general attitude of the travellers that we have met so far although we should note Defoe's impatient dismissal of antiquarianism. All travellers experienced the space between towns as a penance to be endured if they were to arrive at the next centre of comparative civilisation, the distance between Berwick and Edinburgh being the longest and most forbidding. Only Celia Fiennes, in her appreciation of the Tyne valley, suggests that there might be pleasure in the travelling as well as in the arrival. Yet by the time of writing the introduction to Volume 3 of the *Tour* Defoe has modified his view:

I have yet the largest, though not the most populous, part of Britain to give you an account of, nor is it less capable of satisfying the most curious traveller. Though, as in some places things may stand more remote from one another and there may, perhaps, be more waste ground to go over; yet 'tis certain a traveller spends no waste hours if his genius will be satisfied with just observations. The wildest part of the country is full of variety, the most mountainous places have their rarities to oblige the curious and give constant employ to the enquiries of a diligent observer, making the passing over them more pleasant than the traveller could expect, or that the reader perhaps at first sight will think possible.

Defoe's account of his ascent of the Cheviot is worth quoting in full:

Cheviot Hill or Hills are justly esteemed the highest in this part of England, and of Scotland also; and, if I may judge, I think 'tis higher a great deal than the mountain of Mairock in Galloway, which they say is two miles high.

When we came to Wooller we got another guide to lead us to the top of the hill; for, by the way, though there are many hills and reachings for many miles, which are all called Cheviot Hills, yet there is one Pico or Master-Hill, higher than all the rest by a great deal, which, at a distance, looks like the Pico-Teneriffe at the Canaries, and is so high, that I remember it is seen plainly from the Rosemary-Top in the East Riding of Yorkshire, which is near sixty miles. We prepared to clamber up this hill on foot, but our guide laughed at us, and told us we should make a long journey of it that way: But getting a horse himself, told us he would find a way for us to get up on horse-back; so we set out, having five or six country boys and young fellows, who ran on foot, volunteer to go with us; we thought they had only gone for their diversion, as if frequent for boys; but they knew well enough that we should find some occasion to employ them, and so we did, as you shall hear.

Our guide led us very artfully round to a part of the hill, where it was evident, in the winter season, not streams of water, but great rivers came pouring down from the hill in several channels, and those (at least some of them) very broad; they were overgrown on either bank with alder-trees, so close and thick, that we rode under them, as in an arbour. In one of these channels we mounted the hill, as the besiegers approach a fortified town by trenches, and were gotten a great way up, before we were well aware of it.

But, as we mounted, these channels lessened gradually, till at length we had the shelter of the trees no longer; and now we ascended till we began to see some of the high hills, which before we thought very lofty, lying under us, low and humble, as if they were part of the plain below, and yet the main hill seemed to be but beginning, or, as if we were but entering upon it.

As we mounted higher we found the hill steeper than at first, also our horses began to complain, and draw their haunches up heavily, so we went very softly: However, we moved still, and went on, till the height began to look really frightful, for, I must own, I wished myself down again; and now we found use for the young fellows that ran before us; for we began to fear, if our horses should stumble or start, we might roll down the hill together; and we began to talk of alighting, but our guide called out and said, "No, not yet, by and by you shall", and with that he bid the young fellows take our horses by the head-stalls of the bridles, and lead them. They did so, and we rode up higher still, till at length our hearts failed us all together, and we resolved to alight; and though our guide mocked us, yet he could not prevail or persuade us; so we worked it upon our feet, and with labour enough, and sometimes began to talk of going no farther.

We were the more uneasy about mounting higher, because we all had a notion, that when we came to the top, we should be just as upon a pinnacle, that the hill narrowed to a point, and we should have only room enough to stand, with a precipice every way round us; and with these apprehensions, we all sat down upon the ground, and said we would go no farther.

Our guide did not at first understand what we were apprehensive of; but at last by our discourse he perceived the mistake, and then not mocking our fears, he told us, that indeed if it had been so, we had been in the right, but he assured us, there was room enough on the top of the hill to run a race, if we thought fit, and we need not fear any thing of being blown off the precipice, as we had suggested; so he encouraging us we went on, and reached the top of the hill in about half an hour more.

I must acknowledge I was agreeably surprised, when coming to the top of the hill, I saw before me a smooth, and with respect to what we expected a most pleasant plain, of at least half a mile in diameter; and in the middle of it a large pond, or little lake of water, and the ground seeming to descend every way from the edges of the summit to the pond, took off the little terror of the first prospect; for when we walked towards the pond, we could but just see over the edge of the hill; and this little descent inwards, no doubt made the pond, the rain-water all running thither.

One of our company, a good botanist, fell to searching for simples, and, as he said, found some nice plants, which he seemed mightily pleased with. But as that is out of my way, so it is out of the present design. I in particular began to look about me, and to enquire what every place was which I saw more remarkably shewing it self at a distance.

The day happened to be very clear, and to our great satisfaction very calm, otherwise the height we were upon, would not have been without its dangers. We saw plainly here the smoke of the salt-pans at Shields, at the mouth of the Tyne, seven miles below New Castle; and which was south about forty miles. The sea, that is the German ocean, was as if but just at the foot of the hill, and our guide pointed to shew us the Irish Sea: But if he could see it, knowing it in particular, and where exactly to look for it, it was so distant, that I could not say, I was assured I saw it. We saw likewise several hills, which he told us were in England, and others in the west of Scotland, but their names were too many for us to remember, and we had no materials there to take minutes. We saw Berwick east, and the hills called Soutra Hills north, which are in sight of Edinburgh. In a word there was a surprising view of both the united kingdoms, and we were far from repenting the pains we had taken.

Nor were we so afraid now as when we first mounted the sides of the hill, and especially we were made ashamed of those fears, when to our amazement, we saw a clergyman, and another gentleman, and two ladies, all on horse-back, come up to the top of the hill, with a guide also as we had, and without alighting at all, and only to satisfy their curiosity, which they did it seems. This indeed made us look upon one another with a smile, to think how we were frighted, at our first coming up the hill: And thus it is in most things in nature; fear magnifies the object, and represents things frightful at first sight, which are presently made easy when they grow familiar.

Satisfied with this view, and not at all thinking our time or pains ill bestowed, we came down the hill by the same route that we went up; with this remark by the way, that whether on horse-back or on foot we found it much more troublesome, and also tiresome to come down than to go up.

When we were down, our guide carried us not to the town of Wooller, where we were before, but to a single house, which they call Wooller Haugh-head, and is a very good inn, better indeed than we expected, or than we had met with, except at Kelso, for many days journey. Here we had very good provision, very well dressed, and excellent wine. The house is in England, but the people that kept it were Scots; yet every thing was very well done, and we were mighty glad of the refreshment we found there.

Defoe employs all his skill as a novelist in this dramatic but realistic description of his expedition. Having screwed up the tension in his lengthy account of the ascent he deftly deflates his own achievement by recounting the arrival of the clergyman's party sauntering up to the summit as if for a Sunday afternoon picnic.

A Parcel of Dirty Savages

Elizabeth Montagu (1718-1800)) was perhaps the most unlikely coal owner in the history of mining in the north-east. As a girl and young woman she had been the intimate friend of Lady Margaret Hartley, the granddaughter of Defoe's employer Robert Hartley. Later, as a literary bluestocking from London she became the third wife of Edward Montagu whose previous father-in-law, John Rogers, had purchased the East Denton estate and its collieries in 1689 for £10,900. By 1743 Edward Montagu had come to the end of a long legal suit to have Rogers certified as a lunatic, and in the autumn of that year he made his first business trip to Denton to take charge of the business. Having run the business for 15 years as the appointed legal representative Edward Montagu inherited the estate on Rogers's death in 1758, and it subsequently passed to Elizabeth Montagu on Edward's own death in 1775.

As far as I can tell Elizabeth Montagu did not visit Denton until August 1758, shortly after the death of John Rogers. Given Rogers's state of health she may well have thought it tactless or impracticable to stay at Denton during his lifetime, particularly as Edward Montagu's practice, subsequently adopted by Elizabeth in her widowhood, was to make a single protracted visit each year. Edward Montagu did of course write to her from Denton, giving details of the business problems arising from Rogers's long neglect of his estates and, in one letter, telling her of a visit to Gibside:

> I dined this day sennight at Gibside, it was one of the finest summer days I ever saw. It set off to great advantage the whole vale through which the river Tyne runs, which consists of a good deal of rich land. The moors, though not so pleasing to the eye, make abundant amends by the riches of the mines.

Elizabeth Montagu was to be equally utilitarian in her assessment of the landscape and of its inhabitants, writing on her first visit that there was much rich land in the county but giving her view that agricultural methods were behind the times and a couple of years later reporting in a letter to her father:

> I had a very pleasant journey, for fine weather, like a good-natured companion, makes ordinary scenes appear cheerful and pleasant, but from the time I left Hertfordshire till I got to Doncaster the counties I passed through were dreary and barren. But, if those prospects in the other counties were brown, these in Northumberland are bleak, the people in them a parcel of dirty savages, so that I cannot say with the Psalmist that my lot is fallen in a fair ground, it is some comfort it is in a rich one.

This is 'north of Watford Junction' with a vengeance and a letter from her bluestocking friend Elizabeth Carter indicates that others of her London literary circle similarly regarded the north as being beyond the pale. For whatever reason Elizabeth Montagu did not accompany her husband to Denton in the autumn of 1759, leading Mrs Carter to congratulate her on her escape both from the northern winter and from Newcastle society:

Well, but how do you do, and what are you doing, and what are you to do? I long to hear that you are quite delivered from the terror of freezing in the arctic circle; not but your winter in London is much longer, for it lasts till July, but then you have the comfort of spending it among creatures of your own species, and in your own way.

Half a century later Jane Austen confirms that some in the south still considered Newcastle to be beyond the pale when Mrs Bennet complains about the fate of her daughter Lydia:

"It is a delightful thing, to be sure, to have a daughter well married," continued her mother, "but at the same time, Mr Bingley, it is very hard to have her taken such a way from me. They are gone down to Newcastle, a place quite northward, it seems, and there they are to stay".

Should any reader think that such attitudes are historical, and perhaps quaint, a speech by the Conservative peer Lord Howell in the House of Lords on 30th July 2013 may act as a corrective:

In beautiful rural areas [Sussex] there are worries about drilling and fracking, which I think are exaggerated, but also about trucks, deliveries, roads and disturbance, which are quite justified. However, there are large, uninhabited and desolate areas, certainly in parts of the North-east, where there is plenty of room for fracking.

While Elizabeth Montagu never changed her view that London life and society was greatly preferable to that of Newcastle the letters from her first visit already evidence a greater range of feelings than the above quotations might suggest. Her initial apprehension about the journey is tempered with irony:

In about a week we shall set out for the North, where I am to pass about three months in the delectable conversation of stewards and managers of coal mines, and this by courtesy is called good fortune and I am congratulated on it by everyone I meet.

The journey itself however did her good. Despite the fatigue of days on end in a post-chaise she felt much better on arrival than she had on departure. The house at Denton was however unfit for occupation, probably again as a result of Rogers's long illness, so she and her husband took a short lease on Carville Hall on the banks of the Tyne at Wallsend. From there she was able to view the ships sailing up and down the river and look across to the monastery at Jarrow. She must have visited Tynemouth, with regrets that she was not able to do so more often:

> We have a very good turnpike road to the sea-side, where I should pass a great deal of my time if it was not all engrossed by company, but we are in the midst of the largest neighbourhood I ever saw, and some of these gentlemen by means of coal mines have immense fortunes.

Although Carville Hall may have been bearable, Newcastle was not:

> The town of Newcastle is horrible. Like the ways of thrift it is narrow, dark and dirty, some of the streets so steep one is forced to put a drag-chain on the wheels….The streets are some of them so narrow that, if the tallow chandler ostentatiously hangs forth his candles, you have a chance to sweep them into your lap as you drive by, and I do not know how it has happened that I have not yet caught a coach full of red herrings, for we scrape the City wall on which they hang in great abundance.

Nevertheless she was to take an active part in Newcastle's social life:

> I was at a musical entertainment yesterday morning, at a concert last night, at a musical entertainment this morning. I have bespoken a play for tomorrow night, and shall go to a ball on choosing a Mayor on Monday night.

In the same month she writes to Elizabeth Carter to say that she has entered into all the diversions of the town so as not to cause offence, but at the same time acknowledges that desire of pleasure and love of dissipation are as prevalent in Newcastle as in London and, even if the diversions are less elegant and the conversation less polite, retirement from society holds no attractions for her. To judge from an earlier letter the main topic of conversation may well have grated on a sensitive London bluestocking brought up to regard 'tradesman' as a term of contempt:

> Every gentleman in the country, from the least to the greatest, is as solicitous in the pursuit of gain as a tradesman. The conversation always turns upon money; the moment you name a man, you are told what he is worth, the losses he has had, or the profit he has made by coal mines. As my mind is not naturally set to this tune, I should often be glad to change it for a song from one of your Welsh bards.

She was not however reluctant to celebrate their own financial success when it arrived. In January 1765 they opened a major new mine on the Denton estate and a few months later she wrote to Lord Lyttleton:

I assure your Lordship the coal fires which Mr Montagu mentioned were to me *feux de joye*. I believe we have opened a noble source of future plenty, but it is present poverty. We are at present the poorer a great deal, for a mine at first opening has a prodigious swallow; when it begins to disgorge it makes noble amends. Indeed everything is very encouraging to the coal trade. Wood is every day decreasing, so that all the Counties which have not inland coal are to be supplied from the north; the increase of London is a prodigious advantage to the trade, the improvement of mechanics has made our business more easy and more sure, and all the people of fortune who have worked mines have grown rich.

Daniel Defoe could not have expressed it better, and would have agreed wholeheartedly with the sentiment that the growth of London underpinned the commercial prosperity of the other parts of England. After the death of her husband in 1775 Elizabeth Montagu continued to manage and expand the Denton estates, rejoicing in the flow of funds to her bankers in London. Writing to Mrs Carter from Denton Hall she makes clear that her view of the miners remained the same as on her first journey to the north:

I am well situated for airing on the edge of a turnpike road, and the said road commands as good a prospect as any in this part of the country, but the amenity of our southern countries is not to be found here. The people here are little better than savages, and their countenances bear the marks of hard labour and total ignorance. Our pitmen are literally as black as a coal; they earn much more than labourers, their children get a shilling a day at 9 or 10 years old, but they are so barbarous and uncultivated that they know no use of money but to buy much meat and liquor with it. They eat as well as the substantial tradesmen in great towns, but they are ragged and dirty, and their wives are idle and drunken, so that while they live in plenty they present to your view an air of misery, poverty, and oppression. These pitmen marry and multiply in order to be rich, for their children add to their prosperity. They are useful persons to the general commonwealth, but considered separately a strange set of barbarians. As the children are so early sent into the mines I am afraid it will be impossible ever to civilise them, but if I lived here I should attempt it, by establishing some little school amongst them.

A letter written some years later is interesting both in attesting the scale of the Denton business and in suggesting that she had by then achieved greater reconciliation between her literary life and the demands of her business:

> I have now above 500 men at work below ground in the pits and above sixty in a wheatfield reaping, not to speak of the bricks, tiles, the tar manufactory etc going on at the waterside. My late purchased colliery is now going on very successfully.....The fresh air and fine exercise will I hope preserve my health through all fatigues of business. Here I have the satisfaction of finding all my affairs in great order and prosperity, and I enjoy many solid and substantial blessings, but for the pleasures of the imagination and the delights of rural life I cannot enjoy them here. I live in a great beehive, and though as the queen bee I do not work myself yet, like her Majesty, I have care of the collected treasures.

Mrs Montagu was to live on until 1800 but in her later years her nephew Matthew Montagu took most of the responsibility for running the Denton estate, allowing his aunt to live out her life among her remaining friends in her beloved London.

A Man with a Mission

John Wesley (1703-1791) first came to Newcastle in late May 1742. He had already established Methodist communities in London and in Bristol, where he had preached with success to the Kingswood colliers. Lady Huntingdon, a consistent patron of Methodist preachers, suggested that he might find similar success at Newcastle. He realised immediately that there was work to be done:

> We came to Newcastle about six and, after a short refreshment, walked into the town. I was surprised: so much drunkenness, cursing and swearing (even from the mouths of little children) do I never remember to have seen and heard before in so small a compass of time. Surely this place is ripe for Him who 'came not to call the righteous, but sinners to repentance'.

Were he to walk out in the evening on Quayside in the 21st century he might find that much remains unchanged. On this first visit he preached twice in Sandgate on 30th May, gathering a crowd of many hundreds and collecting the first contributions towards the building of the Orphan House, the largest meeting house in England. He was back in December 1742, when he arranged the purchase of the land on which the Orphan House was to be built, and again in March and April 1743 when:

> I met a gentleman in the streets cursing and swearing in so dreadful a manner that I could not but stop him. He soon grew calmer; told me he must treat me with a glass of wine; and that he would come and hear me, only he was afraid I should say something against fighting of cocks.

Wesley no doubt accepted the glass of wine since, while believing both tea and coffee to be bad for health, he happily drank moderate amounts of alcohol. On 8th March he rode to Chowdene south of Gateshead, describing it as 'the very Kingswood of the North', where he noted in particular the children of this mining community:

> Twenty or thirty wild children ran round us, as soon as we came, staring as in amaze. They could not properly be said to be either clothed or naked. One of the largest (a girl of about fifteen) had a piece of a ragged, dirty blanket some way hung about her, and a kind of cap on her head, of the same cloth and colour.

3 weeks later he rode to Plessey, south-west of Blyth, where his diary entry evidences his empathy with the miners:

> I had a great desire to visit a little village called Plessey, about ten measured miles north of Newcastle. It is inhabited by colliers only, and such as had been always in the first rank for savage ignorance and wickedness of every kind. Their grand assembly used to be on the Lord's Day; on which men, women, and children met together, to dance, fight, curse, and swear, and play at chuck, ball, span-farthing, or whatever came next to hand. I felt great compassion for these poor creatures, from the time I heard of them first; and the more because all men seemed to despair of them.

At Chowdene and at Plessey, as at the Sandgate in Newcastle, he preached in the open air to those who gathered around him, often in great numbers. However Wesley's 'great compassion' for the miners did not extend to the forgiveness of those who accepted conversion and then fell back into old habits. Methodist congregations were subject to periodic purges and Wesley records in his journal for 12th April the expulsion of 64 members from the Newcastle congregation since the beginning of the year:

Number	Reason for Expulsion
29	Lightness and carelessness
17	Drunkenness
4	Railing and evil-speaking
3	Quarrelling and brawling
3	Habitual, wilful lying
2	Retailing spirituous liquors
2	Cursing and swearing
2	Habitual Sabbath-breaking
1	Idleness and laziness
1	Beating his wife
64	

Nehemian Curnock, the editor of his Journals, terms this purge "an admirable example of the thoroughness of Wesley's visitations". Others may find in it evidence of intolerance and of an obsession with control. It is interesting to note that over the same period 76 members left the congregation of their own accord for reasons which give a fair summary of the social pressures operating against the Methodists:

Number	Reason for Leaving
14	Their ministers would not give them the sacrament
12	Parental opposition
9	Because they did not wish to be laughed at
9	Opposition of husbands or wives
7	Persuaded against by their acquaintances
5	Because people said such bad things of the Society
5	Master or mistress would not allow them to come
3	Lack of time
3	So as not to lose the allowance given to the poor
2	Too far off
2	Because Thomas Naisbit was in the Society
1	Because people in the street were so rude
1	Because she was afraid of falling into fits
1	Because he would not turn his back on his baptism
1	Because the Methodists were mere Church of England men
1	Because it was time enough to serve God yet
76	

While the last reason, or excuse, is reminiscent of Augustine's famour prayer "Lord give me chastity - but not yet" the first reason, that ministers would not offer communion to Methodists, points to a crucial area of debate within Methodism. Until the end of his life Wesley saw himself as trying to revive the Church of England from within, but the Methodist demand for more frequent administration of communion was continually denied by the church, which was based in its traditional cathedral cities and country parishes and had very few ministers in the new industrial towns. Nearly half a century later Wesley finally ordained the first specifically Methodist ministers, thus precipitating the breach which he had spent his life trying to avoid. Unless "lightness and carelessness" is, as it may well be, a euphemistic catch-all it is surprising that sexual immorality plays no apparent part in any of the departures (voluntary or involuntary). Wesley was always flustered by evidence of sexuality, describing the pictures in Seaton Delaval Hall as being such that "an honest heathen would be ashamed to receive under his own roof, unless he designed his wife and daughters should be common prostitutes". There is no doubt too that sexual love too openly expressed could be a reason for members to leave their congregations. In June 1764 Wesley records as one of the reasons for the decline in the Weardale society that:

Most of the liveliest in the society were the single men and women, and several of these in a little time contracted an inordinate affection for each other, whereby they so grieved the Holy Spirit of God that He in great measure departed from them.

This profoundly inhuman comment comes from a man who effectively abandoned his own wife a mere 2 weeks after their marriage, making it clear to her that his constant journeying and preaching took absolute priority over any claims that she might have had on his time and attention.

Wesley preached in the open air at Sandgate, Plessey and elsewhere because the refusal of Church of England parsons to allow itinerant Methodists to occupy their pulpits forced him into the role of a field-preacher. It was however a role that he came to relish and his practice in going to the people, rather than expecting them to come to him in church, is reminiscent of the way in which early Northumbrian missionaries such as Paulinus and Aidan set aside the trappings of nobility and spoke to the people on their own level. However, if

Wesley was often intolerant of dissent within his flock, the local magistrates could show an equal determination to maintain public order in the face of indecorous demonstrations of Methodist 'enthusiasm'. In July 1743, as a result of a disturbance which took place during one of his preaching sessions at the foot of Sandhill, the Mayor of Newcastle banned him from preaching there. Wesley accepted the decision but argued that *agents provocateurs* had initiated the disturbance and that his preaching actually served the cause of public order:

I preached Jesus, the saviour of sinners. Many sinners of all sorts came and heard. Many were (and are) saved from their sins. The drunkards are sober, the common swearers fear God, the Sabbath-breakers now keep that day holy. These facts are undeniable, the persons being well known and ready at any time to attest them.

A few months later Wesley returned to the topic of religion and social order in a letter to Alderman Ridley:

My soul has been pained day by day, even in walking the streets of Newcastle, at the senseless, shameless wickedness, the ignorant profaneness of the poor men to whom our lives are entrusted. The continual cursing and swearing, the wanton blasphemy of the soldiers in general, must needs be a torture to the sober ear, whether of a Christian or an honest infidel. Can any that either fear God or love their neighbour hear this without concern, especially if they consider the interests of our country, as well as of these unhappy men themselves? For can it be expected that God should be on their side who are daily affronting Him to His face? And if God be not on their side, how little will either their number, or courage, or strength avail?

With the extension of his parish to Newcastle Wesley embarked on fifty years of almost continuous travelling centred on the 'golden triangle' of London, Bristol and Newcastle, riding between 4000 and 8000 miles in each year. In his Journals Wesley generally treats this travelling as routine, but his account of an admittedly exceptional journey to Newcastle in February 1745 is a reminder of the risks inherent in in contemporary travel:

[Friday 22rd] – There was so much snow about Boroughbridge that we could go but very slowly; in so much that the night overtook us when we wanted six or seven miles to the place where we designed to lodge. But we pushed on at a venture across the moor and, about eight, came safe to Sandhutton.

[Saturday 23rd] – We found the roads abundantly worse than they had been the day before, not only because the snows were deeper, which made the causeways in many places unpassable (and turnpike roads were not known in these parts of England till some years after), but likewise because the hard frost, succeeding the thaw, had made all the ground like glass. We were often obliged to walk, it being impossible to ride, and our horses several times fell down while we were leading them, but not once while we were riding them, during the whole journey. It was past eight before we got to Gateshead Fell, which appeared a great pathless waste of white. The snow filling up and covering all the roads, we were at a loss how to proceed, when an honest man of Newcastle overtook and guided us safe into the town.

Whatever the difficulties of the road and whatever drunkenness he observed or insults he received Wesley was always happy to visit Newcastle. His Journal entry for 4th June 1759 is typical:

After preaching I rode on to Newcastle. Certainly, if I did not believe there was another world, I should spend all my time in summer here, as I know no place in Great Britain comparable to it for pleasantness. But I seek another country, and therefore am content to be a wanderer upon earth.

The entries in his Journal for 4th June and 9th June 1790, on the occasion of his final visit, attest that his love of Newcastle endured to the end of his life:

[4th June] – We reached Newcastle. In this and Kingswood [Bristol], were I to do my own will, I should choose to spend the short remainder of my days.
[9th June] – Having dispatched all the business I had to do here, in the evening I took a solemn leave of this lovely people, perhaps never to see them more in this life, and set out early in the morning.

Wesley did not however confine himself to Newcastle and a great part of his interest to us lies in the range of his travels around the region, reaching parts that other travellers had probably never heard of, let alone visited. The itinerary of his 12th visit in July and August 1748 is particularly extensive: Boroughbridge, Newcastle, Morpeth, Widdrington, Alnmouth, Alnwick, Long Horsley, Newcastle, Blanchland, Hindley Hill, Nenthead, Alston, Hindley Hill, Allendale

Town, Newlands, Tanfield Cross, Newcastle, Sunderland, Biddick, Pelton, Spen, Horsley, Newcastle, Morpeth, Alnwick, Tuggal, Berwick, Alnmouth, Widdrington, Newcastle, Leeds. In Widdrington on 18th July he experienced "a delightful evening, and a delightful place, under the shade of tall trees" but on the following day dismissed Alnmouth as "a small seaport town, famous for all kinds of wickedness". In September of the following year he added that Alnmouth was inhabited by "a stupid, drowsy people", their stupidity and drowsiness no doubt reflecting their failure to respond to his preaching with sufficient enthusiasm. Wesley experienced a similar lack of response in Scotland, where conditions were much less favourable to the Methodist revival, and on riding south to Alnwick in June 1757 exclaimed, "Oh what a difference is there between these living stones and the dead, unfeeling multitudes in Scotland!". But, as at Alnmouth there were many times when Wesley experienced similar frustrations in Northumberland:

> When I came to Old Cambus I found notice had been given of my preaching about a mile off. So I took horse without delay and rode to Cockburnspath, where the congregation was waiting. I spoke as plain as I possibly could, but very few appeared to be at all affected. It seems to be with them as with most in the north – they know everything, and feel nothing.

Perhaps his most devastating comment is reserved for Stanhope in County Durham:

> We returned to Stanhope, formerly the seat of several great families, now an inconsiderable village. It is eminent for nothing in this age but a very uncommon degree of wickedness.

What the people of Stanhope had done to deserve this opprobrium is left unstated; probably they were inclined to live in sin. As we have noted Wesley kept up this punishing schedule to the end of his life, making his only visit to Rothbury in June 1782 in the course of a 2 month tour of the north and of Scotland. His journal entry for 17th June gives us another indication of a typical day's travelling and preaching, on the exact day of his 79th birthday and despite having fallen downstairs 2 days previously in Alnwick:

I preached at Rothbury in the Forest, formerly a nest of banditti, now as quiet a place as any in the county. About one I preached at Saugh House, a lone house, twelve miles from Rothbury [about 1 mile east of Cambo]. Though it was sultry hot, the people flocked from all sides; and it was a season of refreshment to many. In the evening I went to Hexham, and preached near the old Priory to an immense multitude. Very many were present again in the morning, and seemed to drink in every word that was spoken.

3 sermons and at least 35 miles riding in one day. Very good going for a man of 79 on a sultry hot summer day, even if the new turnpike road from Hexham to Alnmouth must have made the travelling easier than it had been 40 years earlier. We shall however end our survey of Wesley with his account of a visit to Blanchland 35 years earlier in March 1747, a passage which evidences his ability to respond to both the landscape and the people and which reflects his hopes for the success of his mission:

I rode to Blanchland, about twenty miles from Newcastle. The rough mountains round about were still white with snow. In the midst of them is a small winding valley, through which the Derwent runs. On the edge of this the little town stands, which is indeed little more than a heap of ruins. There seems to have been a large cathedral church, by the vast walls which still remain. I stood in the churchyard, under one side of the building, upon a large tombstone round which, while I was at prayers, all the congregation kneeled down on the grass. They were gathered out of the lead mines from all parts; many from Allendale, six miles off. A row of little children sat under the opposite wall, all quiet and still. The whole congregation drank in every word, with such earnestness in their looks I could not but hope that God will make this wilderness sing for joy.

An Actor's Life in the Early Nineteenth Century

The painter J M W Turner made several visits to Northumberland, including a tour in 1797. He was particularly enthralled by Norham Castle, of which he made several studies. And in 2 recent books Roz Southey has made a convincing case for the proposition that Newcastle was far from being a provincial backwater in its musical life. She has noted among other things the speed with which London hits, such as *The Beggar's Opera*, were staged in Newcastle and the popularity of touring performers. The *Reminiscences* of William Macready (1793-

1873) provide evidence that the same proposition holds good in the theatrical world in the early years of the nineteenth century.

Macready's father was himself an actor-manager with an interest in a string of provincial theatres. One of these was the Theatre Royal at Newcastle and, with his father being temporarily in bankruptcy, William made his first visit as acting manager in the summer of 1809, at the age of 16:

> I remained here about two months, not deriving much advantage, though some experience, from the society of some of the players, and falling desperately in love with one of the actresses – no improbable consequence of the unguarded situation of a boy of sixteen.

He returned at the end of the year for the Christmas season but then had little to do for some time. He spent some weeks at Tynemouth, a place also visited on various occasions by Thomas Bewick:

> Several weeks after this engagement, as it was termed, were passed in solitude at Tynemouth, then a small village, where, with a very few books, I contrived to while away the lonely hours, fishing, bathing, rambling along the shore, meditating on the characters I had acted, and declaiming to the louder waves the various passages from them…..In one of my fishing excursions I was amused and surprised by the sagacity of one of our boatmen. We were at a short distance from the rocky shore, our lines let down to the full depth, when one, pulling up, observed that "it was a good one from its weight". To our surprise it was a very good sized cod-fish, but lean-looking, wasted, and there was a sort of sea-vermin crawling in numbers over its skin. A fish of that size near the shore and lying, as it evidently had been, at the bottom, instantly suggested the cause of its enfeebled state to the sailor. "I should not wonder," said the man, "if he has a gold watch in his belly – let's see," and with his knife opening the stomach, he threw down on the bench a cat of middling size, exclaiming, "Dash my buttons, if it isn't a kitting." It would have been supposed impossible for the fish to have passed so large a mass down its throat; but, being lodged in the stomach, the digestive action of the creature must have been stopped, and the animal remained in its perfect state, the hair of its skin only being ruffled. Our unscientific boatman directly knew that indigestion was the malady of the voracious fish.

Despite considerable improvements in the road system travel in winter could still be dangerous, and Macready was fortunate to reach

96

Newcastle at all when he travelled south from Edinburgh in the second week of January 1814:

> Our journey was long and tedious; the coaches then, except the mails, generally carried six inside, and we had from Edinburgh our full complement. The snow was falling fast, and had already drifted so high between the Ross Inn and Berwick-on-Tweed, that it had been necessary to cut a passage for carriages for some miles. We did not reach Newcastle until nearly two hours after midnight; and fortunate was it for the theatre and ourselves that we had not delayed our journey, for the next day the mails were stopped; nor for more than six weeks was there any conveyance by carriage between Edinburgh and Newcastle. After some weeks a passage was cut through the snow for the guards to carry the mails on horseback, but for a length of time the communications every way were very irregular.

Such circumstances were by no means unprecedented. In 1799 a severe snowstorm affected much of the country and 3 months later, on 27th April, the London Post Office issed a circular asking for help in resolving continuing problems:

> Several mail-coaches being still missing that were obstructed in the snow since the 1st February last, this is to desire you will immediately represent to me an acoount of all spare patent mail-coaches that are in the stage where you travel over, whether they are regular stationed mail-coaches or extra spare coaches, and the exact place where they are, either in barn, field, yard, or coach-house, and the condition they are in, and if they have seats, rugs and windows complete.

As an actor Macready was on tour for much of the year and in these early years he took holidays not only at Tynemouth but also on Lindisfarne, to which he became much attached despite finding it primitive and often lonely. However he was not always by himself, and a brief account of his summer holiday in 1815 details the range of his recreations:

> My summer, spent in company with my sisters, was divided between professional engagements at Carlisle, Dumfries, and Berwick-upon-Tweed, and some holiday weeks in my old favourite retreat of Holy Island, from whence we made excursions to Bamborough Castle, Wark, Norham etc, or frequently dined and drank tea among the rocks or sandy hills under a little tent that I had constructed to supply the want of a

bathing-house – days of enjoyment that I have never ceased to reckon among the pleasures of the past.

Three years later he spent time sightseeing further south in the region, and his account of a visit to a coal mine is worth quoting at length. Like Daniel Defoe on the summit of the Cheviot Macready screws up the tension in a dramatic narrative before puncturing the ballon with gentle satire on his own nervousness :

Some idle days on my hands were given to sightseeing. The old castle, Sunderland Iron Bridge etc, were interesting, but the chief object of my curiosity, when in the North, had always been the working of a coal-mine. I had a letter to the manager or head-man of a mine: the name does not remain with me, but it was the deepest but one in the whole region. Loder, a violinist of great note in his day……, was dining with my father, and, hearing my intention, expressed his wish to accompany me the next morning. Accordingly at the appointed hour next day a chaise took us to the little hamlet at the pit's mouth, about six or seven miles from Newcastle. Arrived there, the manager receiving me very civilly, informed us that we must put on miners' dresses. This was not a very agreeable introduction, but we at once understood its necessity, and there we were two complete miners, save and except the want of smudge upon our faces, which however we did not wait long for. A stout, elderly, steady-looking man was directed to be our guide. The basket was pulled to the pit's mouth, and I must confess to a flutter of the heart when I saw the craft in which we were to make our downward voyage, feeling, like Acres, very much inclined to "run"; but casting a look on my companion, and seeing his face as pale as ashes, restored my courage, and with a hearty laugh I got into one side of the basket, whilst he slowly took his place in the other; our guide slung his thigh into the noose of a chain, and the steam-engine began to lower us down at half-rate pace, which seemed to me what be better termed "double-quick time".

Once or twice in our downward course I looked up aloft, when the aperture through which we had emerged appeared like "a star of smallest magnitude", and our guide, when we had made what seemed a great distance of depth, kept constantly striking against the wall of shaft the particular sort of rough stick he carried. I was wondering what his object could be, perceiving there was some significance in his action, when he enlightened us not very agreeably with the exclamation, "Now then I'll tell ye, when we get half-way doon". It was with a suppressed groan I learned that we were still dangling at such an awful distance from the bottom. But the deepest shaft, like the longest day, will have an end; we reached a solid footing at last, and extricating ourselves from our basket, sat down in a scooped-out recess to "get our sight", as our guide, who was providing himself with a light, directed us before setting out on our tour through this gnome's world of wonders.

A world it seemed to be from the activity pervading it. There were horses with long trains of creels of coal, and their drivers; a steam-engine at work; a pond for the horses to wash in. But a partial view was all we could obtain in the darkness visible by the help of our conductor's lamp. We traversed gallery after gallery, sometimes more than six feet in height; at other times we were obliged to walk in a stooping posture. At given distances through the galleries there were trap-doors, with pulleys and weights, to ensure a frequent circulation of air; under an open shaft was an immense roaring fire, kept up, like the great *lung* of the excavation, for a continual draft of pure air from above. It particularly surprised me to see the process of blasting a huge mass of coal detached, which the miners, naked to their waists, vigorously broke up and deposited in the creels. The air was very thick and close, and heavy on the breath; but the particular oppression I experienced was in the sensation of my ears. In one compartment, as the trap-door shut after and enclosed us, our guide stopped us, and, apparently with great relish, said, "Now I'll show you something," then lighting a match at his lamp, he raised it to the top of the seam, and igniting the gas or fire-damp, in an instant the roof was all on flame. For the uninitiated it was a very nervous minute. "Thank you," said I, "that will do". "Oh, there's no danger," returned he, "d'ye think I'd have lighted it if I did not well know". "I have no doubt," I continued, "but we're perfectly satisfied". Upon which, half grumbling at the effect of his pyrotechnic display, he continued, "Oh, I'll put it out in a minute, ye'll see," and beating the ceiling with his hat, he very soon extinguished every trace of fire. We were some hours below, for our slow walk was one of miles, and at the extreme point of our progress our guide informed us that "we were just under the middle of the Tyne". In some places the heat was very great, and the perspiration flowed profusely down our blackened faces. We were glad to have seen what was to me was a wonderful sight, but at the same time it was not the least part of our enjoyment to take in a good draught of the fresh air of heaven, and to find ourselves standing again on the outside of the earthy crust. After a hearty laugh at the figures we presented to each other, we took the benefit of the cold water set for us, exchanged our miners' suits for our own apparel, and, recompensing our conductor, got merrily into our chaise for our return to Newcastle.

In 1818 or 1819 Macready's father disposed of his interest in the Theatre Royal and this meant that Newcastle was no longer a stop on William Macready's annual tours of the country. Like many successful actors and musicians his life became increasingly centred in London, although he did make a sentimental visit to Newcastle in

March 1841 which we will consider in our final chapter. For now we will leave Macready, noting as we do so that he is the first of our visitors to leave a record of seaside breaks at Tynemouth and on Lindisfarne, the precursors of the holidays to be enjoyed by many working men and women in the following 2 centuries.

CHAPTER 6

NORTHERN SURVEYS

To have been at Newcastle, and men of curiosity too, without seeing a coal-pit, would have been a sin of the most unpardonable nature.

R J Sullivan

On His French Majesty's (not so) Secret Service

The above quotation neatly summarises the eagerness of many eighteenth century leisure travellers to see something of the industrial life of the north of England. Another such traveller, the Rev James Plumptre, describes his descent with a guide into the Heaton colliery:

> He held with his right arm round the chain and directed us with his left; my left was round his right, and I held fast to the chain with my right. I shut my eyes till we reached the bottom, when we stopped suddenly, and I was held by a collier who led me to a seat. I was quite bewildered with the quickness and the novelty of the motion, and possibly some little apprehension, and the darkness of the place, the dim light of the lamps, and the grim figures of the colliers, had a very strange effect.

Esther Moir, to whom I owe these two quotations, rightly observes that travellers like Sullivan and Plumptre were motivated partly by the prospect of the dramatic and often picturesque experience offered by contemporary industry and partly by genuine patriotic pride in the achievements of English technology. As is shown by the example of the 1704 lawyer backing away from an invitation to descend into a pit more was required than mere curiosity to persuade travellers to don uncomfortable and stinking mining clothes and to brave the all too obvious risks of descending into and exploring coal mines. However, if the more enterprising English tourists felt justified pride in the industrial achievements of their country, the French were equally interested in acquiring British industrial know-how in order to narrow the technological gap which had opened up between the two countries. The government of the ancien régime commissioned Gabriel Jars (1732–1769) to travel to Germany, Sweden, Norway, England and Scotland in order to research mining, manufacturing and other industrial technologies with a view to improving the performance and productivity of French industry. Jars was a prominent metallurgist who, on 19th May 1768, became a member of the Académie Royale des Sciences in the same election as Antoine Lavoisier, the father of modern chemistry. He was to die prematurely on 20th August of the following year, his death due to sunstroke brought on by a long hot day's riding in the Auvergne. His younger brother, who was also a metallurgist and had accompanied Gabriel Jars on some of his travels, arranged the posthumous publication of his papers. In his introduction he summarises Jars's approach to his work, making a clear differentiation between serious industrial research and the more dilettante attitude of the leisure travellers whose accounts we have reviewed:

> Travel would be no more than an idle leisure pursuit were one not to take the trouble to observe the progress of industry and of human endeavour, and to bring back to one's own country the fruits of that progress, or at the least some of the benefits that foreigners have discovered how to obtain for themselves.

There are some similarities between this endeavour and the work undertaken by Daniel Defoe at the beginning of the eighteenth century. Both were paid agents of their respective governments but, while Defoe's political mission was secret and deniable, Jars's industrial espionage was conducted with relative openness and benefited from a perhaps surprising degree of cooperation from local industrialists who generally allowed him free access to their works. Although primarily interested in mining and the manufacture of iron and steel he conducted research into many other industries, including pottery, the mining and processing of alum, and the production of salt. Much in his papers is highly technical. He was also a fine draughtsman, producing attractive and detailed illustrations of many of the processes which he describes. In common with Defoe he was keenly aware of the interrelationship between different industries, noting for instance how pottery manufacture at Newcastle depended on the supply of raw materials shipped north as ballast in the colliers returning from London.

Like Lord North in the previous century Jars visited Seaton Sluice where he saw a large steam engine recently installed to provide power for raising coal up the mine shaft. This was almost certainly the machine designed by Joseph Oxley and installed at the Hartley mine in 1763, a couple of years before Jars's visit. It was notoriously unreliable and was out of action when Jars saw it. The machine was subsequently improved by James Watt, who visited Hartley in 1768. However he was able to take a proper view of the harbour works:

> The proprietor of these mines........incurred considerable expense to ensure the safety of the ships which carried his coal. He made a cut forty feet deep through more than 200 yards of rock. This cut forms a sort of canal through which the ships enter and leave when they take on their cargoes of coal. To avoid the risk of ships lying in the harbour being tossed about and damaged by the rising tide vertical grooves are cut into the rock at each end of the cut. By means of a revolving platform, and of pulleys and ropes, these grooves facilitate the lowering of large wooden panels, similar to lock-gates, which break the impact of the waves. This place is called Seaton Sluice, and it is claimed that this cut cost more than ten thousand pounds sterling. In addition, waggonways.......have been built to transport the coal from each mine to the harbour. The same proprietor has an important glass-works on the same site.

The salt-works, seen by Lord North, were another part of the industrial complex at Seaton Sluice. We have noted the description by William Brereton and Daniel Defoe of similar works in North and South Shields. Jars visited the works in Shields and left a detailed account, with accompanying technical drawings to illustrate the construction of the buildings. Having explained the steps taken to ensure a continuous supply of heat to the underside of the salt-pans he noted that the pans were filled with sea-water no less than 9 times before being boiled almost dry. The workers tested the salinity of each incoming high tide and filled the pans only when the salinity level exceeded 3 per cent; the maximum salinity level, rarely achieved, was around 4 per cent. Jars also visited the iron and steel works upstream from Newcastle, particularly the works at Swalwell where he observed the manufacture of anchors, anchor chains, agricultural implements, tools for working wood and stone, and domestic kitchen utensils. In the context of the present work it is however more appropriate to focus on his review of coal-mining, to which he devotes almost an entire chapter of his first volume.

Jars opens his account of the mining industry with a historical discussion of the legal framework for mineral extraction activities, explaining the legislation on the payment of royalties for the exploitation of subterranean resources as well as that relating to the payment of wayleaves for the transport of coal and other material across land owned by other proprietors. In this context he states that the standard term of a mining lease was 21 years, giving the mine-owner adequate time to recoup the considerable capital cost of opening the mine and to assure himself of a good commercial profit. We may recall Elizabeth Montagu's comment that "a mine at first opening has a prodigious swallow; when it begins to disgorge it makes noble amends". Jars put a figure on this, noting that the cost of opening a mine might be anything between £4,000 and £20,000, a huge amount in eighteenth century terms. The first step was to engage the local master-driller to sink one or more exploratory drill shafts to a depth of up to 600 feet, the cost of one such 600 foot shaft being £238–15s–0d (such precision in figures is typical of his work). On receiving a report from the master-driller that there were sufficient exploitable reserves, and that there were no insuperable problems with drainage, the mine-owner would negotiate lease terms before sinking 2 shafts, the first (with a steam-engine at the head) to extract water from the pit, and the second as the main shaft for the extraction of coal and for the miners to descend into the pit. This second shaft was equipped with a *machine à moulettes*, which is probably to be identified with a horse-drawn winding gin, an early type of winding gear of which an example can be seen in the Beamish Museum. Miners used this winding-gear to descend into the pit by clinging on to the ropes attached to the coal baskets.

The height of the underground workings was variable, depending on the thickness of the coal seam, but the minimum workable height was considered to be 2½ feet with thinner seams being ignored. The width of each individual working varied between 5 feet and 15 feet depending on the solidity of the roof. Steam power was becoming increasingly important, and Jars goes into minute technical detail on the design of a new steam-engine installed at the Walker pit to extract water. However, horses remained an essential part of the mining industry. They were needed to operate the winding-gin, to pull trucks along the waggonways leading from the pithead to the staithes, and to pull trucks from the coal-face to the bottom of the main shaft. Jars noted that 20 pit ponies were kept in the pit at Walker:

When the mine workings become somewhat extended several horses are lowered into the pit and will remain there for the rest of their lives. The driest parts of the pit are chosen for their stabling. These horses are used to haul the coal from the most distant parts of the mine to the bottom of the shaft with the winding-gear. To this end wooden waggonways are constructed, just like those built on the surface, on which the horses haul four-wheeled waggons filled with the baskets of coal, and these baskets are then hoisted to the surface by the winding-gear. In those places where no waggonways have yet been built young boys have small sledges on which they place the baskets of coal and then haul the sledges either to the bottom of the shaft or to the nearest horse waggonway.

For the most part Jars shows much more interest in the technology than in the workforce. He takes no notice of their living conditions beyond the gates of the factory or mine but he does give some indication of the working conditions in the mine and of the pay that miners could expect to receive:

Almost all the miners are employed at piecework rates, with these rates varying depending on the thickness of the seam. To illustrate this we can look at an important new pit.....called the Walker pit. Coal is mined from a single seam with a six-foot thickness of good quality coal, lying 600 feet below the surface........The workers start their shift at 2.00am, accompanied by the master miner who allocates the work. Each miner works only 6 or 7 hours in each 24 hours. During this time a miner can dig out from 15 to 25 or even 30 basketfuls of coal. Each basket weighs about 6cwt and for each basketful the miner is paid 5 farthings, in French money about 2½ silver sous. In addition to the miner there are many small boys who stay in the mine from 2.00am to nearly 4.00pm, the time needed to fill the baskets and to guide or haul them to the bottom of the shaft with the assistance of the 20 pit ponies. These boys earn 14 pence a day, or 27 to 28 French sous. The boys who work on the surface, leading the horses which work the winding-gear and for the same length of shift, earn 12 pence or 1 shilling.

Although young boys were to disappear from the mines by the end of the nineteenth century the conditions of work for both men and ponies remained little changed for the best part of the next 2 centuries. It is perhaps a sobering thought that the last surviving pit pony died in July 2011, having spent the last 17 years of his life in retirement after being brought up in 1994 from Ellington colliery, itself destined to be the last deep mine in Northumberland and to close in 2005 as a result of flooding.

Jars took a special interest in the waggonways, both because of the technological innovation involved and because of their importance in the overall commercial structure of mining:

All the mine owners need a secure outlet for their product, especially for its transport by sea. To this end they construct, at very considerable cost, waggonways from their mines to the river in order to transport coal to the warehouses at the water's edge. The cost of construction is however recouped very quickly by the ease with which coal can be transported in all seasons of the year.

To achieve this they undertake a very accurate survey of the ground between the mine and the river and, so far as possible, ensure a steady gradient over the whole distance. Waggonways must never go uphill and must be at least level for the reasons which I shall set out. If there are any small slopes to be negotiated cuttings are made to ensure that the way remains level.

After the gradients have been determined the track itself is marked out, 6 feet wide, and a ditch of this width is then dug, its depth depending on the result of the survey and on the solidity of the ground. All along the way they lay down lengths of oak at right angles to the line of the track, these lengths being 4, 5, 6 or 8 inches square and set at intervals of 2 or 3 feet. These lengths of oak are squared off at each end, with other lengths of wood being fixed with wooden dowels to the squared off sections; these rails are themselves accurately sawn and squared off, being about 6 or 7 inches wide and 4 or 5 inches thick. The rails are laid on both sides of the track along the entire length of the way, normally 4 feet apart which is the inside gauge of the track.

It will be seen that these new ways are simply grid-like frames made of wood. The entire space between the rails is reinforced with stones packed down as firmly as possible to ensure that the track is solid. This is then all covered with sand and gravel, placed in between the rails and built up to about 2 inches from the top of the rails. This helps to preserve the buried lengths of wood and renders the track extremely firm. In addition care is taken to ensure regular maintenance. If there are any dips or streams to be crossed wooden bridges are constructed, care still being taken to lay the 2 rails on both sides of the track at a distance of 4 feet from each other and projecting from the surface of the bridge just as they do from that of the main way. All these rails must be exactly aligned at their ends, sometimes with the assistance of iron bands.

Jars goes into a similar level of detail on the construction of the wagons and on the method of operating the waggonway. A particularly interesting illustration shows a turntable used to effect a change of direction in the way, presumably because the existing technology did not enable the constructors to build curved sections of track.

Gabriel Jars was not the only French scientist to come to Northumberland in the last quarter of the eighteenth century. Monsieur B Faujas Saint Fond (1741-1819), professor of geology at the Museum of Natural History in Paris, visited England and Scotland in 1784, demonstrating right from the start a refreshing independence of mind in his approach to travel:

> I do not intend to descant on the extent, the beauty, or the immense population of London; natural history, the sciences, the arts, and commercial economy more particularly engaged my attention, and will form the prominent features of my journal.

As the title of his journal indicates a principal purpose of his tour was to visit the Hebrides, specifically the island of Staffa with its unusual geological features. The planning for this journey to the north shows that this was a serious scientific expedition:

> As I intended to take advantage of the remainder of the fine season to visit Scotland and the Hebrides I devoted some days to the necessary preparations for my journey, and procured letters of introduction to several persons in Edinburgh and Glasgow, and to the Duke of Argyll, who was then in the north.
> At length all things having been got in readiness, Count Paul Andreani of Milan, William Thornton, an American student in medicine, M de Mercier who had been lately introduced to us as a naturalist and much attached to the study of mineralogy, and myself set out in two post chaises, followed by a third containing our servants.

With the improvements to roads in the north brought about by the turnpike system from 1750 onwards travel from London to Newcastle was by now much easier, and Saint Fond and his companions were able to cover the final 96 miles from Ferrybridge to Newcastle in a single day. Their guide in Newcastle was David Crawford, a local metallurgist and correspondent of the Royal Society who would in 1787 become a leading partner in the opening of a new colliery at Ryton. Under Crawford's guidance the expedition conducted a survey of Newcastle's industry, which is worth quoting in full:

Newcastle stands on the banks of the beautiful river Tyne, which is covered with vessels, and bordered on the right and left with manufactures of every description. Here I remained long enough to enable me to pay due attention to its numerous coal mines, and the multiplied produce of its active industry, under the direction of Mr David Crawford, a lover of natural history, himself, and who was the proprietor of a manufactory, in which gold and silver are extracted from the cinders used in the furnaces of the works in these metals, and also from old crucibles. He purchases these rude materials in Holland, France, and England; and by a particular process, aided by the abundance and cheapness of coals, carries on this business and some other branches of manufacturing, to advantage.

We saw several glass houses, where window-glass, bottles, decanters, drinking glasses &c were made. All these manufactures, though established in buildings of mean appearance, are managed with a simplicity and œconomy that cannot be too much praised. It is a taste for pomp and grandeur which almost always ruins the manufactures in France, and prevents those new ones which we want from being established. In this respect, the Dutch and English are much more prudent, and furnish examples of utility combined with œconomy deserving of imitation.

The Tyne is rendered highly interesting by the number and variety of the manufactures carried on upon its banks. One one hand are seen brickfields, potteries, glass-houses, and chymical works, for making ceruse, minium, vitriol &c. On the other, manufactories in iron, tin and every kind of metal: machines for fabricating brass-wire, plate metal &c. This assemblage of manufactories, rising opposite one another, every where infuses life and activity; and humanity rejoices to see so many useful men finding comfort and happiness in a labour which at the same time contributes to the enjoyment of others, and the good of their country.

The numerous coal mines in the vicinity of Newcastle, form not only immense magazines of fuel for the rest of England, but are also the sources of an extensive and profitable foreign commerce. Vessels loaded with this article for London and different parts of Europe, sail daily from this port. Besides this commerce, the working of these mines gives an incalculable advantage to the British navy. It was in this school that the immortal Capt. Cook was trained. This astonishing navigator sailed thrice round the world, and enriched geography, natural history, and navigation, with great and valuable discoveries. The modest habitation where he was born, in the neighbourhood of Newcastle, is preserved with pious veneration.

The coal mines here are covered with a soil which yields fine pasturage, and the finest products of agriculture. Under this fertile stratum is found a freestone of an excellent quality, and manufactured into grindstones.

The first mine I visited belonged to a private individual, and required an hundred men to work it. Thirty of these were employed above ground, and twenty in the pit. Twenty horses were kept in this profound abyss for drawing the coal through the subterranean passages to the bottom of the mouth of the pit: four more worked the machine which raised the coal, and some others were employed in auxiliary labours.

The following is the order of the mineral substances, as they appear in descending to the coal:

Strata	Feet
Vegetable earth of good quality	2
Beds of rounded calcareous stone, intermixed with rounded pieces of free- stone	15
Grey clay more or less pure	16
Hard quartoze free-stone, with lamellœe of mica	25
Very hard black clay, somewhat bituminous, intermixed with some specks of mica	26
Black clay more bituminous, and partly inflammable; when the foliations of this clay which separates with facility are examined with attention, some prints of fern appear, but they are scarcely discernible	18
Total	102

At this depth the coal is found. The bed is five feet thick in some places: in general it is easily wrought, and large pieces are brought up.

When the bed of black and bituminous clay is penetrated, the coal is found adhering to it; but this is not always the case, for there are other mines in the neighbourhood where free-stone is the covering, and mixes two or three inches in depth with the coal. Some of the mines are upwards of 180 fathoms in depth, and contain different strata of coal.

This mine had a large steam engine for carrying off the water, and working a ventilator. The machine which raises the coal from the pit is very convenient, and is worked with stout horses. To convey the article to the vessels on the river, roads with an almost insensible inclination are made with much art, and the waggons moving by the laws of gravity, proceed as if it were by magic, in the rear of each other till they reach the river. The waggon being emptied, returns by a second road parallel to the first. This contrivance, which is as ingenious as it is economical, soon indemnifies the proprietors for the money they expend in the construction of rail and tram ways.

These extraordinary roads are varied in several ways; but I cannot enter into details. Suffice it to say, that they are all excellently adapted to the purposes of facilitating labour, and of diminishing expences.

The industry of the inhabitants of Newcastle is so active, that they are accustomed to apply it to every object which presents itself. They have turned to profit the pyrites which injures the quality of the coal, but which is abundantly produced in some of the mines. From these they extract vitriol in very large quantities by a process at once simple and economical, which does honour to the intelligence of those who first put it into practice.

The great quantity of coal dust collected at the numerous pits in the neighbourhood of Newcastle, would soon become an incumbrance, were it not for an admirable method adopted of making it into coke, which is used in a great number of manufactories, as a substitiute for charcoal, to which it is in most cases superior, producing a stronger, more equal, and long continued heat.

Coal thus prepared is called in France purified coal, or dephlogisticated coal. The city of Paris uses great quantities of it, and in Lyons it is likewise employed in the copper works. Since the revolution, however, this kind of coal is neglected; and the trees of our finest forests are reduced to ashes.

At just over 100 feet in depth this is a much shallower mine than the Walker pit visited by Jars, although it is interesting to note that 20 pit ponies are required for underground working in both mines. The unique aspect of Faujas St Fond's account is however that the overground waggonway to the river is not, as at Walker, reliant on horse traction but is, according to a modern study, the earliest reported description of a self-acting inclined plane with sets of waggons.

After 4 or 5 days in Newcastle the expedition continued on its way north, with Saint Fond making observations (much abbreviated in Mavor's abridgement) on the geology of the country between Newcastle and Wooler.

A Spell behind Bars

Another visitor with a different, but equally serious, agenda was the English prison reformer John Howard (1726-1790) who made it his life's work to inspect all the prisons of Britain and Ireland as well as those in various overseas countries. He shared many of the attributes of his older contemporary John Wesley, not least the single-minded concentration on his mission and the stamina displayed over many years of travelling. An early biographer discovered among his papers a summary of his journeys over a period of 11 years from 1773 to 1783:

Journeys	Years	Mileage
Great Britain and Ireland	1773-1776	10318
First Foreign Journey	1775	1400
Second Foreign Journey	1776	1700
Third Foreign Journey	1778	4636
Great Britain and Ireland	1779	6490
Fourth Foreign Journey	1781	4465
Great Britain and Ireland	1782	8165
Fifth Foreign Journey	1783	3304
to Ireland		715
to Worcester		238
to Hereford, Chelmsford and Warrington		602
Total Mileage		42033

In common with Wesley Howard usually travelled on horseback. As a reasonably wealthy man he was well able to afford post-chaises but his clothes became so impregnated with the reek of contemporary prisons that he found the resulting odours insufferable in the enclosed space of a chaise.

In his youth Howard had been struck by Wesley's preaching in his home county of Bedfordshire but, as far as we know, he met Wesley only once, in Dublin in June 1787 when both were approaching the end of their lives. They immediately recognised each other as kindred spirits:

Wesley on Howard – I had the pleasure of a conversation with Mr Howard, I think one of the greatest men in Europe. Nothing but the mighty power of God can enable him to go through his difficult and dangerous employments. But what can hurt us, if God is on our side?
Howard on Wesley – I was encouraged by him to go on vigorously with my own designs. I saw in him how much a single man might achieve by zeal and perseverance, and I thought, Why may I not do as much in my way as Mr Wesley has done in his if I am only as assiduous and

persevering? I determined I would pursue my work with more alacrity than ever.

In compiling the successive editions of his great work *The State of the Prisons* Howard made several visits to Newcastle and Northumberland. For each prison he completed his own questionnaire, giving precise details of the names, remuneration and main duties of the gaoler, chaplain and surgeon, and of the number of prisoners incarcerated at the date of each visit. For the main gaol in Newcastle prisoner numbers are recorded as follows:

Date of Visit	Debtors	*Felons*
21 March 1774	6	2
8 January 1775	12	4
15 January 1776	14	3
30 June 1779	13	4
25 March 1782	12	1

Given that the eighteenth century is often seen as a rather rough and lawless age the small numbers of prisoners may surprise us. However it should be remembered that there were at the time no sentences of imprisonment. Felons, or suspected felons, were incarcerated pending trial and would then be released on acquittal or imprisoned temporarily while awaiting execution or transportation. For debtors however imprisonment could often mean a life sentence, as was the case in the early seventeenth century for Huntingdon Beaumont, the inventor of the waggonway. And one of the scandals which Howard set out to remedy was the established practice of exacting fees on the release of prisoners. It was not unusual for debtors who had paid off their original debt, and for suspected felons who had been acquitted at their trial, to remain in prison because of their inability to meet the discharge fees owed to the gaoler and the turnkey. In this respect Newcastle was untypical (at least as regards suspects acquitted in court), as Howard notes in his supplementary remarks where he also finds much else to commend:

In this Newgate, which is the gate at the upper end of the town, all the rooms except the condemned room are upstairs and airy. I always found them remarkably clean, strewed with sand etc. The corporation allow both debtors and felons firing and candles in plenty; and every prisoner

112

has a chaff bed, two blankets, and a coverlet. Debtors and felons are thus accommodated in few other prisons in England..........

The debtors walk on the battery at the top of the gaol, which is 38 feet by 34. There is no court, but one might be made of the vacant ground that lies west of the gaol, at little expense, as the town wall is on one side of it. The debtors' beds are in closets; if on iron bedsteads and in the wards (as in some hospitals) it would be more salutary. No prisoners here have fetters, unless they be riotous. For some years past, prisoners acquitted have been discharged in court; the corporation paid the gaoler's fees if the prisoners were poor....

I was concerned to find that the humane gaoler Crafter was dead. But his successor Mr Harle seems equally worthy of the trust.

Dr Rotheram, a physician in this town, visits the prisoners very assiduously without fee or reward. This is one of the few instances of the kind I have met with.

After noting the details of 3 smaller prisons in Newcastle Howard moves on to the County Gaol at Morpeth, where his remarks reflect harsher conditions tempered by some instances of mercy including, once again, the payment of some discharge fees by the County authorities:

The debtors have six sizeable rooms which are out of repair, and a free ward called the Middle-tower. Some commodious rooms lately built are occupied by the gaoler. Only one court, which is for debtors. Felons are always shut up in the tower. In the women's room I saw (January 1776) two who, the gaoler said, were cast for transportation: one in September 1773, the other in November 1774; but at my visit in 1779 I found they had been humanely released at the assize.

Of the other two rooms, generally appropriated to men-felons, one is a day-room (14 feet 2 inches by 6 feet 9), the other an offensive dungeon, the window only 18 inches by 9. In the latter were three transports (1776) who, upon *suspicion* of *intending* an escape, were chained to the floor. They had not the king's allowance of 2s 6d a week.

Gaol delivery once a year. Assize held at Newcastle, whither prisoners are conveyed; and men and women confined together seven or eight nights in a dirty damp dungeon down 6 steps in the old castle which, having no roof, in a wet season the water is some inches deep. The felons are chained to rings in the wall.

The county for some years paid the gaoler's fees for acquitted prisoners, if poor, and clothed such transports as were quite indigent.

The debtors' court should be allotted to felons, or two courts might be taken from the gaoler's spacious garden.

In Berwick Howard found the town gaol in the same building as the grand town hall built in 1754. He noted that the cells on the ground floor were damp and that the prisoners were therefore housed in 2 long rooms over the main hall. While they did not have access to a court they were permitted to exercise on the roof. The overall impression is that Howard found the prisons of Northumberland to be managed more efficiently and more humanely than those in many other parts of Great Britian.

An Agricultural Missionary

At the time of his tour of the northern counties in 1769 Arthur Young (1741-1820) was a relatively young man who had, by accident rather than by deliberate design, become a gentleman farmer on his family estate at Bradfield near Bury St Edmunds. His own farming endeavours, at Bradfield and elsewhere, were characterised by persistent experimentation and by equally persistent failure to achieve economic viability. Nevertheless he set himself up as an expert on progressive agricultural practice and, by publishing detailed accounts of his lengthy tours of inspection, established a national and European reputation. His legacy as a writer is of far more value to us than his achievement, or lack of achievement, as a practical farmer, so perhaps it is as well that he did not follow his own advice:

> I lay it down as a maxim, that no man can establish or support a reputation in any branch of experimental philosophy, such as shall really descend to posterity, otherwise than by experiment; and that commonly the more a man works, and the less he writes the better, at least the more valuable will be his reputation.

On his arrival in Newcastle Young conformed to the practice of other visitors by viewing and admiring the coal mines, waggonways and other industry. His description of the machinery at Crawley's ironworks to the west of Newcastle is a characteristic blend of detailed observation and ill-informed pontification, concluding with an unexpectedly lyrical passage on the riverine landscape in the vicinity of the island where, a century earlier, the municipality had entertained Lord North to a picnic:

As to the machines for accelerating several operations in the manufacture, the copper rollers for squeezing bars into hoops, and the scissors for cutting bars of iron – the turning cranes for moving anchors into and out of the fire – the beating hammer, lifted by the cogs of a wheel; these are machines of manifest utility, simple in their construction, and all moved by water. But I cannot conceive the necessity of their executing so much of the remaining work by manual labour. I observed eight stout fellows hammering an anchor in spots, which might evidently be struck by a hammer, or hammers, moved by water upon a vast anvil, the anchor to be moved with the utmost ease and quickness, to vary the seat of the strokes. It is idle to object the difficulty of raising such a machine; there are no impossibilities in mechanics: An anchor of 20 tons may, undoubtedly, be managed with as much ease as a pin. In other works beside the anchor-making, I thought I observed a waste of strength.

In the road from Newcastle to the works, upon rising the first hill, there is a most noble view into an extensive vale: cultivated rising enclosures, surrounding a prodigious fine water (the river Tyne), which has the appearance of a lake, several miles long, and of a noble breadth. In the middle a very fine island of an irregular oblong shape, scattered with trees: The whole water enlivened with numerous boats, sailing to and from Newcastle: The river loses itself at each end, under waving hills in a beautiful manner. Upon the whole it has the appearance of one of the finest lakes in the world.

Young's itinerary on his northern tour rivals that of John Wesley described on page 70 above: Newcastle – Gosforth – Morpeth – Alnwick – Belford – Waren - Hetton - Berwick – Wooler – Fenton – Ascent of Cheviot – Rothbury – Cambo – Wallington – Chollerford – Glenwelt and the Roman wall – Cumberland. For each place on this extensive itinerary Young provides a very detailed description of farming practices, clearly structured on the basis of a questionnaire which he filled in for each community. The resulting analysis is far too lengthy to quote in full, but some extracts from Young's findings at Hetton (Horton) give a good flavour of his method:

At Hetton, a few miles west of Belford, the husbandry varies much. The soils are light loams, and rotten black moory ground; let from 1s 6d to 15s an acre, average about 6s 6d. Farms rise from £100 to £700 a year but are, in general, from £200 to £300. Their courses [crop rotation] are:
Turnips – Barley – Clover – Oats, and
Fallow – Wheat – Peas – Wheat

115

They plough 6 times for wheat, sow 2 bushels in October, and do not reap in return above 10 upon an average [*similar details for barley, oats, beans, peas and turnips*].

As to the management of their manure, they stack their hay in general in the farmyard, except what is used for sheep; but know nothing of chopping stubbles for littering the farmyards. They lime a great deal, lay six cartloads on an acre, or 120 bushels, which costs 3s 9d per load, besides the leading. In the burning of lime, one load of coal burns two of lime – they never fold their sheep……..

Their breed of cattle is the short-horned, both for fatting and milking. The product of a cow they reckon at £4 4s, a good one will give them five gallons of milk per day. They feed them in winter upon both hay and straw, of the first of which a cow eats from 1½ to 2 tons, and always feed in a house. Of swine they generally keep one to two cows. Their calves do not such at all but are brought up by hand; three weeks for rearing and six weeks for the butcher. A dairy maid will take care of 12 cows……………..

They constantly salve all sheep in October with tar and butter; two gallons of tar and a firkin of butter, melted together, will do 120 [*sheep*]. They reckon this method keeps them free from the scab, warm in the bad weather, and also makes the wool grow………..

Poor rates in general low, from nothing up to 2s in the pound. The poor women and children in total idleness. They do not drink tea, but smoke tobacco unconscionably. The farmers carry their corn seven miles.

One can visualise Young spreading out his questionnaire on a farmhouse table in order to take down the answers from the farmer, but from time to time being distracted from his schedule and jotting down totally random observations quite out of any logical sequence.

Young was a consistent advocate of progressive farming, which in his day was based on the enclosure of former common land. Later in life he came to see the hardships that many had suffered from the introduction of enclosures, and he belatedly proposed palliative measures. At the time of his northern tour he was however blind to the human consequences of the new agriculture and showed no sympathy for poor people deprived of their hereditary rights to the common land. He identified rather with rich progressive agriculturalists, living exemplars of what he aspired to in his own farming:

The town of Belford, which is a pretty, well-situated place, belongs entirely to Abraham Dickson Esq. That gentleman's father procured a market and two fairs to be established at it; but the spirited conduct of the

116

present owner is what has brought it to the condition, so flourishing, to what it formerly was. Thirteen years ago it did not contain above 100 souls, but they now amount to above six times that number. And this increase has been owing to the excellent means of introducing an industry unknown to former times. Mr Dickson has established a woollen manufacture, which already employs 16 looms, and the spinning business goes on sufficiently to keep them at work; a noble acquisition in a place where a spinning-wheel was not to be seen a few years ago. Another establishment of very great importance was that of a tannery...............The situation of Belford, half way between Alnwick and Berwick, at the distance of 30 miles, was very advantageous for fixing a good inn, with post-chaises and accommodation for travellers. This likewise was executed, and is now found of peculiar use to all travellers and of benefit to the town.

But as a town without good roads to and from it is course but in a paltry condition, Mr Dickson applied himself with great spirit to rendering the road to Belford, north and south, as good as possible. This he effected as far as his influence extended, and would not have left a mile of bad road in the whole country, had others been as solicitous as himself about so important an object.

Coals had formerly been raised around Belford, but the pits exhausted, and the undertaking discontinued for many years. The common report which this active gentleman heard on all sides was that no more coal was advantageously to be had, but common report was not sufficient for him. He tried in several places, and was fortunate enough to find a very beneficial seam, which has since been worked to noble advantage, both to the town and the proprietor.

Discovery of coal led to the burning of lime for the purposes of agriculture, as a manure, in a much larger way than had been usual; and for this work three new lime-kilns were erected, in a most substantial manner, and at a large expense.

Clearly Belford had improved since one of King Charles's courtiers passed that way in 1639:

Belfort nothing like the name either in strength or beauty is the most miserable beggarly sodden town, or town of sods, that ever was made in an afternoon of loam and sticks. In all the town not a loaf of bread, nor a quart of beer, nor a lock of hay, nor a peck of oats, and little shelter for horse or men.

Young's tour took him as far north as Berwick which "has nothing more worthy than its bridge over the Tweed" and to Wooler where he took the chance to follow in the footsteps of Daniel Defoe:

> From Wooler I turned aside to go up Cheviot Hill, whose towering head invited me to the prospect, which could not but suppose he must command. The height of this mountain is prodigiously great, and the view from it on all sides most extensive. I saw Gateshead Fell, near Newcastle, at a distance of 55 miles, and several objects in Scotland, beyond Edinburgh as I was told.

On his journey out of Northumberland into Cumberland Young passed through Glenwelt and Greenhead, where he visited and admired the remains of the Roman wall. He finishes his account of Northumberland with a summary of what he has seen during his stay:

> The farms become large almost immediately on entering it, after the small ones of Yorkshire and Durham; and rise in many parts of it to be as great as any in the kingdom, if not the greatest; but they must be divided into two classes, those which consist of cultivated lands, and others which are chiefly moor farms.
>
> The husbandry of the first is much superior to that of the two preceding counties; and that not only in one or two trifling articles, but in many very important ones. Manuring is carried on with greater spirit; lime is used in larger quantities; and they understand better the management of the farm-yard manure. Hoeing of turnips is a pregnant influence; I found it coming into practice at Gosforth, and all hoed about Morpeth. The potato culture is carried on upon a much larger scale: and, in short, the whole management better, and more spirited.
>
> With the other class, this is not the case. The grand article of their agriculture is the improvement of moors; and a viler or more slovenly husbandry than theirs, in this branch, can nowhere be found. The ploughing up wastes, without a previous inclosure, and breaking up the deepest soils, with paring and burning; the sowing two, three, and even four crops of corn running, upon a ploughing up, and liming; the leaving the exhausted soil to turf itself, in some places, and only scattering a little ray grass in others; the keeping 8000 and 10000 sheep, and never folding. All these are strokes of barbarism, which tend to damp and even extinguish the spirit of improvement, from the infallible want of success, and to the leaving a country, after what is here called improvement, in as miserable and waste a state as before it was begun.
>
> The occupiers of large farms, who are consequently men of considerable substance, are in most parts of England the greatest of all improvers.

Nature takes a new face under their hands; whole counties are converted at once from deserts into finely cultivated countries. But here we meet with no improvements that deserve the name; nothing lasting; three or four tolerable crops, and then the land left as desolate as ever, in the true spirit of a little lousy farmer of £20 a year. Unworthy those who occupy as many hundreds!

While moors are thus *improved*, I do not much wonder at seeing so much waste land in Northumberland. But surely the landlords are strangely remiss, in not introducing better customs; letting no tracks without their being inclosed, and restraining their tenants from exhausting the soil by continued crops; obliging them, at the same time, to lay it down to grass, in a given manner. But this must be done by practising such methods themselves, that the success may justify the proposal. If the farmers of the country are, nevertheless, backward in following such examples, men of large estates can well afford the importation of others, from counties whose cultivators are more informed.

It is very melancholy to ride through such vastly extensive tracks of uncultivated good land, as are found in every part of this county. And it is equally unfortunate that so many men of substance, in the farming way, should tread perpetually in the beaten route, and hire land in so many parts of England at an enormous rent, while such quantities are to be had almost for nothing. This is truly the *cultusque habitusque locorum praediscere*.

Although Young does not say so the Latin tag quoted here comes from the first book of the Georgics, in which Virgil emphasises the need for the farmer to know the nature of his soil and what plants it will bear. Young's negative assessment of moorland farming in the county reflects his background in agricultural East Anglia. One may doubt that Young ever tried to understand the nature and character of the northern moors. In quoting Virgil in the original Latin, and without attribution, he is more concerned both to establish his credentials as a member of the elite and to massage the self-esteem of his readers who would have shared his educational background. William Cobbett, whom we shall consider later in this chapter, took an apparently opposite view:

I have always contended and have now proved that a knowledge of those languages [*Latin and Greek*] is, generally speaking, of no use, and that as the acquiring of that knowledge costs much time and money, it is, generally speaking, *worse than useless*.

Young's more positive assessment of lowland farming is based on his inspection of a few large farms owned by progressive landowners like Abraham Dickson. As a general statement it is not borne out by a more comprehensive survey undertaken 25 years later:

.....a great portion of the county, extending from near Newcastle on both sides of the railway as far as Warkworth, is as little drained and as badly farmed as any district we have yet seen in England, and that the occupiers of the small farms can only eke out a scanty subsistence by careful parsimony, and by employing no labour except that of themselves and their families.

George Culley, the joint author of that report, visited Young's estate at Bradfield in 1784, and his comments on what he saw there provide a scathing riposte to Young's criticisms of northern farming practice:

People that devote their time to writing cannot act or execute. His sheep are scabbed, his cattle ill chose and worse managed; in short he exhibits a sad picture of mismanagement.

We should not however leave Young without remarking his summary of the roads and inns of Northumberland:

Road	Type	Comments
Durham to Newcastle	Turnpike	Good, but parts of it broken
To the Iron Works	Not stated	Very bad
To Morpeth	Turnpike	A pavement for a mile or two out of Newcastle, which is tolerable, all the rest vile.
To Alnwick	Turnpike	Much better than the last
To Belford	Turnpike	Better still
To Wooller	Turnpike	Part tolerable, but some execrable
To Rothbury	Turnpike	Part of it middling; some very good but hilly
Alnwick to Rothbury	Turnpike	Middling; some good
To Wallington	Turnpike	Very good, towards Wallington excellent
To Chollerford Bridge	Turnpike	Excellent. Much indebted is the country to Sir Walter Blacket for the many good roads which lead every way around him

To Glenwelt	Military Road	Excellent
To the River Arden	Cross	Very bad
To Carlisle	Military	As far as Brampton good; but thence to Carlisle cut up by innumerable little paltry one-horse carts

Town	Name	Comments
Newcastle	Not stated	Civil, but extravagantly dear. A boiled fowl, oysters, and one woodcock, 2s 6d a head. Also a roast fowl, a very small haddock, and ten smelts, 2s 6d a head
Alnwick	Angel	Pretty good
Belford	Not stated	Very good
Rothbury	Three Half Moons	Clean, and very civil
Cambo	White Hart	Where you will find a haughty landlady, never to come near her company, send as often as you please
Choller-ford Bridge	George	Very civil, and to a degree cheap. Mutton chops, pickles, potatoes, tarts and cheese, 6d a head
Glenwelt	Angel	Very civil, but not clean, extremely cheap. Boiled fowl with catchup sauce, and roast potatoes, 8d a head

It is interesting to compare the details of inns with those given by earlier travellers on page 65 above.

The Natural History of Northumberland

In 1769, the same year as Arthur Young, Thomas Pennant travelled through Northumberland on his way to Scotland. Pennant (1726-1798), like William Brereton a native of Chester, was a celebrated naturalist who became a Fellow of the Royal Society and was an acquaintance of Buffon and a correspondent of Linnaeus. He set out from Chester on 26 June 1769 with the aim of supplementing his previous academic research with direct observation:

A gentleman well known to the political world in the beginning of the present century made the tour of Europe, and before he reached Abbeville discovered that in order to see a country to best advantage it was infinitely preferable to travel by day than by night.

I cannot help making this applicable to myself who, after publishing three volumes of the *Zoology* of Great Britain, found out that to be able to speak with more precision of the subjects I treated of, it was far more prudent to visit the whole than part of my country. Struck therefore with the reflection of having never seen Scotland, I instantly ordered my baggage to be got ready and in a reasonable time found myself on the banks of the Tweed.

Apart from *British Zoology* (in 3 volumes) and *A History of Quadrupeds* Pennant also published *Indian Zoology* and *Arctic Zoology*, presumably without the benefit of visiting those regions. He did in fact exercise considerable diligence in obtaining information from correspondents, and the boundary between personal observation and reported local knowledge can sometimes be blurred. It may be fair to conclude that he used his local correspondents in the same way that a modern traveller might use a guide book, to point him to what he should take time to see and to provide additional information when he wrote up his books and found that his contemporary notes were inadequate. His account of Newcastle is clearly a blend of personal observation and reported local knowledge:

Newcastle, a large town divided into two unequal parts by the river, and both sides very steep. The lower parts, very dirty and disagreeable, are inhabited by Keelmen and their families, a mutinous race; for which reason the town is always garrisoned. In the upper parts are several handsome well-built streets.

The great business of the place is the coal trade. The collieries lie at different distances, from five to eighteen miles from the river, and the coal is brought down in waggons along rail roads and discharged from covered buildings at the edge of the water into keels or boats that are to convey it on shipboard. These boats are strong, clumsy and round, will carry about 25 tons each; sometimes are navigated with a square sail, but generally are worked with two vast oars. No ships of large burthen come up as high as Newcastle, but are obliged to lie at Shields, a few miles down the river, where stage coaches go thrice every day for the conveniency of passengers. This country is most remarkably populous; Newcastle alone contains near 40,000 inhabitants, and there are at least 400 sail of ships belonging to that town and its port. The effect of the vast commerce of this place is very apparent for many miles around; the country is finely cultivated and bears a most thriving and opulent aspect. Left Newcastle; the country is in general flat; passed by a large stone column with three dials on the capital, with several scripture texts on the sides, called here Pigg's Folly from the founder.

Travelling north from Newcastle Pennant is dismissive of Alnwick Castle, finding the modernisation of both house and gardens inconsistent with its feudal past – "nothing, excepting the numbers of industrious poor that swarm at the gate, excites any one idea of its former circumstances". However, at Belford, he shares Arthur Young's approval of the work of Abraham Dixon:

A stage further is Belford, the seat of Abraham Dixon Esq.; a modern house. The front has a most beautiful simplicity in it: the grounds improved as far as the art of husbandry can reach; the plantations large and flourishing: a new and neat town instead of the former wretched cottages; and an industrious race instead of an idle poor at present fill the estate.

Pennant reserves his most ardent admiration for the humanitarian efforts managed from Bamburgh Castle:

This castle, and the manor belonging to it, was once the property of the Forsters; but purchased by Lord Crew, Bishop of Durham, and with considerable other estates left vested in Trustees to be applied to unconfined charitable uses. Three of these Trustees are a majority: one of them makes this place his residence, and blesses the coast by his judicious and humane application of the Prelate's generous bequest. He has repaired and rendered habitable the great square tower: the part reserved for himself is a large hall and a few smaller apartments; but the rest of the spacious edifice is allotted for purposes which make the heart to glow with joy when thought of. The upper part is an ample granary, from whence corn is dispensed to the poor without distinction, even in the dearest time, at the rate of four shillings a bushel; and the distressed, for many miles round, often experience the conveniency of this benefaction.
Other apartments are fitted up for the reception of shipwrecked sailors; and bedding is provided for thirty, should such a number happen to be cast on shore at the same time. A constant patrol is kept every stormy night along this tempestuous coast, for above eight miles, the length of the manor, by which means numbers of lives have been preserved. Many poor wretches are often found on the shore in a state of insensibility; but by timely relief are soon brought to themselves.
It often happens that ships strike in such a manner on the rocks as to be capable of relief, in case numbers of people could be suddenly assembled.

For that purpose a cannon is fixed on top of the tower which is fired once if the accident happens in such a quarter, twice if in another, and thrice if in such a place. By these signals the country people are directed to the spot they are to fly to, and by this means frequently preserve not only the crew but even the vessel, for machines of different kinds are always in readiness to heave ships out of their perilous situation.

This extended and sympathetic account of humanitarian endeavour is unusual in the travel literature of the period. While at Bamborough Pennant visited the Farne Islands in a coble, "a safe but seemingly hazardous species of boat, long, narrow and flat-bottomed, which is capable of going thro' a high sea, dancing like a cork on the summit of the waves". Pennant was a prominent naturalist and his approach to ornithology was quite different from that of Thomas Kirk and his companions a century earlier:

Touched at the rock called the *Meg*, whitened with the dung of corvorants which almost covered it; their nests were large, made of tang, and excessively fetid.

Rowed next to the *Pinnacles*, an island in the farthest group, so called from some vast columnar rocks at the south end, even at their sides, and flat at their tops, and entirely covered with guillemots and shags. The fowlers pass from one to the other of these columns by means of a narrow board, which they place from top to top, forming a narrow bridge, over such a horrid gap that the very sight of it strikes one with horror.

Landed at a small island, where we found the female Eider ducks at that time sitting. The lower part of their nests was made of sea plants, the upper part was formed of the down which pull off their own breasts, in which their eggs were surrounded and warmly bedded. In some were three, in others five eggs, of a large size and pale olive colour, as smooth and glossy as if varnished over. The nests are built on the beach, among the loose pebbles, not far from the water. The ducks sit very close, nor will they rise till you almost tread on them. The drakes separate themselves from the females during the breeding season. We robbed a few of their nests of the down and, after carefully separating it from the tang, found that the down of one nest weighed only three-quarters of an ounce, but was so elastic as to fill the crown of the largest hat. The people of this island called these St Cuthbert's ducks, from the saint of the islands.

Besides these birds, I observed the following: puffins, called here *Tom Noddies*; auks, here *Skouts*; guillemots; black guillemots; little auks; shiel [shell] ducks; shags; corvorants; black and white gulls; brown and white gulls; herring gulls, which I was told fed sometimes on eggs of other

birds; common gulls, here *Annets*; kittiwakes, or tarrocks; pewit gulls; great terns; sea pies; sea larks, here *Brokets*; jackdaws, which breed in rabbit holes; rock pidgeons; rock larks.
The terns were so numerous that in some places it was difficult to tread without crushing some of the eggs.

On his way north Pennant gained a distant view of the Cheviot Hills which, he was told, were both a breeding ground for green plovers and the winter habitat of great bramblings. Like some other travellers he was not much impressed by Berwick, where he found most of the streets narrow and bad, but he makes an unusual observation on a local industry:

Abundance of wool is exported from this town: eggs in vast abundance collected through all the country, almost as far as Carlisle: they are packed up in boxes, with the thick end downwards, and are sent to London for the use of sugar refiners. I was told that as many are exported as bring in annually the sum fourteen thousand pounds.

From Berwick Pennant rode north into Scotland, the main objective of his tour. He echoes other travellers in noting the bleak aspect of the first few miles on Scottish soil, but remarks also on signs of recent improvement:

The entrance into Scotland has a very unpromising look; for it wanted, for some miles, the cultivation of the parts more distant from England. But the borders were necessarily neglected for, till the accession of James VI, and even long after, the national enmity was kept up, and the borderers of both countries discouraged from improvement, by the barbarous inroads of each nation. This inattention to agriculture continued till lately but, on reaching the small village of Eyton, the scene was greatly altered. The wretched cottages, or rather hovels, of the country were vanishing; good comfortable houses arise in their stead; the lands are enclosing, and yield very good barley, oats and clover; the banks are planting. I speak in the present tense, for there is still a mixture of the old negligence left amidst the recent improvements, which look like the works of a new colony in a wretched impoverished country.

Given the contribution of Scottish thinkers to the European enlightenment some might take umbrage at Pennant's picture of a backward region experiencing the beneficial effects of English colonisation. Yet the passage also reflects a broader eighteenth century belief in progress, the sense that the past is another country and that the future is open. One can argue that this essentially optimistic world-view survived for another 150 years until it became one of the countless casualties of the First World War killing fields of the Somme, Verdun and Passchendaele.

Passing Cattle

In an earlier chapter I regretted the lack of any accounts reflecting the experience of the servants who accompanied the visitors recalled in this book. We similarly lack any contemporary accounts from the Scottish drovers who, year after year, accompanied their herds of black cattle south over the Border on their trek to the English markets. The origins of this trade can be traced back to medieval times, but the pacification of the Border region noted by Pennant had allowed it to thrive to the extent that as many as 100,000 cattle annually came south over the Border by the end of the eighteenth century. The trade continued more or less at this level until the middle of the nineteenth century, at which point it entered on a sharp decline as a result of the rapidly expanding availability of rail transport. Transporting cattle by train slashed the time needed to bring them to market, and ensured that they arrived at their destination in good condition.

Other visitors, even men such as Arthur Young with his specific interest in agriculture, do not remark upon this trade. The herds were certainly not invisible. In his *Tour Thro' The Whole Island* Defoe comments on the vast numbers of Scottish cattle being fattened on the rich pastures of East Anglia before the final leg of their journey to Smithfield. And in the section *July* in *The Shepherd's Calendar* the poet John Clare gave a vivid account of the impact made on local inhabitants by the drovers and their herds. John Byng also met the drovers and their herds as he rode around the country on his many lengthy excursions, although that lively and curmudgeonly tourist is inclined to take notice only when the droves block or churn up the roads, or when the drovers take over most of the accommodation in the town where he has chosen to stay the night. Travellers were however far less likely to meet the drovers in Northumberland than on the roads further south. Most visitors followed the Great North Road from Newcastle to Berwick, and this was not a droving route. The droves came south from Falkirk and Hawick across the Cheviot range, many of them heading for the great cattle fair at Stagshaw Bank just north of Morpeth. For the drovers this route, or rather this nexus of routes, was far more direct and offered various other advantages noted by Walter Scott in his story *The Two Drovers*:

> The Highlanders in particular are masters of this difficult trade of driving, which seems to suit them as well as the trade of war. It affords exercise for all their habits of patient endurance and active exertion. They are required to know perfectly the drove-roads, which lie over the wildest tracts of the country, and to avoid as much as possible the highways, which distress the feet of the bullocks, and the turnpikes, which annoy the spirit of the drover; whereas on the broad green or grey track, which leads across the pathless moor, the herd not only move at their ease and without taxation, but, if they mind their business, may pick up a mouthful of food by the way. At night, the drovers usually sleep along with their cattle, let the weather be what it will; and many of these hardy men do not once rest under a roof during a journey on foot from Lochaber to Lincolnshire. They are paid very highly, for the trust reposed is of the last importance, as it depends on their prudence, vigilance, and honesty, whether the cattle reach the final market in good order, and afford a profit to the grazier. But, as they maintain themselves at their own expense, they are especially economical in that particular.

Scott's account is as near as one can get to the experience of the drovers. His own grandfather followed that trade, so that Scott can be presumed to know what he was talking about. One might have expected to find contemporary tales of droving in the Scottish folk tradition, but I have not been able to track down any songs specifically linked to the long drove south. By an irony of musical history the richest tradition of droving songs can now be found among the Scottish, and particularly Irish, emigrants to Alberta and other parts of Western Canada, where the genre is known as Cowboy Celtic. However we should perhaps close this section with a beautiful blessing known as *The Herding Rune*, collected on South Uist by Alexander Carmichael:

> Travel ye moorland, Travel ye townland, Travel ye gently far and wide,
> The protection of God and Columba encompass your going and coming,
> And about you be the milk maid with the smooth white palms,
> Bridget of the clustering hair, golden brown.

And yet, there is an additional tailpiece to this short excursus on droving. Dogs were essential tools of the drover's trade as they guided the herds on their southward trek. But many drovers then took employment on English farms, spending several weeks on this work in order to earn some additional income before they began their return journey. The dogs were now surplus to requirements and were therefore sent on their way home, following their southward route in reverse and obtaining food at the same 'stances'.

A Political Progress

The last visitor to be considered in this chapter is William Cobbett (1763-1835) who visited Northumberland for the first and only time in his life in the autumn of 1832, arriving in Newcastle on 21st September and leaving Alnwick on 8th October to travel via Berwick en route to Edinburgh. During this period he visited North and South Shields, Sunderland, Durham, Morpeth and Hexham.

Cobbett was a conservative Radical, a consistent champion of small farmers and agricultural labourers against the new capitalists who maximised their income from the land by enclosures and by squeezing the income of those who worked on the farms. Such radicalism was unusual in an age when parliamentary politics was dominated by the aristocracy and by big money, so that Cobbett won the trust and support of very many people who would otherwise have taken no interest in politics (particularly as they were denied the right to vote). His conservatism shows through in his wish to return to a golden age when paternalistic farmers shared their houses and meals with those who worked on their land, with none of the profits being sucked out to fill the pockets of newly rich investors based in London and other big cities. He is now best known as the author of *Rural Rides*, a collection of journalistic essays written at various times over the years from 1821 to 1834. These essays, written for publication in his *Political Register*, mix wonderfully evocative descriptions of the (mainly) English agricultural landscape with vituperative invective against his political opponents and the evils of the new financial system. Undoubtedly he is at his best in the earlier years when he repeatedly criss-crosses the south of England between Kent and Gloucestershire. By the time that he came north in 1832, now by stage coach rather on his own horse, he had become a political celebrity with a marked tendency to bask in his own glory. The accounts of his *Rides* into the north of England and Scotland contain numerous accounts of banquets held in his honour, with verbatim transcriptions of fulsome welcome addresses complete with lengthy lists of signatories. Nevertheless he took time to look at Northumberland and his initial judgement that it is a meat-producing rather than a bread-producing county shows a finer perception of regional variation in agriculture than we find in the writing of Arthur Young:

> This then is not a country of farmers, but a country of graziers; a country of pasture, and not a country of the plough; and those who formerly managed the land here were not husbandmen, but herdsmen.

Cobbett was impressed with Newcastle ("this fine, opulent, solid, beautiful, and important town") and also by the stir and bustle of the shipping on the Tyne when he took the river boat for the 8 mile journey down to North Shields on 25th September. On the following day he took the half-hourly steamboat service to South Shields on his way to Sunderland. On the 27th he travelled to Durham, then returned to Newcastle on the 28th. Each evening he gave a lecture, typically lasting for at least 2 hours; that given in the play-house on the 28th was his third in Newcastle in the space of a week. At the age of 69 Cobbett had both stamina and an enthusiastic audience. From Newcastle Cobbett went to Morpeth, with some idiosyncratic observations on the changes in the agricultural scene along the way:

> In coming from Newcastle to Morpeth we came over land vastly inferior to that on the eastern coast. The farms appear to produce much less; the pastures are not nearly so good; and, which is very curious, the cows *change their shape*, as well as their *colour*. They get to be swag-backed, pin-haunched, their tails thick and rough, their heads coarse, their faces broad, ribs flat, and horns thick and rather long. This is very curious that, in so few miles, we should have nearly lost the beautiful Holderness cows, and got in their stead these ordinary-looking things, like those of the commons and forests of Surrey and Hampshire. I saw some little West Highland oxen as I came along, which, when fat, weigh about a third part as much as the Nottingham hog of which I bought the ham; that is to say, about fifteen score, or three hundred pounds. The beef of them is very good; and I should suppose that they will fatten upon food which will not fatten a Devonshire, a Herefordshire, a Lincolnshire, or a Durham ox.

The presence of Highland cattle in the town was almost certainly linked to the important cattle market which Cobbett noted. He was less impressed with the modern jail in the Gothic style, regarding it as a sad sign of the times that the largest new building should be a prison rather than a church or monastery. In his *English* Journey of 1933 J B Priestley made a similar observation about 2 enormous bank offices dominating the Coventry skyline. For most of the way from Morpeth Cobbett found the land bleak and poor, with few trees, but all changed as he approached Hexham:

> As I approached this town, along a valley down which runs a small river that soon after empties itself into the Tyne, the land became good, the ash trees more lofty, and green as in June; the other trees proportionately large and fine; and when I got down into the vale of Hexham itself, there I found the oak tree, certain proof of a milder atmosphere; for the oak, though amongst the hardest woods, is amongst the tenderest of plants known as natives of our country. Here everything assumes a different appearance. The Tyne, the southern and northern branches of which meet a few miles above Hexham, runs close by this ancient and celebrated town, all round which the ground rises gradually away towards the hills, crowned here and there with the remains of those castles which were formerly found necessary for the defence of this rich and valuable valley which, from tip of hill to tip of hill, varies perhaps from four to seven miles wide, and which contains as fine cornfields as those of Wiltshire and fields of turnips, of both kinds, the largest, finest, and best cultivated that my eyes ever beheld.

On 1st October Cobbett took a post-chaise to travel from Hexham to Newcastle. Again he admires the countryside and the agriculture, and adds comments on the accommodation and life of the agricultural labourers, whose living conditions are a constant theme in the *Rural Rides*:

> The sides of the Tyne are very fine: cornfields, woods, pastures, villages; a church every four miles, or thereabouts; cows and sheep beautiful; oak trees, though none very large; and, in short, a fertile and beautiful country, wanting only the gardens and vine-covered cottages that so beautify the countries in the South and the West. All the buildings are of stone. Here are coal-works and railways every now and then. The working people seem to be very well off; their dwellings solid and clean, and their furniture good; but the little gardens and orchards are wanting. The farms are all large, and the people who work on them either live in the farmhouse or in buildings appertaining to the farmhouse; and they are all

well fed, and have no temptation to acts like those which sprang up out of the ill-treatment of the labourers in the South.

A major theme of the final chapter of this book will be the coming of the railway, a historical development that effected an irreversible change in the dynamics of travel. At the beginning of October 1832 Cobbett sees the first signs of this future alongside the persistence of past practices:

> They have begun to make a railway from Carlisle to Newcastle, and I saw them at work at it as I came along. There are great lead mines not far from Hexham, and I saw a great number of little one-horse carts bringing down the pigs of lead to the point where the Tyne becomes navigable to Newcastle.

The need to transport coal and lead more quickly over long distances was the principal reason why investors were prepared to put up money to finance the construction of this major project, and some years later to undertake the branch line from Haltwhistle to Alston in the heart of the lead-mining area. Bringing lead down to the river in small carts and then in small boats down to Newcastle had been a slow and laborious task, but the only practicable way before the completion of the new railway.

After a second lecture tour to North Shields and Sunderland Cobbett set out north from Newcastle on 7th October to travel to Alnwick. Again he found little to commend in the country on either side of the Great North Road. On the 8th he left Alnwick en route for Edinburgh, with a savage parting shot at the Duke of Northumberland:

> From Alnwick to Belford, which is about fourteen miles, we first leave behind us, with every feeling of contempt which haughtiness and emptiness can excite in the human mind, the endless turrets and lions of the descendant of Smithson, commonly called Percy, whose father Canning and Ellis and Frere so unmercifully ridiculed under the name of 'Duke Smithson' in a poem entitled *The Duke and the Taxing-man*, the Duke having committed the sin of endeavouring to evade Pitt's assessed taxes.

Tax avoidance by the wealthy obviously dates back at least to the initial introduction of Income Tax in 1799. Little has changed. The Duke was the son of Hugh Smithson, and had acquired the peerage by

131

marrying the heiress. Here is the opening of the poem, an example of political satire cast in ballad form:

> Whilome there liv'd in fair Englonde
>   A Duke of peerless wealth,
> And mickle care he took of her
>   Old Constitution's health.
>
> Full fifty thousand pounds and more
>   To him his vassals paid,
> But ne to King, ne Countree, he
>   Would yield th'assessment made.

From Alnwick Cobbett moved swiftly north to Scotland, hardly pausing to draw breath at Berwick. We should perhaps leave him with his final eulogy on Newcastle:

> This Newcastle is really and truly the London of the North. It has all the solidity of the city of London, all its appearances of industry and real wealth, all its prospects of permanency; and there is only this difference in the people that at Newcastle they are all of one breed and of one stamp, whereas London is inhabited by persons from every part of the kingdom, not omitting a considerable number from the sister kingdom! As to which has the best population, I am naturally shy about delivering a very decided opinion; but this I will say, that a better race than that at Newcastle and its vicinity, I am quite satisfied there is not upon this earth. Here you find all the good qualities, public and private; and, which is a great thing to say, you find them in every class.

Cobbett's language reflects the love of Newcastle expressed by John Wesley. While Wesley's praise was entirely genuine, based on a lifetime's experience of visiting the North, Cobbett's is somewhat suspect. Like many politicians he had the habit of eulogising his immediate audience, and in *Rural Rides* he pays similar tributes to towns and populations up and down the country. But his concern with all classes, particularly the labourers, brings him much closer to Wesley. From a modern perspective his approach is probably more attractive, for while Wesley hoped to improve the lot of the working class by converting them away from drinking, swearing and fighting, Cobbett's more positive and practical wish was to ensure that they had decent accommodation and food, and their fair share of the fruits of the land.

CHAPTER 7

IN TIME AND SPACE ALONG THE WALL

Could my circumstances allow it, there is nothing wherein I should take more pleasure (next to the performance of necessary duties) than in a leisurely journey along the Picts wall, with those preparatory queries wherewith I am pretty well furnished.

Bishop Nicolson, Letter of 17th June 1708 to Ralph Thoresby

In the Footsteps of William Camden

The antiquaries who travelled to Northumberland in the eighteenth century stand apart in several respects from most of the other visitors whom we have met. For them Northumberland and the other northern counties formed the destination of their travels rather than a stage on a journey to Scotland or elsewhere. They were equipped with a historical perspective not shared by all, and a survey of the Wall necessarily involved visiting those remote and wild parts of the county which lay well off the beaten track. And, unlike other travellers, their determination to explore the ruins of a historically significant past places them firmly in the mainstream of the story of the development of modern tourism, with its emphasis on the marketing of heritage sites.

We ended the previous chapter by considering William Cobbett's visit of 1832. To pick up the story of the antiquaries on the Roman Wall we need to step back to 1695 when the young Edmund Gibson (1669-1748) published his new translation of William Camden's *Britannia*, Camden's text being supplemented by new material provided by contemporary scholars. This format proved enduringly successful. Gibson published a revised 2nd edition in 1722, with important new material on the Wall, and further editions followed in 1753 and 1772. For his version of 1789 the new editor Richard Gough provided his own translation of Camden's Latin text and, like Gibson before him, made full use of the best contemporary scholarship, while retaining Gibson's basic format of original text with supplementary essays. A poem published in 1724 gives us some insight into the impact of Gibson's work on the community of scholars:

> For tho' we here had lived some Ages past;
> We liv'd as Strangers on some Island cast,
> And scarce knew where we stood, till Gibson drew
> *Britannia's Map*, and plac'd her all in View.

Given our previous encounter with Daniel Defoe it is interesting to note the poet's assumption that *Robinson Crusoe*, published 5 years earlier in 1719, is already an instantly recognisable reference point, with Gibson being characterised as a new Crusoe engaged in the exploration and mapping of his island.

For his edition of 1695 Gibson obtained supplementary information on the Roman Wall in Northumberland from William Nicolson (1655-1727), Dean (later Bishop) of Carlisle. Nicolson's letter of 25th January 1693 to his fellow antiquary Ralph Thoresby tells us precisely when and how Gibson made his approach:

> I had last week a long letter from him, giving me some account of the undertaking, and what prospect he had of help. I have promised to contribute the little I am able and, particularly, have engaged to communicate what remarks I have relating to the Roman and Saxon antiquities throughout the whole province of York, besides the county of Northumberland, for which I am more especially concerned.

We also know from a later letter of 7th May 1694 that Nicolson had by then completed his contribution:

> A deal of my spare hours were employed in finishing that county of Northumberland, which I have now sent up to our friend Gibson, in such a dress as I had leisure to put upon it.

Despite his undoubted antiquarian expertise Nicolson has little to say about the Wall itself. He does however take issue with Camden's estimate of its original height as 15 feet, preferring the older estimate of 12 feet given by Bede in his *History of the English Church and People*:

> Bede's account of the Roman Wall is very likely fair and true. For in some places on the wastes, where there has not been any extraordinary

fortifications, several fragments come near that height, and none exceed it. His breadth also (at eight feet) is accurate enough. For, wherever you measure it now, you will always find it above seven.

Nicolson's omission to define 'that height' reveals his assumption of a readership of fellow antiquaries with the works of Bede at their fingertips. We should however acknowledge that he bases his conclusions both on his own survey and on the reported observations of Bede who lived 900 years earlier at a time when the Wall was in a far better state of preservation. The most recent research, based on the angle of the steps extant in the milecastle at Poltross Burn (Gilsland), supports Nicolson's estimate of an inner height of 12 feet. The importance of personal observation is also evident in Nicolson's sceptical riposte to Camden's account of the medicinal plants supposedly introduced by the Romans:

As to the medicinal plants Mr Nicolson (to whom we owe these observations upon the Wall) has made a very diligent search, but could never meet with any form of plants growing along the Wall, which is not as plentiful in some other part of the country.

This new spirit of on the ground, if not yet ground-breaking, research was also exemplified by Christopher Hunter (1675-1757), a doctor practising initially at Stockton-on-Tees and later at Durham, with a lifelong interest in antiquities. He made more than one visit to the Wall and to related Roman sites as far north as the fort at High Rochester outside Otterburn. His most interesting contribution is that he calls the Wall unequivocally Hadrian's Wall. Bede and Camden both took the view that the Wall had been built around 400 AD to protect the province after the withdrawal of the Roman forces, while the 18th century consensus ascribed its building to the emperor Severus around 200 AD. Hunter had the correct answer but, frustratingly, does not tell us how he got there.

In 1722 Gibson published his 2nd edition of Britannia, replacing Nicolson's notes with some *Observations upon the Picts Wall* written by Robert Smith (1682-1750), a relative of Dr John Smith, treasurer of Durham cathedral and editor of Bede. Robert Smith almost certainly penned his notes to assist his older relative with his edition of Bede, not with any intention that they should be passed to Gibson for inclusion in his new edition of *Britannia*. Gibson's editorial practice does appear somewhat haphazard. He probably failed to get the best out of Nicolson by not providing him with adequate briefing on the scope of the project, and his use of Smith's unrevised notes over a decade after they had been written is hardly evidence of commitment to the best contemporary scholarship. This does not however mean that Smith's observations are without interest. In 1708 he surveyed the whole of the Wall between Newcastle and Carlisle, and then in May 1709 he journeyed along the stretch between Newcastle and Wallsend. The only part not surveyed, and where there was probably little to see even then, was the section running west from Carlisle to Bowness-on-Solway. Where he did go he combines precise archaeological observation with sensitivity to the landscape setting:

> From the top of the Thirlwall bank to Seven-sheals [Sewingshields], for eight or nine miles together, the wall runs over the summits of steep, rugged, bare and inaccessible rocks on the north side,being built only at eight, six, five, four, and very often at scarce two yards of distance from the very precipice…..This is a very dismal country, but more especially on the north side, being all wild fells and moors, full of mosses and loughs.

As he approached Newcastle the landscape becomes more enclosed, more in keeping with the early eighteenth century ideal:

> From this Walltown……for eight miles together all the way to Newcastle, the wall runs over the top of a great deal of very high ground, but all finely inclosed; and the country, on both sides, yields a pleasing prospect by the great plenty and variety of corn, meadow, and pasture grounds.

The Lucid Springs of Truth - Antiquarianism and Ideology

The most important eighteenth century study of the Wall, John Horsley's *Britannia Romana* (1733), lies outside the scope of the present work since Horsley (1684-1732) was not a visitor to the region but a minister in Morpeth. As a scholarly account Horsley's work held the field until at least the middle of the nineteenth century and remains a key reference work for modern archaeologists. In his Preface he replies to objections by insisting that truth is always valuable in itself, irrespective of its practical usefulness, and by reminding his readers that the history of Roman Britain is the history of our own country. Study of the Roman past is not therefore to be regarded as the serendipitous and ultimately trivial pursuit of amateur antiquarians, but as central to the quest for our national identity.

In making this point Horsley echoes William Camden in his concern to move away from the prevalent dilettantism which encouraged the collection of curiosities, and instead to ground antiquarian studies in their broader historical context. It is no accident that this renewed interest in history and national identity should come to the fore in the years after the union of England and Scotland. Alexander Gordon (1692-1754), who visited the Wall in 1724, as part of his general survey of the Roman remains of North Britain, was prompted to do this by the comment of William Stukeley that the Scots had failed to take any interest in their Roman heritage. Gordon was a colourful character who had previously toured Italy to acquire works of art on behalf of rich patrons. While there he had made use of his good tenor voice to appear on the operatic stage in Messina and Naples. He made his first visit to the Wall in 1724 in the company of his then patron Sir John Clerk (1676-1755), 2nd baronet of Penicuik. Clerk, who was able to use his family's wealth from coal mining to fund his antiquarian interests, was also a prominent figure in contemporary politics. Trained as a lawyer in Leiden he entered the Scottish parliament and established a reputation for his understanding of public finance. This qualified him to serve as one of the 31 Scottish commissioners for the Treaty of Union, where a major issue was the compensation to be paid to the Scots in return for their assumption of part of the English National Debt. His visit to the Wall was preceded by a tour of Tyneside collieries to research the most modern ideas in colliery management. It is unfortunate that his journal of that tour has never been published. Alexander Gordon did however publish the *Itinerarium Septentrionale* in which he devotes considerable space to a survey of the Wall. In his preface he produces a rhetorical flourish on the lasting splendour of what we now know as Hadrian's Wall and the Antonine Wall:

> For who can, even to this day, take a view of those stupendous Walls made cross the island from sea to sea by sundry emperors and their lieutenants but must confess that (China excepted) the whole world cannot shew a greater sight of amazing grandeur than what the Romans have left behind them in Cumberland, Northumberland and Scotland?

His actual survey however was, both literally and metaphorically, a pedestrian affair, as is illustrated by the following typical passage:

> Near Harlow Hill the turf wall comes within 175 paces of Severus's. About 100 paces further west of this place the same stone wall appears very conspicuous, being about 9 foot high, though the square stones or outfacings of the wall are not above two courses entire.
> About 162 paces from Severus's wall the rampart of stone and earth on the north side of Hadrian's vallum appears very plainly, and both continue thus remarkable for 134 paces.

Eric Birley rather unkindly dismisses Gordon's work as having "more in common with popular journalism than with methodical study". The phrase 'popular journalism' applied to Gordon's prose calls to mind Voltaire's dismissal of the Holy Roman Empire as neither holy, nor Roman, nor an empire. However it is probably a fair assessment that Gordon tried to appear more of a scholar than he was and thus fell between two stools, failing to satisfy either the serious archaeologist or the common reader. His book was however to achieve a rather dubious literary immortality in the hands of Mr Jonathan Oldbuck as he travelled in the diligence to Queensferry:

> The coach had continued in motion for a mile or two before the stranger had completely repossessed himself of his equanimity, as was manifested by the doleful ejaculations which he made from time to time on the too great probability, or even certainty, of their missing the flood-tide. By degrees, however, his wrath subsided; he wiped his brows, relaxed his frown, and undoing the parcel in his hand, produced his folio, on which he gazed from time to time with the knowing look of an amateur, admiring its height and condition, and ascertaining, by a minute and individual inspection of each leaf, that the volume was uninjured and entire from title-page to colophon. His fellow-traveller took the liberty of inquiring the subject of his studies. He lifted up his eyes with something of a sarcastic glance, as if he supposed the young querist would not relish, or perhaps understand, his answer, and pronouned the book to be Sandy Gordon's "Itinerarium Septentrionale", - a book illustrative of the Roman remains in Scotland. The querist, unappalled by this learned title, proceeded to put several questions, which indicated that he had made good use of a good education, and although not possessed of minute information on the subject of antiquities, had yet acquaintance enough with the classics to render him an interested and intelligent auditor when they were enlarged upon. The elder traveller, observing with pleasure the capacity of his temporary companion to understand and answer him,

plunged, nothing loath, into a sea of discussion concerning urns, vases, votive altars, Roman camps, and the rules of castrametation.

After a heavy dose of Gordon it is a relief to turn to the antiquary who unwittingly inspired his quest for Scotland's Roman heritage. William Stukeley (1687-1765) opens his *Itinerarium Curiosum* with an epigraph from Martial, "I, fuge, sed poteras tutior esse domi" – go on then, speed on your journey, although you would be much safer if you stayed at home, and then launches into a rhetorical preface that merits inclusion in any anthology of eighteenth century prose:

> If ruminating upon antiquities at home be commendable, travelling at home for that purpose can want no defence; it is still coming nearer the lucid springs of truth. The satisfaction of viewing realities has led infinite numbers of its admirers through the labours and dangers of strange countries, through oceans, immoderate heats and colds, over rugged mountains, barren sands and deserts, savage inhabitants, and a million of perils; and the world is filled with accounts of them. We export yearly our own treasures into foreign parts, by the genteel and fashionable *tours* of France and Italy, and import ship-loads of books relating to their antiquities and history (it is well if we bring back nothing worse) whilst our own country lies like a neglected province. Like untoward children, we look back with contempt upon our own mother. The ancient Albion, the valiant Britain, the renowned England, big with all the blessings of indulgent nature, fruitful in strengths of genius, in the great, the wise, the magnanimous, the learned and the fair, is postponed to all nations. Her immense wealth, traffic, industry; her flowing streams, her fertile plains, her delightful elevations, pleasant prospects, curious antiquities, flourishing cities, commodious inns, courteous inhabitants, her temperate air, her glorious show of liberty, every gift of providence that can make her the envy and the desirable mistress of the whole earth, is slighted and disregarded.
>
> You, Sir, to whom I pretend not to talk in this manner, well know that I had a desire by the present work, however mean, to rouse up the spirit of the Curious among us, to look about them and admire their ancient furniture: to show them we have rarities of domestic growth. What I offer them is an account of my journeyings hitherto, but little indeed, and with expedition enough, with accuracy no more than may be expected from a traveller; for truth in every particular, I can vouch only for my own share, strangers must owe somewhat to informations. I can assure you I endeavoured as much as possible not to be deceived, nor to deceive the reader. It was ever my opinion that a more intimate knowledge of Britain more becomes us, is more useful and as worthy a part of education for our

young nobility and gentry as the view of any transmarine parts. And if I have learnt by seeing some places, men and manners, or have any judgment in things, it is not impossible to make a classic journey on this side the streights of Dover.

Stukeley was the greatest antiquary of his day, and it is interesting to find him echoing Celia Fiennes's plea to the educated classes to pay full attention to English history and archaeology. In his work on Avebury and Stonehenge he pioneered techniques of field archaeology, excavation and accurate recording which were far in advance of anything else achieved before the nineteenth century. His reputation as an archaeologist was not in fact not properly established until the twentieth century. His more lasting influence was on popular culture. He buried sound archaeological work in increasingly bizarre religious theories about Druidism, thus paving the way for the Welsh eisteddfods and for the midsummer celebrations at Stonehenge. In suggesting that young English gentlemen should forego the pleasures of the continental Grand Tour in order to visit Northumberland and the other parts of Britain he was of course totally unsuccessful. One critic has acidly remarked the gilded youth who embarked on the European Grand Tour were far less interested in art than in 'the glory of the Roman whores'.

Stukeley made his tour of the Wall in 1725 in the company of the well-known Yorkshire antiquary Roger Gale, whose sister was later to become Stukeley's second wife. This was the last of his summer expeditions before he settled down as an in Stamford and London as an Anglican clergyman with a well-merited reputation for intellectual eccentricity. His tour of the Wall was not an occasion for detailed archaeological work such as he had undertaken at Avebury, but he shows a fine understanding of the interrelationship between the wall and the vallum and of the military advantages of building the wall on the north side of the Tyne valley rather than using the river as the line of the frontier. His influence on contemporary research was limited by the fact that his notes remained in manuscript for half a century, eventually being published posthumously in 1776 as the *Iter Boreale* and bound together in the same volume as the 2nd edition of the *Itinerarium Curiosum*. Like most gentleman antiquaries he was able to lift his eyes from the Wall itself to observe other curiosities, as in a description of Newcastle which slides into some more general comments:

This is a very large and populous town. The Picts wall ran along by the north side of the road from Corbridge hither, upon a northerm declivity all the way, and in a strait line, on the north side of Newcastle. The present castle was built where the Roman *castrum* was, and the Roman bridge: that and the walls of the town, the churches, and oldest houses, are raised from the plunder of the Roman wall, which ought to be have been preserved as the noblest monument in Europe: it seems to have gone across the present town, from the west gate to Pandon gate; and lately, about the meeting-house, they dug up foundations of it: near Pandon gate was found a seal-ring, now in Mr Warburton's possession.

One of the church steeples in this town is of a very ingenious model, the original of one near London bridge. The bridge here is very long, has houses on it: the arches and piers are rather larger than those of London bridge. There is a ground-plot of the town lately made by an artist. In some parts of this country, the ordinary people make a good sort of ale called *hather*, that is, ling ale, by boiling the tops of the Heather plant to a wort: then I suppose they put wormwood to it, and ferment it. The coal in this country, and which is universally diffused through it, dips many ways, as the falls of valleys, or ducts of rivers, occasionally divert its primary bent; but the main dip of it is to the south-east....Immense are the quantities of coals transported from this focus of our kingdom; and the trade thereof is a perpetual source of seamen for our navy. They speak very broad, so that, as one walks the streets, one can scarce understand the common people, but are apt to fancy one's self in a foreign country. The perpetual clouds of smoke hovering in the air makes everything look black, as at London, and the falling of it down must needs enrich all the ground round about.

Heather Ale, or Fraoch, is still made and is a most refreshing drink. Although a serious antiquary Stukeley, like Celia Fiennes, was also fascinated by new technology, as is evidenced by his visit to the newly constructed Tanfield railway where he left the first known description of the Causey Arch, completed in the year of his visit:

The manner of conveying the coals down to the river side from the pits is very ingenious: a cart-way is made by a frame of timber, on which the wheels of the carts run without horses, with great celerity; so that they are forced to moderate their descent by a piece of wood like a lever applied to one of the wheels. The manner of rowing their great barges is here also very particular, and not unworthy of remark: four men manage the whole; three to a great and long oar, that push it forward; and one to another such a-stern, that assists the other motion, but at the same time steers the keel,

141

and corrects the bias the other gives it. They observe that horses kept under-ground in the coal-mines for two or three years, as sometimes they do, have their hair very fine and sleek, and as short almost as that of a mouse. We saw Colonel Lyddal's coal-works at Tanfield, where he carries the road over valleys filled up with earth, 100 foot high, 300 foot broad at bottom: other valleys as large have a stone bridge laid across: in other places hills are cut through for half a mile together; and in this manner a road is made, and frames of timber laid, for five miles, to the river side, where coals were delivered at 5s the chauldron.

I have mentioned Stukeley's work at Avebury. This is important, not only for the archaeological techniques which he pioneered, but also for his conscious decision to undertake his survey in order to record a monument that was being destroyed year by year to provide building stone for the local community. In modern terms that this was an exercise in rescue archaeology. Stukeley had a clear perception of the obligation of the antiquary to preserve the memory of the past for the benefit of future generations, and this is linked to his belief that knowledge of history is central to the understanding of our national identity. Riding along the Wall he did not have the time to practise rescue archaeology, but his awareness of the potential for irreparable loss is clearly shown 30 years later at a time when he was able to gain the ear of the Princess Augusta, the Princess Dowager, to express his concern about the pillaging of the Wall for road-stone in the wake of the 1745 Jacobite uprising. He asked the Princess to use her influence to press for legislation to halt the damage. His indignation might have been even stronger had he realised that the army was using a substantial stretch of the Wall west from Heddon as the base layer for the new Military Road from Newcastle to Carlisle. As with his plea for the youth of the English elite to spend their leisure and their money in Britain rather than in Europe Stukeley's demand for legislation to protect ancient monuments fell on deaf ears. It was not until 1928 that parts of the Wall first came into public ownership.

75 Years On – Walking the Wall in 1801

On 18th May 1768 the novelist Tobias Smollett, writing to a London apothecary Robert Cotton, commended his wife's plans for her convalescence:

142

I hear Mrs Cotton intends to try the Effect of a Sea Voyage to Newcastle, and I very much approve of her Intention, for I know nothing more likely to set her up.

We may hope that Mrs Cotton's voyage led to the recovery of her health. Others were not so fortunate in their experience of the sea. In 1754 another writer Oliver Goldsmith (1730-1774) embarked on a voyage from Edinburgh to Bordeaux:

You may see by the top of the letter that I am at Leyden; but of my journey hither you must be informed. Sometime after the receipt of your last, I embarked for Bourdeaux, on board a Scotch ship called the St Andrews, Capt John Wall, master. The ship made a tolerable appearance and, as another inducement, I was let to know that six agreeable passengers were to be my company. Well, we were but two days at sea when a storm drove us into a city of England called Newcastle-upon-Tyne. We all went ashore to refresh us after the fatigue of our voyage. Seven men and I were one day on shore, and on the following evening as we were all very merry the room door bursts open, enters a serjeant and twelve grenadiers with their bayonets screwed, and puts us all under the King's arrest. It seems my company were Scotchmen in the French service, and had been in Scotland to enlist soldiers for the French army. I endeavoured all I could to prove my innocence; however I remained in prison with the rest a fortnight, and with difficulty got off even then.

Goldsmith was nevertheless lucky in his misfortune. The Scotch ship had sailed without him while he was in prison, and he later learned that all on board had perished when it was wrecked at the mouth of the Garonne. While Goldsmith's arrival at the port of Newcastle was unplanned, another visitor, the Reverend John Skinner (1772 – 1839), the Rector of Camerton in Somerset, chose the sea route for his journey from London to Newcastle. He boarded a Newcastle trader in the Pool of London at 8.00am on the morning of Wednesday 19th August 1801 but, with adverse winds, it was not until late on the Sunday afternoon that his ship finally cleared the Thames estuary to sail north past Harwich. The subsequent voyage was uneventful and Skinner disembarked at Tynemouth on Friday 28th August, again at 8.00am, after a journey lasting exactly 9 days. Travelling by stage-coach would have been faster and more reliable.

Only a few weeks earlier William Hutton (1723-1815) had set out from Birmingham to visit the Wall. Hutton disdained any mode of transport other than his own two feet and, leaving his home on Saturday 4th July, arrived in Penrith on the Friday the 17th, having covered after walking 230 miles with rest days in Liverpool and Heysham. Up to this point he had been accompanied by his daughter, who describes their daily routine:

> I rode on a pillion behind a servant; and our mode of travelling was this. My Father informed himself at night how he could get out of the house the next morning, before the servants were stirring. He rose at four o'clock, walked to the end of the next stage, breakfasted, and waited for me. I set out at seven; and, when I arrived at the same inn, breakfasted also. When my Father had rested two hours, he set off again. When my horse had fed properly, I followed; passed my Father on the road, arrived before him at the next inn, and bespoke dinner and beds.

At Penrith Catherine and her father temporarily parted company. She continued on horseback to Keswick and, after a brief tour through the Lakes, rode to Hest Bank, a small sea-bathing resort north of Heysham which they had passed through on their journey north and agreed to be the place of rendez-vous on their return. Hutton headed for Carlisle to begin his walk along the Wall.

While Skinner's main purpose in coming north was also to visit the Wall he took the opportunity to fit in a fortnight's tour of east Northumberland and a week's tour of the Lakes before and after his survey of the Wall itself. He could well spare the time since he had lent his house, and no doubt his clerical duties, to another clergyman whose own rectory was being rebuilt after a fire. After disembarking at Tynemouth he set out immediately on his personal exploration:

> From hence to Shields I walked nearly a mile on a high bank rising eighty or a hundred feet above the river. The greater part of the town of North Shields is on a level with the water below. The houses are irregular and are confined, the streets being only sufficiently wide to admit a cart, and miserably dirty. All manner of nastiness obstructing the passage, but what more disgusted me was the butchers' shops where lambs were killing before the door. A sight of this kind I should always wish to avoid, but where the street is only fourteen or fifteen feet wide it cannot be done easily.

Skinner is inclined to sniff those not so genteel as himself. The inhabitants of Sunderland "cannot be expected to to have much time or taste for improvements" and the industrial landscape between Shields and Newcastle was dispiriting:

Walked this morning [30th August] to Newcastle, eight miles to the West of this place; the road to it by no means abounds in picturesque objects; coal works and rope houses bespeak the activities and commercial enterprises of the inhabitants, but there are a few gentlemen's seats to adorn the country. One indeed I observed to the right, about a mile from Newcastle; a good, substantial stone-built building belonging to Mr Matthew White.

Skinner had taken the boat to travel north but, once in the region, he shared Hutton's preference for exploring on foot. His antiquarian interests took him first to Tynemouth where he described and sketched the ruins of the priory. He then heard of the hermitage at Warkworth, combining antiquarian lore with the charms of the picturesque and of Gothic romanticism. Leaving his portmanteau at the inn in Shields he took a knapsack and set out on foot at noon on 31st August, reaching Blyth that evening after bathing on the beach north of Seaton Sluice. This impromptu dip proved unwise since he felt and looked very unwell afterwards and was therefore turned away by the innkeepers in Blyth, only finding a bed for the night with great difficulty. Still feeling off colour the next morning he hired a boy to carry his knapsack and walked along the shore to Newbiggin, exploring about a mile beyond the town before returning to pass a much more comfortable evening:

Returning, I made a sketch of the church and spent a very pleasant evening at the Inn where there is a boarding table kept for the company who come here to bathe at a guinea a week lodging. Included in the village are other lodging-houses apparently very comfortably fitted up let at the rate of six shillings a room. For a retired watering-place I think one cannot see a more pleasant situation; the sand is the finest imaginable, the air healthy, and the living very reasonable. The greatest inconvenience is the distance from a post-town, Morpeth being nearly eight miles off. Three bathing machines are kept here, and I understand that sometimes there is a great deal of company from Newcastle and the neighbourhood.

On the following day Skinner continued his antiquarian perambulation, visiting the church at Woodhorn, the church and castle at Bothel before heading for the hermitage::

Leaving Bothel, I proceeded northwards to Warkworth. In my way I passed Widdrington where stood a castle in ancient times belonging to a family of that name; one of these is rendered immortal in the song of Chevy Chase. The old ruin was about twenty years ago entirely demolished and a modern mansion in castellated form erected on the spot. From thence to Warkworth I experienced a very dreary and uncomfortable walk, as the rain which had fallen very heavily earlier in the day occasioned the road to become very dirty and slippery. However I was fortunate enough to get my knapsack carried by a man on horseback for the last five miles which was a great relief and saved my linen from a complete wetting which it was not in my power to avoid, for when I arrived at the place of my destination there was not a dry thread on my back and I was obliged to immediately to go to bed. This day's stage was about twenty miles.

Skinner was clearly not used to getting wet and, as at Blyth, felt not at all well on the following morning. This gave him the opportunity to finish the drawings he had sketched on the previous day, before visiting the castle and the hermitage in the afternoon. He was so enchanted with the hermitage that he prolonged his stay in Warkworth by 2 further days, spending a whole morning in transcribing all 806 lines of a ballad printed in Percy's *Reliques of Ancient English Poetry* recounting the legend of the hermit. By the third day the Duke's servant responsible for escorting visitors was clearly tiring of Skinner's presence since he gave him both the keys of the hermitage and the boat and let him go to spend most of the day there by himself.

On 7th September Skinner started on his return walk to Shields. It is worth quoting his journal entry for this day in full:

My knapsack proving too heavy, I forwarded it by the Shields carrier and only took a change of linen with me. The weather was more favourable, and I left my Inn at Warkworth, and proceeding along the banks of the Coquet to the west experienced a very interesting walk for eight miles to Felton, a small place standing on the Northern road. I had been informed of an ancient Abbey some miles up the river which occasioned my present deviation instead of returning direct to Shields. As it was too far to reach this evening I determined to take up my abode in my present quarters, and was more induced in this determination by the civility and attention of my host who had been a soldier in the American War where he had lost an arm and an eye. After dinner he accompanied me a little tour round the village and along the side of the river. Being a good trout fisher, every turning and shallow of the stream possessed some particular attraction to his mind, and I was much amused by his conversation and remarks which were far above what I should have expected from one in his station, - what is more bespoke a good heart. In the evening on my return to the Inn I found a party assembled from the harvest field, and having procured a blind fiddler, were preparing for a dance. As my object is to observe everything, I went upstairs and saw a great many Scotch reels danced with great life and spirit however different they might have been in grace and elegance, but the dancers not breaking up till past one o'clock, from necessity I was obliged to sit up in the parlour, the scene of amusement being too close to the room allotted for my sleeping apartment.

I have met with a very sensible man who I at first took to be a clergyman but afterwards found he was steward to a Mr Davidson a gentleman in the neighbourhood. On mentioning my intention of viewing the ruins of Brinkburn Abbey, he readily offered to accompany me the next morning; as he was well acquainted with the place. I accepted his proposal with pleasure. N.B. There is is a very large society in this part of the country amongst gentlemen of extensive property.

Mr Davidson's steward, a Mr Atkinson, accompanied Skinner on his walk the next day to and from Brinkburn Abbey where he made a couple of sketches of the building and some notes on its architecture and setting. On the way there they crossed the Devil's Causeway, the old Roman road from Corbridge to Berwick first put on the map by John Warburton in 1716. They returned to Felton at 6pm after an outing lasting 9 hours. On the following day Skinner walked back to the Tyne, following the turnpike as far as Morpeth and a cross-road thereafter:

I did not stop at Morpeth, but taking the road to the left of the bridge endeavoured to make the shortest cut to Shields, but afterwards regretted I did not continue the turnpike to Newcastle, a few miles further but I am convinced less fatiguing than the mirey road I chose. After walking about seven miles I was obliged to rest at a small ale-house by the roadside for nearly an hour. I have heard more of the Northumbrian dialect than I had before met with; it appears to be Scotch. A little girl was rocking a child in a cradle in the house, and on my enquiring whether the host was at home and whose child it was, she told me "the bairn" belonged to her mistress; that "the guid man" was dead; that the mistress was "ganged down the burn and would not be hame yet"; that "the laddie and lassie before the door" were her mistress's and many other expressions perfectly Scottish.

I arrived at Shields a little after six in the evening and took up my quarters at the Inn I had before put up at; indeed I was not a little glad to get to bed after a walk of above 28 miles. I forgot to mention a singular quarrel I was witness to between two butchers returning from Morpeth market; the expressions they made use of, and the manner in which they conducted their abuse reminded me of Horace's voyage and will not bear repetition, but poor human nature did not appear to advantage I must confess.

Skinner was now ready for his exploration of the Wall but, after 2 very long days on foot, was perhaps not overly disappointed to have to postpone his departure for 24 hours. The carrier from Warkworth had not yet arrived with his knapsack. It was therefore on September 11th that he set off to walk 4 miles along the Newcastle turnpike before he "turned down to the left to a small place consisting of a few houses inhabited by colliers called Wallsend". Skinner doesn't tell us how he managed his luggage for the tour along the Wall. It is probable that he carried his knapsack with his notebooks, ink, pens and a change of linen, and arranged for his portmanteau to be sent ahead. The portmanteau only resurfaces in his Journal when he mentions forwarding it from Carlisle to Keswick after he had completed his exploration of the Wall itself. Hutton however was not encumbered with any surplus baggage when he set out on his walk from Birmingham:

> I was dressed in black, a kind of religious travelling warrant, but divested of assuming airs; and had a budget of the same colour and materials, much like a dragoon's cartridge-box, or post-man's letter pouch, in which were deposited the maps of Cumberland, Northumberland and the Wall, with its appendages, all three taken out of Gough's edition of the Britannia; also Warburton's map of the Wall, with my own remarks, &c.
> To this little pocket I fastened with a strap an umbrella in a green case, for I was not likely to have a six weeks' tour without wet, and slung it over that shoulder which was the least tired. – And now, July the 4th, 1801, we began our march.

In fact Hutton appears not even to have included any change of clothing in his budget or knapsack. Even if his daughter Catherine carried some spare linen for him in her luggage he would have been wearing the same clothes from the time he left Penrith on 17th July until he met up with Catherine again at Hest Bank on the 29th. And she cannot have taken very much since there would not have been much spare capacity on a horse that was already carrying her servant and herself.

Hutton started his tour from Carlisle but his account starts from Wallsend to avoid the duplication of detail that would have been inevitable if he had published a full journal of his out and back expedition. This makes it easier for us to compare their observations as both accounts follow the Wall in the same direction from east to west. Skinner is very much the antiquary, seizing any opportunity to investigate the ruins on the ground:

> Just about where the footpath leads into the turnpike at Byker Hill, they are now employed in digging up the foundations of the Wall to clear the ground of the stones. This gave me an opportunity of seeing it more plainly, for hitherto I had only observed a kind of earth-mound here, and I could trace the position of the stones at the bottom. Some of them were very large, but as there are quarries on the spot they had not far to carry them.

Faced by such evidence of deliberate destruction Skinner adopts a tone of religious resignation, admitting that the Antiquary may regret the disappearance of the remains "but still in the course of things it must be so, and the whole globe itself must dissolve and like the baseless fabric of a vision leave not a trace behind".

Hutton by contrast leaves his Shakespeare at home and comments caustically on the diggings which Skinner had observed:

> Byker's Hill. A hedge now runs in the Ditch, a part of which, this year, for the first time is levelled and converted into a bed of potatoes, which the proprietors will allow gratis, during three years, to any one who will level and improve the ground. This is the taste of the neighbourhood for the grandest piece of antiquity in the whole Island.

Further along, just short of Chollerford, Hutton took particular exception to the action of a Mr Henry Tulip, whom he named and shamed for demolishing a long stretch of the Wall in order to erect a new farmhouse:

> I desired the servant with whom I conversed, "to give my compliments to Mr Tulip, and request him to desist, or he would wound the whole body of Antiquaries. As he was putting an end to the most noble monument of Antiquity in the whole Island, they would feel every stroke. If the Wall was of *no* estimation, he must have a mean opinion of me, who would

travel six hundred miles to see it; and if it *was*, he could never merit my thanks for destroying it".

"Should he reply, 'The property is mine, and I have a right to direct it as I please', it is an argument I can regret, but not refute".

It is possible that Hutton's protest had some effect since a short section of the Wall still remains in place on Mr Tulip's old property. Equally likely is that the stones in that section were surplus to his building requirements.

What marks Hutton out from his predecessors and contemporaries is his very personal, even idiosyncratic, approach to the Wall and his desire to share his feelings about it with his readers. In the Preface to his *History* he makes his position clear:

> There are few pursuits, in the compass of letters, more dry than that of Antiquity. The Antiquary feeds upon withered husks, which none can relish but himself; nor does he seem to possess the art of dressing up his dried morsel to suit the palate of a reader, for his language is often as dry as his subject; as if the smile was an enemy to Truth. Mere dull description, like a burnt cinder, is dead matter. If he designs a *treat*, why not infuse a little spice to suit the taste of his guest? ……………
>
> I would enliven truth with the smile, with the anecdote; and while I travel the long and dreary Wall, would have you travel with me, though by your own fire-side; would have you see, and feel, as I do; and make the journey influence your passions, as mine are influenced……………
>
> Perhaps, I am the first man that ever travelled the whole length of this Wall, and probably the last that will ever attempt it. Who then will say, he has, like me, travelled it twice?
>
> Old people are much inclined to accuse youth of their follies; but on this head silence will become me, lest I should be asked, 'What can exceed the folly of that man, who, at seventy-eight, walked six hundred miles to see a shattered Wall!'

Hutton's emotional approach to the Wall was based on his conviction that, in walking along it, he was treading in the footsteps of Agricola, Hadrian and Severus, the men whom he believed to have been its architects and builders. His narrative is often intensely personal, as in the following passages:

> At the twenty-fourth mile-stone, I still have Severus's trench, and what remains of the Wall, on my right, and Hadrian's works on my left, with

the military way on which I tread, only twelve yards wide, between, which fills up the space. Thus am I hemmed in by dignity, upon the best of roads, upon elevated ground, with extensive prospects, in a country thickly inhabited, surrounded with commons, or with inclosures of fifty or a hundred acres each, but without trees or hedges, and where the face of the earth seems shaved to the quick. Yet in this solitary place, where foot seldom treads, I enjoy the company of three valuable friends, Agricola, Hadrian, and Severus.

I now travel over a large common, still upon the Wall, with its trench nearly complete. But what was my surprise when I beheld, thirty yards on my left, the united works of Agricola and Hadrian, almost perfect! I climbed over a stone wall to examine the wonder; measured the whole in every direction; surveyed them with surprise, with delight, was fascinated, and unable to proceed; forgot I was upon a wild common, a stranger, and the evening approaching. I had the grandest works under my eye, of the greatest men of the age in which they lived, and of the most eminent nation then existing; all which had suffered but little during the long course of sixteen hundred years. Even hunger and fatigue were lost in the grandeur before me. If a man writes a book upon a turnpike road, he cannot be expected to move quick; but, lost in astonishment, I was not able to move at all.

This emphasis on the importance of personal response has attracted later walkers and readers. Hunter Davies, whose equally idiosyncratic *A Walk Along the Wall* is probably the most popular modern account, hunted down a copy of Hutton's *History* and took it as his companion, thus walking the Wall with Hutton in much the same way that Hutton had walked with Agricola, Hadrian and Severus. A recent academic study by Claire Nesbitt and Divya Tolia-Kelly also stresses the centrality of Hutton's personal response to the monument. They note how, for Hutton, "the Wall and its landscape…..embodied the spirit of their creators" and became a place in time where Hutton could meet with the past.

It was well for Hutton that he had his Roman friends since, both for him and for Skinner, modern friends were often hard to find. From Heddon on the Wall to Harlow Hill Skinner was pursued by a man who took him to be a spy, and on the way to Chesters he had other problems:

151

I must remark by the way that civility to strangers by no means appears to be a characteristic of the country people of Northumberland more than in Wales. At one cottage I passed this morning close to the Wall, I saw a woman at her door with a sheep dog by her side. As I approached nearer, she shut herself in the house and endeavoured to set the dog on me; had I not been armed with a stick, in all probability I might have been bitten. At the Chesters I have just been speaking of, it was not much bettter, for the farmer who was in the field with his reapers did not attempt to call off his dog when he was running to me, and it was some time before I could persuade him that my intentions were pacific in visiting these parts. How absurd is the idea of Arcadian simplicity and benevolence in the lower orders. Whenever *I* have made any observations I am sure it has been quite the reverse, and the more uninformed the people, the more brutal and selfish I have always found them.

Hutton encountered similar responses on several occasions, being taken for a Methodist preacher, a spy employed by the Government, and an exciseman. Two passages are of particular contemporary relevance:

[Birdoswald] When I entered the house of Mr Bowman, who is the proprietor, and occupier, of these once imperial premises, I was received with that coldness which indicates an unwelcome guest, bordering upon a dismission; for an ink-bottle and book are suspicious emblems. But, as information was the grand point in view, I could not, for trifles, give up my design; an expert angler will play with his fish till he can catch him.
With patience, with my small stock of rhetoric, and, above all, the simplicity of my pursuit, which was a powerful argument, we became exceedingly friendly; so that the family were not only unwilling to let me go, but obliged me to promise a visit on my return. They gave me their best; they wished it better. I had been, it seems, taken for a person employed by Government to examine private property, for the advancement of taxation.

[Bank Head] I entered a farm-house for intelligence; I was treated with great shyness, till they understood my pursuit. It appeared, they had taken me for a surveyor of land, preparatory to inclosing the commons.

Enclosures were of course bitterly contested during this period. Whatever their benefits for progressive agriculture they destroyed the historical rights of ordinary people to use common lands for pasturage and as a source of fuel and fodder. As for taxation one should remember that Pitt's government had introduced the first Income Tax in 1799 and tax surveyors were no doubt making their rounds to assess the annual value of those estates whose owners were likely to be liable to the tax.

I do not think that we should regard either Hutton or Skinner as unduly thin-skinned or as suffering from persecution mania. Strangers were an unusual sight in the areas which they visited, and any natural suspicions would have been exacerbated by their habit of dress and by their decision to cover the ground on foot. Clerical garb, and the notebooks, pens and ink that any surveyor would have carried as a matter of course – it is hardly surprising that their appearance put the locals on their guard. But had they been on horseback they might have aroused less hostility. Gentlemen did not walk. We may recall Miss Bingley's disgust at Elizabeth Bennet's walking from her home to Netherfield:

> To walk thre miles, or four miles, or five miles, or whatever it is, above her ancles in dirt, and alone, quite alone! what could she mean by it? It seems to me to shew an abominable sort of conceited independence, a most country town indifference to decorum.

Karl Philipp Moritz, who visited England in 1782, reported a similar reaction:

> A traveller on foot in this country seems, however, to be considered as a sort of wild man, or an out-of-the-way being, who is stared at, pitied, suspected, and shunned by every body that meets him. At least this has hitherto been my case, on the road from Richmond to Windsor. My host could not sufficiently express his surprise, that I intended to to venture to walk as far as Oxford, and still further.

Hutton and Skinner were perhaps lucky to meet with no more than suspicion and empty threats. In the 1740's a geometer or surveyor, one of a team responsible for the first full cartographic survey of France, had been murdered by suspicious locals in the wild region of the Ardèche. However, given the level of suspicion evident in their accounts, it is hardly surprising that there were times when they found it difficult to obtain accommodation. Had they travelled on horseback and with a servant, like respectable gentlemen, innkeepers would have welcomed them with open arms, sure of extracting a generous payment for accommodation and food. We have however already noted Skinner's problems in obtaining a bed for the night at Blyth when he arrived on foot and obviously unwell. He also walked out of the first inn at Harlow Hill, convinced that the landlord had been warned against him by the man who had followed him all the way from Heddon. There was a happier outcome for Hutton when he asked for a bed at Twice Brewed:

A more dreary country than this in which I now am, can scarcely be conceived. I do not wonder it shocked Camden. The country itself would frighten him, without the Troopers.

As the evening was approaching, and nature called loudly for support and rest, neither of which could be found among the rocks; I was obliged to retreat into the military road, to the only public house, at three miles distance, known by no other name than that of *Twice Brewed*.

"Can you favour me with a bed?"

"I cannot tell till the company comes."

"What, is it club-night?"

"Yes, a club of carriers."

A pudding was then turned out, about as big as a pork measure; and a piece of beef out of the copper, perhaps equal to half a calf.

"You must be so kind as to indulge me with a bed. I will be satisfied with any thing."

"I cannot, except you will sleep with this man" (pointing to a poor sick traveller who had fallen ill upon the road).

"That will be inconvenient."

"Will you consent to sleep with this boy?" (about ten). "Yes".

Having completed our bargain, and supped, fifteen carriers approached, each with a one-horse cart, and sat down to the pudding and beef, which I soon perceived were not too large. I was the only one admitted; and watched them with attention, being highly diverted. Every piece went down as if there was no barricade in the throat. One of those pieces was more than I have seen eaten at a meal by a moderate person. They convinced me that eating was the "chief end of man". The tankard too, like a bowl lading water out of the well, was *often emptied, often filled*.

My landlady, however, swerved from her agreement; for she found me a *whole* bed to my wish.

CHAPTER 8

HIGHWAYS AND BYWAYS

On Tuesday night we came hither. Yesterday I took some care of myself, and today I am *quite polite*. I have been taking a view of all that could be shown me, and find that all very near to nothing. You have often heard me complain of finding myself disappointed by books of travels, I am afraid travel itself will end likewise in disappointment. One town, one country is very like another. Civilized nations have the same customs, and barbarous nations have the same nature. There are indeed minute discriminations both of places and of manners, which perhaps are not unworthy of curiosity, but which a traveller seldom stays long enough to investigate and compare. The dull utterly neglect them, the acute see a little, and supply the rest by fancy and conjecture.

Samuel Johnson, letter dated 12th August 1773 written at Newcastle

Scots Coming South

At the end of the last chapter we left Hutton safely in the company of the carriers on their overnight halt at Twice Brewed. Before that we saw Skinner entrusting his knapsack to the carrier operating between Warkworth and North Shields. Carriers were the long-distance lorry drivers of their day, responsible for transporting goods and packets between the different towns. Like the drovers they tended to avoid the turnpikes and the associated tolls. Although a constant feature of the transport system in the age before the railway they have only a shadowy existence in our story. We may however note the account of one fictional character who set out from Glasgow to follow the traditional route taken by Scots hoping to find fame and fortune in London:

There is no such convenience as a waggon in this country, and my finances were too weak to support the expence of hiring a horse. I determined therefore to set out with the carriers, who transport goods from one place to another on horseback; and this scheme I accordingly put into execution on the first day of November 1739, sitting upon a pack-saddle between two baskets, one of which contained my goods in a knapsack. But, by the time we arrived at Newcastle-upon-Tyne, I was so fatigued with the tediousness of the carriage, and benumbed with the

155

coldness of the weather, that I resolved to travel the rest of my journey on foot, rather than proceed in such a disagreeable manner.

Once at Newcastle Roderick Random puts up at an unnamed inn and is almost persuaded by the hostler to take passage to London in a collier rather than face the long winter walk to London. This however being a picaresque novel he providentially bumps into an old school-friend, and the two of them set out for London on foot. After five days and various adventures they catch up with the regular waggon trundling between Newcastle and London and are able to take places in this for the rest of their journey south. Once arrived in London Roderick is able to secure the post of surgeon's mate on the ill-fated naval expedition to Carthagena.

Smollett's contemporaries regarded this novel as in large measure autobiographical. We know that Smollett (1721-1771) studied surgery at the university in Glasgow and that he travelled to London in 1739 at the age of 18 to seek his fortune there, subsequently taking part in the expedition to Carthagena. We do not however have any evidence of how he travelled to London, although it is wholly possible that he did use the carriers to take him as far as Newcastle. This would indeed have been slow and uncomfortable. Smollett does not however mention the advantages of this mode of travel: safety in numbers, absolute certainty of navigation across wild country, and the guarantee of accommodation and food each evening. Many Scots must have travelled this way to seek employment in England, but they did not leave diaries for us to follow them on their journeys. Smollett himself returned to Scotland in 1755 to see his mother and to visit Glasgow, with a subsequent tour in 1766 when he arrived in Edinburgh in June and then revisited the area around Loch Lomond where he had spent his childhood. Some of these experiences are reflected in his 1771 novel *Humphrey Clinker*:

I have now reached the northern extremity of England, and see, close to my chamber window, the Tweed glide through the arches of that bridge which connects this suburb to the town of Berwick. Yorkshire you have seen, and therefore I shall say nothing of that opulent province. The city of Durham appears like a confused heap of stones and brick, accumulated so as to cover a mountain, round which a river winds its brawling course. The streets are generally narrow, dark, and unpleasant, and many of them almost impassable in consequence of their declivity. The cathedral is a huge gloomy pile; but the clergy are well lodged. The bishop lives in a princely manner – the golden prebends keep plentiful tables – and, I am told, there is some good sociable company in the place; but the country, when viewed from the top of Gateshead Fell, which extends to Newcastle, exhibits the highest scene of cultivation that I ever beheld. As for Newcastle, it lies mostly in a bottom, on the banks of the Tyne, and makes an appearance still more disagreeable than that of Durham; but it is rendered populous and rich by industry and commerce; and the country lying on both sides the river, above the town, yields a delightful prospect of agriculture and plantation. Morpeth and Alnwick are neat pretty towns, and this last is famous for the castle which has belonged so many ages to the noble house of Percy, earls of Northumberland.

As Smollett was well aware the flood of economic migrants moving south from Scotland provoked resentment in the local population:

From Doncaster northwards, all the windows of all the inns are scrawled with doggerel rhymes, in abuse of the Scottish nation; and what surprised me very much, I did not perceive one line written by way of recrimination. Curious to hear what Lismahago would say on this subject, I pointed out to him a very scurrilous epigram against his countrymen, which was engraved on one of the windows of the parlour where we sat – He read it with the most starched composure; and when I asked his opinion of the poetry – 'It is vara terse and vara poignant', said he, 'but, with the help of a wat dishclout, it might be rendered more clear and parspicuous'.

A notably cantankerous travel writer, Smollett was equally cutting about the English:

She (Tabitha) was so little acquainted with the geography of the island, that she imagined we could not go to Scotland but by sea.......if the truth must be told, the South Britons in general are wofully ignorant in this particular. What between want of curiosity, and traditional sarcasms, the effect of ancient animosity, the people at the other end of the island know as little of Scotland as of Japan. If I had never been in Wales, I should have been more struck with the manifest difference in appearance between the peasants and commonalty on the different sides of the Tweed. The boors of Northumberland are lusty fellows, fresh complexioned, cleanly, and well-clothed.

Robert Burns (1759-1796) was another Scottish writer who came briefly to Northumberland. In 1787, at the age of 28, he set out with

157

his friend Robert Ainslie. Leaving Edinburgh on 5th May they made a short excursion into Northumblerland on Monday 7th May when they crossed the Tweed from Coldstream to Cornhill. Burns's travel journal is terse and uninformative:

> Coldstream – went over to England – Cornhill – glorious river Tweed – clear and majestic – fine bridge – dine at Coldm. with Mr Ainslie and Mr Foreman.

The visit to Coldstream was to pay a social call on Robert Ainslie's family. The fine bridge that made possible their outing into England had been built only 4 years before their visit. From Coldstream the two travellers made the tour of the Border abbey towns before riding on Friday 18th May to Berwick, "an idle town, but rudely picturesque". From there they returned once more into Scotland where they parted company. Burns continued the tour by himself and, a few days later, rode south again::

> Sunday – 27th May – Cross Tweed an[d] traverse the moors thro' a wild country till I reach Alnwick – Alnwick castle, a seat of the Duke of Northumberland, furnished in a most princely manner – A Mr Wilkin, an Agent of His grace's, shows us the house & policies – Mr W a discreet, sensible, ingenious man –
> Monday – Come, still through byways, [to] Warworth [sic] where we dine – hermitage & old castle – Warkworth situated very picturesque with Coquet-Island, a small rocky spot the seat of an old monastery, facing it a little in the sea; and the small but romantic river Coquet running through it – Sleep at Morpeth a pleasant little town, and on next day to Newcastle – Meet with a very agreeable sensible fellow, a Mr Chattox, a Scotchman, who shows us a great many civilities and who dines & sups with us.

From Newcastle Burns rode west to Carlisle via Hexham, flirting outrageously on the way with a couple of sisters who suggested that he elope to Gretna Green with the unmarried one. In a letter dated 1st June Burns is far more frank about this episode than in his journal:

> I hae dander'd owre a' the kintra frae Dumbar to Selcraig, and hae forgather'd wi' monie a guid fallow, and monie a weelfar'd hizzie. – I met wi' twa dink quines in particlar, ane o' them a sonsie, fine fodgel lass, baith braw and bonie; the tither was a clean-shankit, straught, tight weelfar'd winch, as blythe's a lintwhite on a flowerie thorn, and as sweet and modest's a new blawn plumrose in a hazle shaw. – They were baith bred

to mainers by the beuk, and onie ane o' them has as muckle smeddum and rumblegumption as the half o' some Presbytries that you and I baith ken. – They play'd me sik a deevil of a' shavie that I daur say if my harigals were turn'd out, ye wad se twa nicks I' the heart o' me like the marks o' a kail-whittle in a castock. –

I was gaun to write you a lang pystle, but Gude forgie me, I gat myself sae noutouriously bitchify'd the day after kail-time that I can hardly stoiter but and ben.

Burns had in fact spent considerable energy on the Scottish side of the border in flirting with the daughters of his various hosts, no doubt leaving one or more sore hearts in his wake.

Dear Sister

No Irish travellers enter our story, although there were doubtless many Irish migrant workers employed in Tyneside industry and later on the construction of the railway network. These men have not left any record of their experiences. We do however have the letters of Bishop Richard Pococke (1704-1765), born in Southampton of English descent but with a career in the Protestant Church of Ireland. He became Bishop of Ossory in 1756, subsequently being translated to Meath shortly before his death in 1765. His ecclesiastical appointments left him considerable leisure and he became an inveterate traveller, spending much time in the decade from 1733 to 1742 in tours of Europe and the Middle East. He also toured extensively in England, Wales and Scotland and his visits to Northumberland in 1760 came immediately before and after an extended stay in Scotland. He recorded his impressions in letters to his sister Elizabeth in Newbury.

Pococke made his first brief entry into Northumberland on 17th May when he travelled down from Alston to Haltwhistle and then visited Thirlwall Castle, Birdoswald and Naworth Castle before following the Military Way west to Brampton and back into Cumberland. He returned to the Border region at the end of September.. On the 23rd he visited Flodden, Etal and Ford Castle and then, like Robert Burns 27 years later, came to Cornhill:

> .....a considerable village, very near the Tweed. They have here a water like that of the Epsom wells, from which they extract a salt; it is esteemed

159

good in nephritick and scorbutic disorders. Near it is a cold bath, which they use much when they drink the water.

After another diversion into the Scottish borders he returned to Northumberland on the 27th, visiting Wooler ("a poor town mostly of thatched houses") and then admiring the productive sheep walks on the Cheviot hills and praising the quality of the mutton produced there. Two days later he visited Wooler Haugh Head, a "place much frequented for drinking goat's whey". Like Celia Fiennes in 1698 Pococke was obviously much interested in health resorts. Moving further south he found Alnwick to be a most handsome town and put on record his approval of the castle:

> The castle of Alnwick, the ancient place of residence of the Percys, Earls of Northumberland, is one of the grandest and most entire in Britain. It is built round a small court with an enclosure on every side except to the north and west, and is defended by towers. To the west it is fortified by a large enclosure in which are the stable offices, to the right of the second court are the kitchen offices and those for servants. In the inner court are two grand rooms fitted up in the finest Gothic style. The dining room is adorned with small arches, and the drawing room in a most elegant taste of arches intersecting one another, and the ceilings of both are richly ornamented. The ornaments in the office are plain Gothic. The Earl has made a Gothic gateway to the south, by which the common entrance is to be entirely clear of the town, and the grand gateway is to be closed. He is also making a park, one of the gates of which is almost built, purposing to take up his constant summer residence here.

After Alnwick he found Rothbury disappointing, although his comments are nevertheless worth quoting:

> Rothbury is a poor town of two streets which are not paved, and the houses are mostly thatched; they cover them with sods for warmth, and thatch with heath, which will last thirty years. There are turnpike roads from it to Hexham, Newcastle, Morpeth, and Alnwick, which make it a thoroughfare from all the villages to the west and north and from Ellesden, for there is no other town this way to the west or north; the rise of the Coquet which is pronounc'd Cocket, being the bounds of Scotland at about twelve miles distance. It is a market town and they have some fairs chiefly for black cattle; and wool is sent from this place to Newcastle. They have several shops and handicrafts exercised here, particularly that of hatters............The parsonage house is an old tower-castle with an addition to it. Near it, the late incumbent Dr Sharp,

160

prebendary of Durham, built a round tower about 30 feet high, with battlements at top from which, they say, there is a prospect of the sea. Most part of the town belongs to the Earl of Northumberland. Dr Sharp's immediate predecessor, Tomlinson, founded a free school, with a salary of £20 a year and a house, to teach all the children of the parish to read, write, arithmetic, and Latin.

The tower, which still stands on the hill above the town, is also mentioned in a somewhat later survey of the County:

Whitton, a small village, is almost close to Rothbury. Here, in a spendid edifice, called Whitton Tower, which had formerly been a castle, the Rector of Rothbury resides. It has been beautified, at a great expense, by the various Rectors, has an extensive fish-pond near it, and is surrounded by thriving plantations. South from it is an observatory, which commands a most extensive and richly-variegated prospect. It was built by Dr Sharpe, in a season of scarcity, to give employment to the poor, and is still called "The Doctor's Folly". – Well would it be for mankind, were folly always to exert itself in similar acts of benevolence.

Pococke was noted for his philanthropic work in Ireland and, since he clearly approved of Tomlinson's foundation of the free school, it is perhaps slightly surprising that he did not make more of Dr Sharp's imaginative blend of benevolence with amateur scientific endeavour. The tower-castle mentioned by both writers is a fourteenth century vicar's pele which, like the better-known example at Corbridge, provided the vicar and his flock with protection from raiding reivers. The fairs for black cattle take us back to the days of the drovers and have long since disappeared, but the general picture of Rothbury as a small commercial centre acting as hub to a large hinterland remains recognisable to this day.

From Rothbury Pococke rode to Corbridge and then north along Watling Street to Risingham (Woodburn) where he transcribed Roman inscriptions and made hurried notes on a variety of topics:

They find medals here; I saw one of large brass of Maximian, and another of the Low Empire. There were some inscriptions that lay close to the river, and were washed away, but probably copied among the several inscriptions which Camden has given from this place, by which it appears that the god Mogon was worshipped here, according to a tradition he mentions among the inhabitants; there is a lower bank between the

161

rampart and the river. The folk on this side Woodburn are a good sort of people, but in Redesdale they are sharper probably owing to the ancient Scotch incursions. And in Tynedale they seem to be a people of great simplicity. We proceeded over dismal heaths, two miles to the curious bridge of one arch over the Rede, it is about one 3d of a circle, turned with a double arch, and two tiers of stone only over them for the battlement.

This magpie collection of disconnected and undigested scraps is a characteristic element in the writings of eighteenth century antiquaries. Not having learned to specialise they took an interest in everything, and on the whole their work is richer for it. Like most of his colleagues Pococke does not restrict his remarks to objects of purely antiquarian interest, but shares their interest in contemporary matters such as the development of the waggonways:

We then came most of the way by the coal wagon-roads, in which it is curious to see the wagons go down the hills without any horse or man to draw them; only a man to stop the wheels when it is too steep, the horse being tied behind, and when they come on a level he is taken off and draws, the wheels are of cast iron with a rim round within which hinders them from going off the frame and they are made a little hollow from that rim to the outside. I came to Newcastle on Tine.

This description of a flanged wheel is clearly based on the same habit of close observation that Pococke employed when deciphering Roman inscriptions. From Newcastle he made excursions to Seaton Delaval, where he visited and described Vanburgh's hall, and to Tynemouth where his observations take in history, architecture, contemporary naval defence arrangements, the hazards of navigation in the Tyne estuary leading to the building of lighthouses, the shipping of coal, and the popularity of the village for sea bathing and the drinking of salt water. In Newcastle itself he notes the glass-houses at Ouseburn, Abraham Crowley's ironworks at Winlaton, the processing of lead and the export of Berwick salmon. He leaves one of the last accounts of the old Tyne bridge which was to collapse 11 years later in the Great Flood of November 1771:

This place is also a great thoroughfare to Scotland, so that it is every way the fourth town for trade in England, after London, Bristol and Liverpool. There is a large bridge over the Tyne, half of it belongs to Durham, and the other part to Newcastle, and is divided by a gate. They have shops in

162

each side of the bridge. It leads to the suburb of Gateshead in the Bishoprick of Durhm, which is much inhabited by colliers. Here is a beautiful Gothic chapel with seven single windows in front, a fine door case, and two ornamental niches in two stories on each side. It was a Popish mass-house and destroyed by the mob in 1745, and is now in ruins.

D'un château l'autre

Sixteen years later another antiquary William Hutchinson (1732-1814) travelled around Northumberland, publishing in 1778 a 2 volume account of his tour. Hutchinson practised as a solicitor in Barnard Castle but, as with Richard Pococke, his professional career left him ample leisure to travel and pursue his antiquarian interests. A committed freemason he wrote *The Spirit of Masonry* (1775) and detailed descriptions of Cumberland and Durham in addition to his work on Northumberland.

Writing a 'Blue Guide' *avant la lettre* Hutchinson, uniquely among our visitors, aimed at comprehensive coverage of the county. His personal observations cover more towns and villages than those of any other visitor, while in his antiquarian commentary he acknowledges his substantial borrowings from earlier English and Scottish authors. Rather too often the sheer delight in antiquarian learning swamps his personal observation, most obviously so in his description of Berwick towards the start of the second volume. Here he devotes 4 pages to his view of the town, and a further 61 pages to the historical background. His predilection for prolix footnotes extending over 2 or more pages calls to mind the description of a Victorian commentary on Virgil as 'a thin stream of text meandering through verdant meadows of commentary'.

Entering Northumberland from Alston Hutchinson heads straight for Featherstone Castle, shuddering at the view of "one vast expanse of waste and barrenness", but recovering his spirits with the progress of cultivation as he approached Bellister Castle and Haltwhistle. His spirits were however raised only to be swiftly dashed by the inexplicable absence of a workman from his post when a gentleman such as Hutchinson, the undoubted possessor of a valuable life, required his presence:

We proceeded towards Haltwezell in hopes to pass the river by the ferry-boat; but the boatman, who thinks himself a competent judge of the necessity there is for his attendance, was not to be found; and we were obliged to pass the ford, which is broad and deep, with a bottom of very large stones over which a horse, breast deep in the water, unaccustomed to the passage, incessantly falters or stumbles. Those circumstances would have been greatly aggravated by our ignorance of the place, had we not met with a person to conduct us – Instances of well applied charity characterize this age; it would not be one of the least to give a stipend to an attendant at such fords as these, by which many valuable lives would be saved - Is it not shocking that a traveller should be exposed to infinite perils by the stupidity or folly of a boatman who presumers to determine on a matter of such moment as the fate of his fellow-creature! A wretch whose character, perhaps, is one of those humiliating subjects, which serve to reduce self-estimation and human vanity by showing how near man in the lowest class is to the brute creation.

This was not Hutchinson's only grievance about the facilities afforded to travellers in Northumberland:

From Risingham to Elsdon the traveller, in all the perplexities of a rainy and desolate country, must proved a patient christian if he forbears to execrate the want of guide-posts, and the neglect of those whose duty it is to remedy the delay, fatigue, hazard and anxiety of the stranger, whose stars infatuate him to engage in the labyrinths and wilds of such a country.

Unsurprisingly however Hutchinson expresses admiring approval of the benevolent work of the Duke and Duchess of Northumberland, and is delighted when he finds an inn where he can meet people of his own class:

The inn at Chollerford tempted our stay; a spacious room, built for the resort of the neighbouring gentlemen, afforded us a pleasing view upon the river; whilst excellent accommodation indulged us with that degree of satisfaction which truly consitutes the traveller's ease.

As he rides from town to town and village to village Hutchinson pays particular attention to all marks of antiquity, most especially the numerous castles which are such a characteristic feature of the county. Like other travellers he spent considerable time in following the route of the Roman Wall, although his comments here are mainly derivative, a fact which he readily acknowledges. Elsewhere he displays a strain of picturesque melancholy, as in his description of Prudhoe:

We passed over the ferry-boat at Ovingham, from whence we had a fine view of the castle of Prudhoe. The river beneath us washed the margin of a level of corn-land, above which arose the the precipitous cliffs on which the castle is erected, in the form of a half-moon, crowned with the remains of the fortress, of an aspect awfully majestic. Over these the rising grounds behind, clothed with woods, and the thick groves on each flank, seemed to cast a solemn mantle. The scene struck me with the image of mourning royalty, weeping in ashes for the dissolution of Empire, and lamenting the cruel vicissitudes of Fortune, in which all its honours are extinguished, and nothing but memorials of calamity left behind.

If I am right in suspecting a contemporary reference here to Burgoyne's defeat at Saratoga in 1777, and to the probable loss of the American colonies, this would suggest that Hutchinson's memory of the visit was coloured retrospectively by the events of the following year. And in the description of the castle on its 'precipitous cliffs' it is almost as if he had seen an advance copy of William Turner's painting of the same scene in 1825, a painting which similarly exaggerates the elevation of the castle.

In contrast to castles and old churches industrial areas, such as Allenheads, are 'dark and deplorable', although his fascination with the new technology of the waggonways does result in one passage where he manages to describe manual work without a shudder:

From the mines the coals are sent to the places of lading in large unwieldy carriages or waggons, of the form of a common mill-hopper, carried on four wheels of iron, the felloes or rims of which are hollow so as to run upon strings of wood adapted thereto, with which the rows are laid. By this means these carriages on an easy descent run without horses, and sometimes with that rapidity that a piece of wood, called a tiller, is obliged to be applied to one wheel, and pressed thereon by the weight of the attendant who sits on it to retard the motion: by the friction of which frequently the tiller and sometimes the carriage is set on fire.

At other times Hutchinson studiously overlooks the messy details, using the sight of industry as the text for a sermon on the value and necessity of human endeavour:

Approaching the sea-coast we viewed Newbiggin, a fine bay for shipping, secured from the stormy quarters by high rocky promontories and capable of receiving vessels of 60 tons burthen. The town is small, and chiefly inhabited by fishermen. The whole coast is enlivened by trade, and opulence is dispensed on every side by the hand of industry. Human nature is capable of vast works; the capacity of man is infinite, the further it is exerted, the more is discovered for the advancement of its occupation. The more our faculties are employed, the nearer we approach to a similarity of the divine being in whose image man was created in the beginning. To let our time elapse whilst our rational powers sleep in indolence is highly criminal; it is a prodigality of all others the worst, denying birth to those good works we owe to ourselves, and to mankind at large. In the bay ships ride in six or seven fathom of water.

The last sentence reverts abruptly to the description of Newbiggin which Hutchinson had cut short in his desire to preach, but the effect is somewhat surrealistic. Perhaps preaching is what Hutchinson would have best liked to do in life, if we assume that it did feature in the vision of his ideal existence inserted into the description of Alnwick Abbey – a world away from the life of industry and trade eulogised at Newbiggin:

Solemn situations like this, and the ruins of religious houses, always affect my mind with a degree of languishment. Such a seclusion, such a retirement, would have filled my wish. The life of the ecclesiastic is most desirable, and seems calculated to be the happiest. No natural tendency to indolence and ease prompts this determination; but the serenity of a churchman's life, under the entire preclusion of all worldly concerns, affords that tranquillity of mind so necessary to contemplation and study, to philosophic researches, and divine meditation – without the poison of ambition, some minds can enjoy a mediocrity with content – without an impertinent wish to intermeddle with public affairs, some men can fit within the little mansion, busied only in pious duties and contemplations; and amidst domestic peace, living each day in gratitude for the enjoyment of the rural beauties of some sylvan scene, the plain, the mead, the grotto, and the stream – call it luxuty: but the busy world incessantly rolls the heavy wheels of care too near my threshold.

This fantasy of ecclesiastical contentment is remarkable for the complete absence of any parishioners, so perhaps it did not include any time spent in the pulpit. One reason for the rise of Methodism was the willingness of the Methodist ministers to reach out to the large majority of the population ignored by the comfortably-beneficed Anglican clergy, particularly those endowed with good livings attached to aristocratic estates such as Alnwick Castle.

Before reaching Alnwick Hutchinson had visited Lindisfarne, leaving the island as the tide began to cover the causeway:

We continued upon the island so long, in reviewing these venerable remains, as almost to forget we had yet to visit many scenes in this county, as worthy the observation of the Antiquarian and Traveller, as those present to us: and we calculated our departure so ill, that the tide had begun to return, before we entered upon the sands. We thought ourselves secure indeed against all dangers, by having a farmer from the neighbouring shore for our guide, who had brought over butter that morning for the inhabitants. The tide approached in a singular manner, not flowing forward in waves, but the water increased imperceptibly, by oozing through the sands. At first the passage seemed a tract of wet sand, but presently it became a shining plain of level water, unruffled by any influx, reflecting in the most beautiful manner the variegated landskips of the adjoining shores. Our guide rode upon one of those methodical beasts, which keeps up an invariable motion with a kind of mechanical exactness, in spite of every approaching emergency. We expressed our anxiety at the increasing waters, yet not daring to leave our guide, on account of the intercepting gullies, and the apprehension of quicksands, of the situation and nature of which we were totally ignorant. He was unaltered, except in his dialogue, which now was filled with the circumstances of a late Traveller's death, who perished in the passage, wandering on the sands till he could not extricate himself from the surrounding floods. This was no pleasing narrative to us, who were now dashing through the increasing waters up to our horses' girths; our guide's constancy of countenance and unmoved mind affording us no very agreeable contemplation. I wish to prevent strangers engaging in so disagreeable a project, tho' ours was attended with no other circumstance than anxiety and impatiency of mind; yet had we attempted to make this passage without a guide, it is impossible to determine what would have been our lot.

Hutchinson and his companion appear to have been entirely lacking in any sense of humour. The farmer, who probably made the crossing several times a week, was no doubt enjoying their discomfiture. The dangers were however real enough, as the following incident demonstrates:

This [chapter] we will conclude by recording the fate that befell a postboy who was charged with the conveyance of the mail for London which left Edinburgh on Saturday the 20th November 1725. This mail, after reaching

Berwick in safety and proceeding thence, was never again heard of. A notice issued by the Post Office at the time ran as follows: "A most diligent search has been made; but neither the boy, the horse, nor the packet has yet been heard of. The boy, after passing Goswick, having a part of the sands to ride which divide the Holy Island from the mainland, it is supposed he has missed his way and rode towards the sea, where he and his horse have both perished". The explanation here suggested is not at all improbable, in view of the fact that November is a month given to fogs, when a rider might readily go astray crossing treacherous sands.

At his most lyrical Hutchinson can still impress, reminding us that this was the age of the picturesque when travellers began to appreciate the natural landscape in ways largely unavailable to earlier writers. His description of the scenery around Nunsbrough is worth quoting in full. Nunsbrough is longer on the map but information given on page 115 of Tomlinson's *Comprehensive Guide to Northumberland* enables us to place Hutchinson's panorama in the double horseshoe of Devil's Water at Linnelswood Bridge, 7 miles south east of Hexham:

Nunsbrough, where lays the most picturesque, though confined landskip, the whole county of Northumberland exhibits. We ascended to the brink of the precipice, near 200 feet high, from whence we looked down upon a sequestered vale, almost insulated by the brook, consisting of a fine level plot of corn land, of about eight acres, in the exact form of a horseshoe; the brook passing over a rugged rocky bottom, under the shadow of lofty hills, in various broken streams was seen on each hand, foaming from fall to fall, which gave a beautiful contrast to the deep hue of the groves. From the brook, the hills to the left arise precipitous, clothed with a fine hanging wood, then glowing with a full sunshine; to the right, the steeps laying from the sun, and in the deep shade, were broken, and scattered over in wild irregularity with brushwood, and here and there a grotesque and knotty tree presented itself impending from the precipice; in front, a fine eminence of brown rock lifted its rugged brow, and closed the circle, dividing the waters with a promontory a few yards wide. In the clefts, and on the little levels of the rock, some shrubs grow; on its crown stood ripened corn, margined with hedge-row trees, through which a cottage was discovered; and by its foot a winding road escaped the eye in intercepting woods; the rays of light fell happily upon the cliffs, and brightened their colouring. To the right and left, the more distant brook shewed itself in deep and rocky dells, embowered by lofty oaks. To the right hand, the hill which surmounts the wood is topped with a plain of grass ground, on whose brink stands a farmhold, accessible by a narrow path winding up the steep, from whence the woods make a beautiful curvature; the distant back ground is composed of heath lands. On the left, woodlands were seen on the circus, winding on the mazy channel of the brook, here and there intercepted by heathy eminences; the back ground very distant, and tinged with a misty azure. To grace the little enchanted vale, reapers were busy with the harvest: in some parts the furrows looked like waving gold; in others they were embossed with upset sheafs. This is the finest natural theatre I ever saw; the circle is almost geometrically just; the plain would have suited those exhibitions of which we read, with an anxious curiosity, in the histories of the Ancients; they would have given it life, taken away the rusticity, and made it noble. When we descended to the vale below, it appeared only to want some of the sacred rites, to improve its solemnity, and compound the idea of hallowedness with greatness. One possessed of a true taste for natural beauties is apt to be wound up to a pitch of enthusiasm at such scenes as these; where every subject that can compose a rural prospect are thus fortunately adjusted and disposed. It is not possible for me to write with temperance on such a subject.

Despite the precipitous cliffs, the wild irregularity of the view, and the grotesque and knotty trees, this remains essentially a man-made rural landscape, but the urge to improve the prospect by the addition of antiquarian elements is very much in line with the tradition of picturesque drawing. On this occasion Hutchinson does manage to see the reapers, though only as conveniently distant and sanitised figures in a landscape. Humanity en masse and close up was far from picturesque, as in the following Dickensian cameo of darkness visible in the wilder parts of the Cheviot range:

This is a deplorable part of the country for a stranger to be benighted in; the heavy vapours which frequently envelop the hills the whole day as frequently attend the advance of night into the vale, as it happened to us, and brings on a darkness truly to be felt; whilst there is no house, inhabitant, or passenger for miles to direct your way.
We were thankful when we gained sight of the Inn at Wooler Haugh; the court-yard, which we descended into from the road, was crowded indeed with waggons and carriages, and the lights in the stables shewed there were several guests in the house, but of what quality and denomination we could not divine. When we alighted the hostler looked to be in some confusion; but we did not devise the reason, being willing not to premise any thing to our disadvantage at that time of night, in the rain, and in a country not known to any of us. We were met by a jolly hostess at the door, who desired us, with all the courtesy of a civil publican, to walk in. We were introduced to the kitchen, and required to air our clothes till the people got lights and prepared a room. It was now time to consider the

scene; the kitchen smelled rank of cooking, for there was as much bustle as if they were preparing a hecatomb. The room was populous to a degree, for the mistress and two jolly nymphs her daughters stickled in the cookery whilst there went backward and forward, in and out, hostlers, livery servants, carriers, and savages of various denominations, in the utmost confusion; carrying, seeking, fetching, or calling for innumerable matters, like the confusion of Babel, in the greatest agitation and emergency. When we had leisure to think we were at a loss to conceive what had occasioned this hurricane, in which we had so awkwardly involved ourselves, at this little house under a hill in the wilds of Wooler. But outward objects embarrassed all thinking to that degree that our minds remained overwhelmed in what the eye communicated, or what distracted the ear; and like fellows that were fascinated we forbore to make our escape. The table was covered with mangled joints of victuals; above us, before us, on this hand, and on that, was the noise of tumultuous companies, creating that discordance of sounds which distracts an Inn at a fair: - hallowing, laughing, ringing of bells, beating on tables, menaces, oaths, female titterations, and music were in the composition. My companion in a whisper says, "Where the devil have we got to?" I would have told him, if it had been in my power. I found myself totally embarrassed, till at length this horrid discordance roused me, and on expressing uneasiness at not being shown to our apartment, we were told the room was clearing of its present possessors, who were going to bed. Startled at such intelligence, we began to doubt what would be our accommodations, and that we might have occasion to displace the same race of visitants a second time, before we could possess any beds. In defiance of the weather, a night as dark as Erebus, and a road unknown, we thought it more prudent to set forward for Wooler town, distant near two miles, and accordingly left this place to the sportsmen who occupied it on their moor shooting parties, and to the carriers and horrid wretches who barricadoed it without.

At the Black Bull Inn in Wooler we ended the anxieties of the evening in comfortable lodgings, and every accommodation a traveller could hope for.

Townscapes could be equally unappealing. Hutchinson found the streets of North Shields to be "narrow, dirty, populous and noisy" but, once on a boat in the river and able to survey matters from a safe distance, he embarks on a lengthy sermon on the progress of maritime science, beginning as follows:

We took a boat to examine this busy scene upon the water. The sight of so many vessels, and such a concourse of people, is very pleasing. It

170

consequently brings to one's mind reflections on the powers of human faculties. The genius of man is infinite; if we could be taught for 1000 years we should discover at that period, from the learning we had acquired, that we had an infinity of subjects yet to learn: for the more knowledge man attains, the wider circle of objects unattained opens upon him. As the scale of numerical calculation is without end, as the variations of musical genius are infinite, so is man's genius. By the use of letters we have accumulated the learning of ages; yet after the conclusion of a few centuries all our acquisitions will perhaps appear to posterity as but minute members of the science of mankind. Before the use of letters, with the fall of empires, the accumulated knowledge of ages expired with them; but henceforth it will not be so.

Hutchinson concluded his tour in Newcastle, and it is perhaps fair to finish with 2 short passages in which he bestows concise praise on institutions that still form part of the cultural fabric of the city:

(St Nicholas Church) – The tower or steeple is 194 feet in height, highly ornamented; four images of no mean sculpture decorate the lower part of the tower. The top of the tower is very elegant, it is ornamented with fine pinnacles of tabernacle-work, from the corner spring intersecting bows or arches, supporting in the middle a light and open lanthorn, graced with pinnacles of extraordinary beauty. The whole has the most uncommon and pleasing appearance, not unlike a magnificent imperial crown. It is justly allowed by all travellers to be the finest piece of masonry of the kind in Europe.
(The Tomlinson Library) – Above the vestry is a library, to which Dr Tomlinson, a late Vicar, at his death, made a great addition by a donation of his valuable books. But of what utility (comparatively speaking) was this library until the late munificent Sir Walter Blackett (over whose name every worthy burgess will for one age at least drop a tear, whilst his experienced benevolence gives the estimate of his loss, and on whose immortal character future ages will contemplate with veneration and Joy) the great modern patron of Newcastle, gave an annual stipend of £25 for ever for a librarian.

Hutchinson's comprehensive survey provided prospective travellers with a detailed checklist of what he considered to be worth visiting throughout the county of Northumberland. That this was in line with the spirit of the age is acknowledged by the anonymous author of *The Border Tour*, although he has his doubts about the practicability of using Hutchinson's two substantial volumes as a travel companion:

Lord Byron has denominated this age, the "age of cant", - more truly might it be denominated the "age of travels". The improvement of the public roads, the adaptation of the power of steam to purposes of navigation, and the increase of commerce and manufactures by which riches are so generally diffused, have made the British nation a nation of travellers. The inhabitant of Cheapside cannot be gathered to his fathers in peace, until he has toiled to the summit of Cheviot, and gazed on the waters which flow beside the lovely ruins of Dryburgh......
It is not to be doubted that these numerous wanderers are often at a loss to what objects to direct their attention, in the various places they visit. Hutchinson and Redpath's histories, invaluable as works of reference, are scarcely suitable companions in a post-chaise; nor is there any volume of description sufficiently portable for a traveller in search of the picturesque. Shut out from these sources of information the casual traveller has often to rely upon what may be communicated to him by the waiter of an inn, and if that person be, as is no unusual case, either surly or ignorant, he is not allowed to view scenes in the immediate neighbourhood which would delight his taste by their beauty, or rouse his enthusiasm by the knowledge that on them patriots of other ages had reared their victorious arms.

Although *The Border Tour* is undoubtedly a handier travel companion it would be dangerous to put too much trust in it when finding one's way around the County. The most egregious of several geographical errors is the advice to visit Flodden Field at a location 10 miles south-east of Berwick, which conjures visions of a naval battle otherwise unremarked by historians.

The Turnpike Age

The author of *The Border Tour* is however entirely accurate in highlighting the improvement of the public roads as a major factor in the transport revolution of the eighteenth century. As far as the North East is concerned this change started late. Except for a couple of short stretches around Whitehaven there were no turnpikes north of the Humber in 1740. By 1750 the greater part of the road from York to Edinburgh had been turnpiked, although with some unimproved stretches north and south of Berwick. By 1770 the main road network across Northumberland had been converted to the turnpike system. The experience of several centuries had shown that local parish councils had neither the will, the funds, nor the expertise to maintain roads in a proper condition. The turnpike system combined the privatisation of the main road network with the introduction of the new technologies of road building pioneered by such men as Telford and Macadam.

We can get some idea of what was involved by considering the project to build the short turnpike from Newcastle to North Shields. The initial stage was for a group of entrepreneurs to back the project with their own funds, and to seek authorisation by way of an Act of Parliament which, in the case of the North Shields Turnpike, was passed in 1748. In time-honoured form the Act opens with a preamble reciting the purpose for which it is passed:

> Whereas the road leading from North Shields in the County of Northumberland to the Town of Newcastle upon Tyne, is in the Winter Season, in divers places, by reason of the many heavy Carriages passing thereon, become so deep and ruinous, that Travellers cannot pass without great Danger, and the said Road cannot, by the ordinary Course provided by the Laws now in being for repairing the Highways of this Kingdom, be effectually amended and kept in good Repair.........to the Intent that the said Road may, with all convenient Speed, be effectually amended, and hereafter kept in good and sufficient Repair.

The Act did not of itself relieve parish councils of their traditional responsibility for upkeep of the road, but it is likely that the trustees of the turnpike used the provision in the Act which allowed councils to pay an annual contribution in lieu of carrying out the work. This would have formed part of the income of the trust, the balance coming from the tolls levied at the main gates on the road itself and at the side gates situated on minor roads leading into the main thoroughfare:

CATEGORY	TOLL
For every coach, chariot, landau, berlin, chaise, hearse, calash or other carriage, drawn by six or more horses, mares, geldings, or mules	1 shilling
As above – drawn by four horses etc	8 pence
As above – drawn by two horses etc	6 pence
As above – drawn by one horse etc	3 pence
For every waggon, wain, cart or carriage drawn by six or more horses, mares, geldings, or mules	1 shilling

As above – drawn by four horses etc	8 pence
As above – drawn by two horses etc	6 pence
As above – drawn by one horse etc	3 pence
For every horse, mare, gelding, mule, ass or beast of burden, laden or unladen, and not drawing	1 penny
For every drove of oxen, or neat cattle	6 pence per score, and so in proportion for any greater or less number
For every drove of calves, hogs, sheep, lambs or goats	3 pence per score, and so in proportion for any greater or less number

The trustees were empowered to compound with regular users of the road, effectively offering annual season tickets. Statutory exemptions were provided for horses and passenger transport on election days, for local residents attending Sunday worship and funerals, for local agricultural traffic, for post-horses, for soldiers on duty, and for horses, carts or waggons travelling with vagrants sent by legal passes. Such exemptions provide an interesting insight into the minds of eighteenth century legislators considering what should be classed as essential travel.

Any taxing Act is of course subject to avoidance and evasion. Transport operators who detached horses or other draft animals on the approach to toll gates were liable to a fine of 20 shillings. A similar fine could be imposed on operators bypassing the toll gates through adjoining land, and in this case the person allowing their land to be used as a bypass was subject to a separate fine, also of 20 shillings. It was the difficulty of policing adjoining lands that led to the 1753 road from Newcastle to Carlisle being built by the military. Entrepreneurs would not have been willing to finance a long stretch of road with low traffic volumes and ample scope for avoiding the payment of tolls.

The strength of the coal owners lobby is evidenced by the provision relating to waggonways:

Nothing in this Act contained shall extend, or be construed to extend, to prevent the Owners or Occupiers of any Colliery or Collieries from laying a Waggonway or Ways along or cross any Part of the said Road, but that such Owners and Occupiers of such Collieries as aforesaid, shall and may have the same Liberty to make, repair, and such Waggon-way and Waggon-ways in, along, or cross the said Road, as they, or any of them, could or might have done, in case this Act had not been made.

Read literally this suggests that a mine owner could have constructed a new waggonway straight along the main track of the new road. In fact there was probably a large overlap of interest between the mine owners and the turnpike entrepreneurs so that any potential conflicts of interest could be handled at meetings of the turnpike trustees. The provision does however highlight the fact that the waggonways were seen as economically more important to the region than the new road.

The building of turnpikes created a revolution in speed of transport. In 1750 the fastest stage-coach took 132 hours on the journey from London to Newcastle, with a further 98 hours to reach Edinburgh. In 1811 the time from London to Newcastle had been reduced to 84¼ hours, with only a further 28¼ hours from there to Edinburgh. Over the whole stretch from London to Edinburgh the time required had been reduced from nearly 10 days to just under 5 days. The coming of the railway in the mid nineteenth century would of course slash journey times further and lead to the demise of the stage-coach, but in the first half of that century the north of England had probably never seemed so close to those living in London or in Scotland.

Holidays in the North

The antiquarian endeavour did not come to an end with the passing of the eighteenth century. Antiquarians did however become increasingly more specialised in their interests, exchanging their views in papers to learned societies and in specialist publications. It is perhaps time therefore to bid farewell to the antiquaries and to conclude this chapter with a brief account of a couple of holiday journeys which show the lighter side of touring in Northumberland.

In 1786 Thomas Thornton (1757-1823) of Thornville Royal in Yorkshire, and Colonel of the West York Regiment of Militia, set out on a sporting tour of Northumberland and Scotland. His father,

Colonel William Thornton, a staunch supporter of the Hanoverian monarchy, had raised at his won expense a troop of 100 soldiers who fought at Falkirk and Culloden. When Colonel William and his wife went to Court King George II paid him a handsome compliment:

> Mr Thornton, I have been told of your services to your country, and your attachment to my family, and have held myself obliged to you for both; but I was never able to appreciate the degree of the obligation till I had seen the lady you left behind you.

Colonel Thomas Thornton's tour was a serious expedition, requiring the purchase and provisioning of 2 boats which sailed north from the Ouse to Forres in Scotland, loaded with hunting equipment and a plentiful supply of porter, ale and small beer. Thornton himself, accompanied by 2 friends and by George Garrard, an artist recommended by William Gilpin and hired to accompany and illustrate the tour, rode north from Yorkshire to Durham:

> As we approached nearer, we perceived the language of the people to differ considerably from those we had passed, their pronunciation being of that disagreeable species termed guttural. In point of complexion, too, they are much more swarthy; but found, from some shrewd remarks, that they were by no means deficient in sense.

Thornton was in a hurry to get to an area where he could start killing (his word) fish and other game, but had to pass through Newcastle first. A brief description of the ride there is followed by a longer comment on the races, probably the only event which could have detained him in the town for more than the time necessary to eat dinner and bait the horses:

> Leave Durham. Day warm, with a fine Italian sky. The ride from hence to Newcastle is pleasant, but short, and we were well pleased to catch a new and unexpected view of the Tyne above the town, forming an elegant and easy sweep, and busy with shipping. The descent to the bridge had that effect on my companion which it must always produce on strangers, and his admiration had scarcely ceased, when we arrived at Brodie's. It certainly is a most abominable entrance.
>
> Being the time of the races, the town was quite alive, and, from the accounts of my northern friends (who were partial in this, as well as in some other instances), expected to find them well worth seeing; but was disappointed, as they appeared but very moderate; not that they were ill

attended, but the racing part is in the most uncomfortable style imaginable. No *stand* unless an erection of coarse boards (but which neither protects the company from wind nor weather, and where every squall endangers the necks of the occupiers) can be esteemed such. Cock-fighting seems likely to flourish more here than in most parts of England, and this favourite amusement was everywhere the general topic of conversation.

They stopped overnight at Morpeth in a good, old-fashioned inn containing 'all the necessary requisites' and here he sent for Mr King, a dog-breeder, who had previously supplied him with some setters:

Found him uncommonly well, for a man of his years, which proves that air and exercise tend not only to preserve health but, by that vigour which they give the constitution, promote longevity.

Thornton was well qualified to judge of a man's physical fitness. He was himself famously athletic and could jump his own height of 5 foot 9 inches, and on one occasion jumped 6 five-bar gates in as many minutes. He had also won a walking race by covering 4 miles in 32 minutes.

Making an early start from Morpeth they took breakfast at Weldon Mill. Continuing north they entered the country described by Hutchinson in the passage quoted earlier in this chapter:

…we proceeded, by a very bad road, with what dispatch it would admit, and, as we advanced, the country improved upon us. Got in good time to Wooller-Haugh-Head, an uninteresting town, and the inn as dreadful as the surrounding scenes are enchanting; but, having experienced so severe a stage, we were obliged to rest quietly for some hours. – Dined early, and Mr P and myself, mounting our hackneys, rode briskly on, leaving Milfield Plain to our right, in order to gain an hour or two's fishing in the pleasing waters of Teviot.

Thornton's destination was the Highlands and he did not therefore delay in Northumberland. Having left Darlington on 6th June the party halted overnight at Durham, Newcastle, Morpeth and in the Cheviots. On 10th June they moved north into Scotland, executing further slaughter of fish and birds en route:

177

June 10 – Morning hazy. Proceeded by Mindrum, whose situation, among these uncommonly beautiful hills, the Cheviot, are unequalled in verdure by any I ever saw. These hills are covered with sheep, and all they want to make the prospect the most charming imaginable is wood and water.................Mr P also with his gun killed several beautiful white birds, which proved to be kittiwakes. The young of this bird are a favourite whet in North Britain, being served up a little before dinner to procure an appetite; but, from their rank smell and taste, they seemed to me more likely to have a contrary effect. I was told of a stranger who was set down, for the first time, to this kind of relish, as he supposed; but, after demolishing half a dozen, with much impatience, he declared that he had "eaten sax, and didna find himself a bit *more* hungry"...........Came over a cross road, very hilly, and distressing to the carriage-horses, after which passed through a charming country, having the Cheviot or Teviot dales and hills behind us, and the country around Kelso, a very beautiful one, in our front. As we took a cross road, and had no guide, I cannot ascertain where we entered Scotland; but was informed that a rivulet between Mindrum and Kelso, crossed by a bridge, is the boundary.

Thornton was not alone in his distaste for the Scottish (and Icelandic) habit of eating sea birds. The Edwardian naturalist Rev C A Johns had much the same reaction to the experience of eating an oyster-catcher:

> I was once induced, on the recommendation of a friend, to have one served up for dinner as an agreeable variation from the bacon and herrings which mainly constitute the dietary of a Scottish fishing-village inn. But I did not repeat the experiment, preferring fish pure and simple to fish served up through the medium of a fowl.

A review of Thornton's book appeared in the Edinburgh Review of 1805, written by Walter Scott (1771-1832), who was decidedly unimpressed:

> The performance is termed a Sporting Tour, not because it conveys to the reader any information, new or old, upon the habits of the animals unfortunate enough to be distinguished as *game*, nor even upon the modes to be adopted in destroying them *secundum artem*; but because it contains a long, minute and prolix account of every grouse and black-cock which had the honour to fall by the gun of our literary sportsman – of every pike which gorged his bait – of every bird which was pounced by his hawks – of every blunder which was made by his servants – and of every bottle which was drunk by himself and his friends. Now this, we apprehend, exceeds the license given to sportsmen. We allow them all the pleasure

which they can procure in an active and exhilarating amusement; nay, we permit them to rehearse the exploits of the field, lake and moor, as long as the audience are engaged in devouring and digesting the spoils of the campaign; but not one minute longer.

Walter Scott himself was a frequent visitor to Northumberland and we have already seen how he drew on that experience for episodes in his Waverley novels. His visit to Gilsland in the autumn of 1797 was of great personal importance, as he then met Charlotte Carpenter to whom he would be married by Christmas of the same year. But in his regular travels between Edinburgh and London he often took the sea route, preferring this to the tedium of the Great North Road. With the introduction of steam packets travel by sea became faster and safer than in the days of sail. His most detailed account of a stay in Northumberland dates from an early visit in August 1791, in the company of his uncle Captain Robert Scott of Kelso. They were probably staying at Langleeford in the Harthope valley:

Behold a letter from the mountains; for I am very snugly settled here, in a farmer's house, about six miles from Wooler, in the very centre of the Cheviot hills, in one of the wildest and most romantic situations which your imagination, fertile upon the subject of cottages, ever suggested. And what the deuce are you about there? methinks I hear you say. Why, sir, of all things in the world – drinking goat's whey – not that I stood in the least need of it, but my uncle having a slight cold, and being a little tired of home, asked me last Sunday evening if I would like to go with him to Wooler, and I answering in the affirmative, next morning's sun beheld us on our journey, through a pass in the Cheviots, upon the back of two special nags, and man Thomas behind with a portmanteau, and two fishing-rods fastened across his back, much in the style of St Andrew's Cross. Upon reaching Wooler we found the accommodations so bad that we were forced to use some interest to get lodgings here, where we are most delightfully appointed indeed. To add to my satisfaction, we are amidst places renowned by feats of former days; each hill is crowned with a tower, or camp, or cairn, and in no situtation can you be near more fields of battle: Flodden, Otterburn, Chevy Chase, Ford Castle, Chillingham Castle, Copland Castle, and many another scene of blood, are within the compass of a forenoon's ride.

If the child is father to the man then we can see in this letter a clear anticipation of Scott's later historical romances. As a young man his romantic imagination was also engaged elsewhere, along with a youthful passion for hunting that Thornton would have recognised:

My uncle drinks the whey here, as I do ever since I understood it was brought to his bedside every morning at six, by a very pretty dairymaid. So much for my residence: all the day we shoot, fish, walk and ride; dine and sup upon fish struggling from the stream, and the most delicious heath-fed mutton, barn-door fowls, poys [pies], milk-cheese, &c all in perfection; and so much simplicity resides among these hills, that a pen, which could write at least, was not to be found about the house, though belonging to a considerable farmer, till I shot the crow with whose quill I write this epistle.

In the following year Scott returned to Northumberland, riding through Hexham and the hills and taking note of all the Roman inscriptions that he could find. Despite his own familiarity with the Scottish border he still found the Northumberland speech strange to his ear:

The inhabitants of this country speak an odd dialect of the Saxon, approaching nearly that of Chaucer, and have retained some customs peculiar to themselves….Their ignorance is surprising to a Scotchman. It is common for the traders in cattle, which business is carried on to a great extent, to carry all letters received in the course of trade to the parish church, where the clerk reads them aloud after service, and answers them according to circumstances.

Having started this chapter with Tobias Smollett and Robert Burns it is fitting to have brought it to a conclusion with the young Walter Scott, another Scottish writer similarly engaged in exploring Northumberland as a visitor from the north.

CHAPTER 9

THE COMING OF THE RAILWAY

If my journals should remain legible, or be perused at the end of 200 years, there will even then be little curious in them relative to travel, or the people, because our island is now so explored, our roads (in general) are so fine, and our speed has reached the summit.

John Byng

Social Calls

Byng is the most consistently readable diarist of travel in England and Wales during the last quarter of the 18th century. It is therefore disappointing that he never crossed the Tyne, as his accounts of the daily experience of travel would have added many colourful details to our picture. The publication of his complete travel diaries in 1934 has ensured his literary survival, much against his own expectations. He was of course also mistaken in his confident assertion that 'our speed has reached the summit'. While the development of the turnpike network had made road travel both faster and safer the absolute rate of progress was still limited to the speed of the horse. Sir Robert Carey's achievement of riding from London to Edinburgh in 70 hours was probably not surpassed by any traveller before the substantial completion of the railway line to the north in 1840s.

In Chapter 5 we looked at the actor manager William Macready and his reminiscences of work and holidays in Northumberland in the decade from 1809 to 1818. With the severing of his connection with the Newcastle Theatre Macready did not return to the town until March 1841 when he made a nostalgic visit, admiring the new developments in Grey Street and Grainger Town while mourning the dilapidation of streets that had been dear to him in his younger days:

Peregrine Ellison called, and walked with me over the new streets, pointing out the old map by sundry relics, such as the school where Lord Eldon was brought up, the Forth, Waldie's house etc. The market, the Philosophical Institution – *open to everybody* – (bravissimo!) and the general appearance interested and pleased me very much, but I was sorry too to see the old streets, which used to look so handsome and lively, neglected, squalid, and forsaken.

But in terms of the experience of travel the following brief note brings home to us the fact that we have now moved into a very different world from that described in our previous chapters:

Intended to post to South Shields and cross the ferry to Tynemouth, but stopped and turned the post boy and made him go to Newcastle, from thence to take the railway. Was half an hour before the train started; lunched, wrote a note for Miss Martineau……. Went by railway to North Shields. Walked to Tynemouth, and inquiring at the post office Miss Martineau's address, called on her, sending up my note; she was very glad to see me.

The railway from Newcastle to North Shields had been opened only on 22nd June 1839, yet less than 2 years later Macready treats taking the train, with a quick snack while waiting for its departure, as an entirely routine and unremarkable travel option.

Harriet Martineau (1802-1876), whom Macready visited, was a radical nonconformist writer who had taken lodgings in Tynemouth early in 1840 for the sake of her health. There she stayed for nearly 5 years, confined indoors for much of the time. She benefited from a window looking across the Tyne estuary to the sea and to South Shields, and her landlady had kindly given her a telescope through which she could observe life outside. Above all she had many friends who would come to visit her when she felt well enough and it was the railway that made it easy for them to come to Tynemouth. How easy is explained in her letter of 29th July 1844 to Richard Monckton Milnes:

I wonder whether you will be at the York meeting, & whether you know how near York is to us, since the opening of the railroad from Darlington. It is only 12 hours now from London.

And in another letter she makes abundantly clear her enjoyment of the life seen from her window:

Your cannon has long vanished from the fort; but the fort remains; & the glorious old sea, finer every day. I have no words for the enjoyment of what I see of it from my window. I have no prospect of leaving my two rooms; but my window-seat (which I have cushioned and made a couch of) is enough for any body with eyes. Besides the sea & the rocks, I have a fine green field, with shady hollows, larks, cows, & a frisky young colt, the castle with the red soldiers, fine gardens and fine pig sties, & a cottage below, with some capital "blackguard" children. Then there is Shields, the other way; but I always forget to look on that side.

And, as her biographer R K Webb makes clear, Martineau was not an armchair philanthropist and reformer, but someone who was prepared to take very practical steps to ameliorate current social problems. She was very concerned about water supply and drainage. She persuaded a reluctant Duke of Northumberland to order the construction of 2 main drains in Tynemouth, and provided twenty pounds of her own money to go towards the cost of house drains linked into the new sewers. She also had a well dug in her own garden, which "kept the maids from bad company" as they no longer needed to walk some distance to fetch water, and take the opportunity thus offered of flirting with the soldiers of the Tynemouth garrison.

She is thoroughly Victorian in her decision to do something immediately rather than to wait for the day when the state would take responsibility for a fully professional drainage scheme. The introduction of sexual morality into such a project is equally typical of the times. As the letter quoted above makes clear Martineau herself liked looking at the redcoats from her window, yet she felt it appropriate to deprive the maids of an opportunity to meet them; their reaction is inevitably not recorded. However Martineau herself did not remain in Tynemouth to enjoy the benefits of her philanthropy. In the summer and autumn of 1844 she finally recovered her health, partly at least in consequence of consulting practitioners of mesmerism, and in 1845 she moved to Ambleside on Windermere where she commissioned the building of a new house for herself. William Macready visited her in this new home where "he was taken for walks and views and continual conversation – and strained his back planting a couple of oaks".

Trains and Boats and Cows

With Macready and Martineau we have touched on the branch line from Newcastle to Tynemouth and on the progress of the railway from London to Gateshead. A slightly earlier railway, on which construction work had begun in 1830, still runs from Newcastle to

Carlisle. The first public traffic started in March 1835 on the section between Blaydon and Hexham, and on 18th June 1838 the first train of 13 carriages covered entire length of the line from Carlisle Canal to Gateshead, the extension from Blaydon to Newcastle being opened by October 1839. In 1835 a very early traveller on the initial section from Blaydon to Newcastle was George Head (1782-1855):

Sixteen miles of the Newcastle and Carlisle Railroad are already completed; and carriages attendant upon the trains daily ply to the small village of Bleadon, on the south bank of the Tyne, four miles from Newcastle; - from Bleadon passengers are conveyed by steam to Hexham. Those to whose lot it has previously fallen to travel this mountainous road, can appreciate the agreeable change between the former laborious journey up one steep hill and down the next, and a level plane; - to form an adequate idea of the beautiful scenery on the way, the traveller must be at the pains of gliding through it himself.

On passing through Newcastle, I took occasion, by way of an evening's excursion, to pursue this picturesque route........I proceeded half the distance to Hexham, and returned by the homeward train, which stopped, for the exchange of passengers, midway. The curiosity of the townspeople was still in full force, but arrangements for the auxiliary wheel-carriages to and from Bleadon were insufficient to meet the demand: the few engaged in the service were loaded without moderation, not being subject, as far as I could perceive, to any sort of regulation.

The first four miles of the railroad were not hitherto completed, the line of its continuation to the westward not yet being decided on; proposals have since been made, and are about to be carried into execution, to extend it along the south bank of the Tyne to South Shields; thence along the line of coast to Sunderland.

Besides the aforesaid sixteen miles of ground, already finished, the whole work, though slowly, is steadily progressing: the last twenty miles, from Haltwhistle to Carlisle, are in a forward state; the sixteen miles in the middle laid out, and on the point of being taken in hand...

On arriving at Bleadon, the train being ready, we immediately departed: several farmers' carts composed part of our cargo; the horses of which were accommodated with standing-room on a large railed platform, constructed on purpose. Besides seats in covered and open carriages, disposed in the usual manner, benches were fixed aloft, on the top of the covered vehicles, on which those who preferred airy travelling were at liberty to sit, back to back, and look about them; curiosity, however, once gratified in this respect, he certainly consults economy rather than taste who repeats the experiment; for it is impossible, owing to the rapid motion, and the smoke and cinders which fly backwards from the engine, to open more than a quarter of an eye at any one instant of time during a whole journey.

Smoke and cinders were not the only hazards for those sitting on top of the covered vehicles. The unfortunate blacksmith George Turnbull was killed on 3rd September 1846 when he stood up to call out to workmen to pick up his hat, not realising that the train was about to pass under a bridge. As a consequence these *al fresco* seating arrangements were terminated. For Head the marvels of the new technology outweigh the discomfort of the smoke and cinders, but no doubt he travelled in a covered first class carriage. One suspects that the horses were terrified.

Head also writes of the boat journey from Newcastle to Shields and of the ferry crossing between North and South Shields:

A voyage from Newcastle to Shields by the regular steam-packets, which depart every half-hour throughout the day, is cheap and disagreeable. For the charge of sixpence, although the ordinary time of the passage is an hour and a half, it sometimes happens that the traveller is accommodated with quarters on board, in regions of dirt and smoke, for a couple of hours more; nay, not unfrequently, little pains being taken by the authorities to clear the channel, half a dozen of these small vessels may be seen together in the middle of the river, quietly reposing on a sandbank. In the latter predicament I had the misfortune to remain for more than an hour, and was indeed truly glad when, after having landed, I found myself, bag and baggage, with a porter at my heels, on the very excellent raft, float, ferry-boat, or whatever may be its proper denomination, which plies between North and South Shields.

I never met with a more commodious vehicle of transport across a river than this, into which a person literally canter on horseback, or drive in his gig or his carriage, without the slightest danger or inconvenience to man or beast. It is, in fact, a double steamer or twin-boat, carrying her paddles out of sight in the middle, having two engines, and two funnels, and being in every respect the same as two steamers lashed together. On each of the landing-places on the north and south side of the river a machine is contrived to form a level platform from the shore to the vessel: it is moveable on castors, and slides up and down an inclined plane into the water, according to the height of the tide; - to make accommodation more commodious, cross pieces of thick matted rope are laid across, which effectually prevent cattle from slipping. Embarkation and disembarkation are thus rendered as easy as such a process can be; the machine plies at as

185

frequent intervals as possible throughout the day, and the passage-money for one individual is no more than a penny.

The regular ferry crossing at this point dates back at least to Elizabethan times, and it is likely that the Romans had crossed the Tyne near here to establish a link between their forts at Arbeia and Segedunum. Another very old institution was the right of the freemen of Newcastle to pasture cows on the town moor. Head gives a splendid account of this ritual, a fitting supplement to the accounts of other animal matters covered in a previous chapter:

Among other municipal privileges in the city of Newcastle, every freeman claims property, as far as it goes, in the town moors; that is to say, he is entitled to the pasturage of two cows, - not upon brown, sour, unhealthy herbage, such as characterizes the ordinary description of common, where geese, having walked and fed, "consumed all before them, and poisoned all behind them", the rest of the grass may be had for nothing; but over an extent of several hundred acres of excellent, rich, meadow land, immediately contiguous to the town.

To ensure regularity amid the diversity of private interests consequent upon the clashing of ownership, two herdsmen are appointed by the corporation, to collect the herd twice a day, at milking time, and drive them into the precincts of the town, where they are met on their return, or find their way of themselves to their several owners. At the periods above stated, five or six hundred, or more, of these matronly animals may be seen daily on their march homewards, in two grand divisions, the one of which enters the town by Percy-street, and the other by Gallowgate.

It was on the occasion of a morning's walk on the northern outskirts, that I first became acquainted with these particulars, my attention was then led to what I conceived an unusual number of cows on the open land in question: and not only were the herd remarkable as to numbers, but a restless, uneasy spirit prevailed among them, which, in order to understand, required explanation. The herdsman was at that time engaged in the duties of his station, diligently threading the extremity of his line, and compelling every loitering and wandering cow to join her companions. Thus he cantered along, mounted on his galloway, while, at a distance, farther than the eye could reach, the eccentricities of his course were marked by the short, sharp, barkings of a dog, his faithful attendant and aide-de-camp.

The sagacious leaders of the herd in the foreground, those whose disposition I had remarked, aware of the well-known sound, urged by their swelling udders towards their homes, yet restrained by a sense of propriety to await the word of command, were patiently, or rather impatiently, lowing; and not only testifying, by their various looks and actions, their extreme eagerness to proceed on their way, but exemplifying the difficulties that always exist in the path of duty, when opposed by natural inclination. Sometimes they hastily caught a bite of grass, and tossed it pettishly into the air at the bite of a fly, then wistfully stretched their necks across the moor to see if their refractory sisters were coming; and then again they would butt at each other in disappointment and sheer vexation. It really was extraordinary perfection of discipline, by dint of which these cows collected together of their own accord in the front, and remained in a state of moral restraint full twenty minutes, under pressing anxiety to march, yet not one daring to set foot on the adjacent turnpike-road, although unrestricted by fence of any sort, without a boy to guard them, or any other kind of let or hindrance whatever.

In the meantime, as the ground to be traversed was of considerable extent, the herdsman was not without his share of trouble, nevertheless, having settled his affairs on the frontier, on he came galloping along with his dog; he had left behind him many of the herd, and the foremost, as it by intuitive knowledge or mutual understanding, already began to divide, pairing off into the two grand divisions before mentioned, and falling naturally, as it were, into their respective lines of march. I accompanied the eastern division homewards, therefore know not the proceedings of the others; they no doubt conducted themselves precisely the same as these. It was extraordinary to witness how all, nearly two hundred in number, immediately on their arrival in the town, instinctively broke off into detachments, each departing through the cross streets as occasion required, and these again subdividing into twos and threes; sometimes one single cow, unattended, might be seen stepping leisurely along, unmolested by men or boys, quietly chewing the cud, placing her feet tenderly on the uneven paving-stones, and daintily picking her way, through intricate streets and lanes, to her place of abode.

Cows still graze the moor, but no longer wend their way homeward through the streets of Newcastle.

Two Visitors from Germany

In Chapter 6 we saw how foreign visitors such as Gabriel Jars and M.Faujas St Fond brought their own perspective to travel in Northumberland. We can now consider two German visitors who came to the county in the early years of the railway era. Frederick von Raumer (1781-1873) visited England in 1835 and again in 1841, the earlier visit being more interesting for our account, while Johann Georg Kohl (1808-1878) made his tour in 1844. The sight of railways in action made a vivid impact on both these visitors, von Raumer in particular being exhilarated by the sheer power of the machine and by the concomitant domination of the landscape:

> From Wakefield I proceeded to Leeds, but did not make a long stay, as I wished to go by the rail-road to Selby; but here, even, the steam-engine rests on Sundays: I had, therefore, no alternative between setting out on Saturday or waiting till Monday.
> In front stands the fiery dragon, groaning, snorting, and foaming till the twenty carriages are lashed to his tail; when he sets forward with the utmost ease and rapidity over the horizontal plane. Mountains have been levelled, valleys raised, and in the gloom of the vaulted tunnel the dragon throws out fire and flames. Yet, in spite of all the force, and all the noise, one man guides the monster at his will.

Kohl, surveying the scene in the county of Durham, marvelled at the sight of a fully-fledged railway network, constructed in such a short space of years:

> The country lying to the south of the "coaly Tyne" is intersected by railroads even more than that lying to the north of the river. Here are railroads to Shields, to Sunderland, to Stanhope, and to many other places. Durham may indeed be said to be of all counties in England the one in which there have been constructed the greatest number of railroads of small extent. This gives to the country an aspect remarkably new and surprising in the eyes of a continentalist. In all directions he sees small trains in motion, small locomotives with two or three passenger carriages, for, as the intercourse is between places at no very great distance from each other, the trains can probably run frequently, but on that very account, perhaps, are obliged to content themselves with a small number of passengers at a time. If, however, the passenger trains are small, the trains of coal waggons are all the longer, and to one who could take a bird's eye view of the country, it would seem to swarm like an ant-hill, with locomotives, hurrying trains, and long lines of coal waggons..........
> Notwithstanding this abundance of small railroads, the great one, between Newcastle and Durham, and which eventually is to connect those towns with London, was not yet complete, and I could avail myself of its services only for a part of the journey.........
> The coal trains are of astonishing length. In some I counted as many as fifty waggons. Each waggon contains two tons and a half of coals, and the whole weight of the loaded waggon is four tons. A train of this kind, therefore, must weigh 200 tons, and with this astonishing load behind

them, equal to the cargo of a small vessel, the steam engines start at a rapid pace.

These observations are entirely credible, as Fawcett's history of the Newcastle & Carlisle railway makes clear. He refers to newspaper reports from 1837, the first about a train comprising 73 wagons and weighing 330 tons, the second about a train of 100 wagons and weighing 450 tons.

Kohl was able to follow George Head's excursion from Blaydon to Hexham and, since the railway was now complete, on to Carlisle. Whereas von Raumer perceived the railway as dominating the landscape Kohl saw how it had connected previously separated communities:

> As I saw nothing of Northumberland but the Tyne valley through which I flew along the last named of these railroads, I was disposed to set the county down for one of the most beautiful and delightful countries in the world. I never was upon any railway which afforded so agreeable a trip............
> Handsome villages, stately groves, teeming fields, busy towns, and here and there a hill or a group of rocks, crowned with the remains of some ancient castle famed in the chronicles of border warfare, passed in quick succession before us. The most remarkable town along the whole line is Hexham, the most interesting castle that of Prudhoe. Hexham was already a famous station in the time of the Romans, and its history down to the troubles arising from the Jacobean insurrections, is a stormy and warlike one; but collieries and railroads have an astonishing effect in pacifying a country.

The Newcastle & Carlisle railway was never an express line. Nevertheless the 1844 timetable shows that some services covered the whole route in just 3 hours despite making numerous stops on the way. By contrast the fastest coach service in 1834, just 10 years earlier, had taken 7½ hours for the same route. This telescoping of time and distance brought about an apparently minor, but in fact fundamental, change with the abolition of local time in 1841. Up to then Carlisle time had been 12 minutes behind Newcastle and London time, but the demands of operating a unified railway timetable required the harmonisation of times across the railway network. England was indeed being unified in ways that could not have been foreseen even a decade earlier.

Von Raumer and Kohl were interested in far more than the railway. On his 1835 von Raumer did the traditional whistle-stop tour of Newcastle and Shields:

On the 4th of August, therefore, I saw…..the coal-mine in Walbottle, the glass and iron works at Leamington, the paper manufactory at Scotswood, the glass manufactory in Newcastle, and the steam-engine manufactory of Mr Stevenson [sic].

On the 5th of August I went with Mr Potter on board the steamer, to the harbour of Shields, and to Tynemouth, and viewed whatever was remarkable in Newcastle. One part of the town is old and, as it were, still in the state of a chrysalis, while in the other new buildings are springing up, and great improvements making. Everywhere is life, work, and activity. Many of the buildings, - for instance, the Museum, the Post Office, &c, are conformable to the rules of classical architecture. Some parts are like Prague.

In Shields, the ruins of an ancient monastery are situated on a high promontory, which runs into the sea: another proof how skilfully the monks chose the site for their abodes, and how sensible they were to the beauties of nature.

And in 1844 Kohl visited the Royal Arcade, sadly demolished during the later reconstruction of central Newcastle led by T Dan Smith:

Of the buildings of Newcastle, none surprised me more than the Newsroom, which bears about the same relative importance to similar institutions in Germany, that a double *Times* does to a Leipzig or Frankfort paper. The room in question is a noble hall of a semicircular form, and its large and lofty dimensions are calculated to awake the idea rather of a temple than of a reading-room. Under the same roof are two banks, the post-office, club-rooms, the stamp-office, &c, and the whole building bears the name of the Royal Arcade.

What is perhaps more thought-provoking, given the folk history that has built up around the struggles between the pitmen and the mine owners, is the substantial agreement between von Raumer and Kohl on the prosperous condition of the miners and their families:

[von Raumer] Every coal-miner receives, 1st, gratis, a plot of ground, chiefly for planting potatoes; 2nd, a dwelling; 3rd, daily wages. I found the dwellings beyond my expectation, very neat and cleanly, bright windows, and behind each some indication of prosperity and ornament. The daily wages of boys, whose work is very easy – driving the horses, for instance – is about one shilling, and rises, in proportion to the labour, to six shillings; on an average they may be stated at four shillings a day. When we consider that provisions and manufactured goods are now as cheap in England as in Germany, that the miners have nothing to pay for house-rent, fuel, and potatoes, and that their wages are without comparison higher than in any country on the Continent, it is evident that this part of the population of England is better off, and enjoys a higher degree of prosperity than anywhere else. It is not unusual for them to have meat on their table twice in a day; and that old and young eat only the finest wheaten bread is a matter of course. Among more than 200 children, I did not see one sickly, beggarly, or deformed; all strong and hearty, with rosy cheeks, and except where a streak of coal crossed the face, remarkably fair and handsome.

[Kohl] The men appeared to quite as much advantage as their dwellings. They were as well clad as men of moderate wishes could desire to be, and when I saw a number of the young men together, they at first appeared to me, to be a party of sailors in holiday attire just come ashore.......Like the manufacturing labourers, however, the colliers are a riotous and discontented race, and any unpopular measure on the part of their employers soon leads to a "strike", which passes with all the rapidity of a bad example from one work to another, and soon becomes general.

The colliers are not more famed in England for their insubordination than for the hardness of their work, which equals in severity any labour assigned to slaves in other countries. I had, therefore, expected to see a wretched, sickly race, and was surprised to find the very reverse. I visited a church and a Sunday school, and there, as everywhere else where I saw the people grouped together, they appeared to me to be cheerful and healthy, always neatly, and often luxuriously dressed. Their wages are probably higher than those paid to any other description of miners in Europe. They live rent-free, have nothing to pay for fuel or light, have small kitchen-gardens attached to their houses, and the lowest wages paid them are two shillings a day, for which they remain at work in the pit for at least eight hours. There are of course many persons engaged on higher terms. Thus a common coal hewer can earn as much as five shillings a day. The dangers to which they are constantly exposed are partly the cause of the high wages paid them, but five shillings a day for so simple an occupation as that of hewing coals, must be considered good pay, even in England. The average earnings of the common labourers in the collieries about Newcastle, are from three to four shillings daily. Yet strange to say, they are by no means a contented race, are continually combining against their employers, and hang together much as was formerly the case with the clans of Scotland. This I attribute partly to the

191

fact that most of the workmen are extremely young. Half of them are under twenty and of the remainder few are much beyond thirty. Such young men are naturally inconsiderate of the consequences to which their rashness may lead.

If this was such a simple and well-paid occupation Kohl might perhaps have asked how it was that so few miners carried on working beyond the age of thirty. Nevertheless the observations of Kohl and von Raumer suggest that there are, as usual, at least two sides to any story.

Like Jars and Faujas St Fond before them Kohl and von Raumer were interested in English industrial processes. A good example is Kohl's description of a visit to a rope manufactory, probably that on the north bank of the Tyne to the south of Byker. The description of the massive ropes destined for the railroads reminds us that in the early days of the railway many inclined sections of track still relied on fixed engines to pull wagons up slopes, this being the case even on several sections of the Stocton and Darlington line:

Of the different manufactories of Newcastle, I had time, on the following morning, to visit only one, namely, a rope-walk. I might, no doubt, have seen a similar establishment, in many of the English towns through which I had passed, but somehow or other I had never seen any thing of the kind. The place was "a mile and a bittock" from Newcastle, as my Northumbrian informant told me, nevertheless, I contrived to run out and see a good deal of it before the Durham train started.
Not only the marine of England, but many of her manufactories likewise, require hempen ropes of all possible forms and dimensions, from the thinnest packthread to huge cables of more than eighteen inches in diameter. Sometimes the ropes must be round, at other square, and sometimes even flat. I saw one rope, three miles long, that was intended for the Edinburgh railroad, and similar ropes for other railroads. In these great English ropewalks, it need hardly be said that every thing is not made out of the hand and the apron, as I have seen in our German ropewalks; machinery and contrivances of a peculiar kind have, on the contrary, been found requisite. I took a particular interest in observing the preparation of the large flat and cornered ropes, of which a great many are used in different kinds of machinery, and likewise in many of the collieries. Their form is given to these ropes by immense pressure, after they have been well softened in warm water.
Of nearly equal interest was the machine by which round ropes of the requisite length and thickness are prepared. This machine is a combination of large and small iron wheels and spindles. At first a

number of small spindles are supplied with Russian hemp, which they spin into thin threads. These threads are taken up by a second division of spindles, that spin the separate threads together. This operation is repeated several times, till the threads grow into ropes, and till at last the huge cable is seen to twist itself into existence, around the last iron spindle, a fellow of enormous dimensions.

I mentioned just now a rope three miles in length, intended for the Edinburgh railroad. This hempen colossus weighed fifteen tons, about enough to form the cargo of one of the Newcastle coal barges, called "keels". The hemp used in these works is almost all Russian, and so is the tar, which is obtained chiefly from Archangel. These afford agreeable reminiscences to England of her discovery of that part of Russia in the 16th century, for well may the first arrival of the English in Archangel be classed with the important maritime discoveries of that age. In return for all this hemp and tar, England how sends to Russia, the ingenious rope-machines of which I have been speaking, for I was told that several of them had been sent thither only a short time previously.

Both our German visitors echo Defoe in their appreciation of the complex interrelationship of industry in the North East. Kohl notes in particular the use of rubbish from the mines in the construction of roads, bridle-paths and footpaths, with excellent drainage resulting in firm and dry surfaces. And von Raumer combines economics and philosophy in his analysis of the superiority of English industry:

Further, the English manufacturer, who has much larger capital at his command, has more left, as he pays lower interest than the German. Lastly, - and this is a most important point (which is very striking in the environs of Newcastle) – local circumstances, and the union of different kinds of trade, are productive of such extraordinary advantages, that wages seem wholly unimportant. By way of example, I will mention only a few particulars. The stream bears down the ships without exertion; the tide carries them up without greater expense. The colliers often bring back manure for the farmers from London, or old iron to be re-melted, and this instead of the necessary ballast. The strata of earth between which the coals lie are elsewhere thrown aside as useless: here immense brick kilns are employed in using them up. The purification of the air in the mines, which in other places is so expensive, is here effected by burning coal, the cost of which is hardly worth taking into account. Whole rows of loaded waggons roll down the inclined planes, and at the same time draw up the empty ones on an adjoining plane; where a countless multitude of men and horses and a great length of time would be required, a few workmen are here sufficient. Therefore, though the payment [of wages] is the very highest, there is in England an extraordinary saving of labour, time, and money, and the English manufacturer does not require protecting duties, on account either of heavy taxes or higher wages – not to mention that, for other reasons, such duties are never of any use. If any person denies all this, nothing more would be necessary to refute him than to bring him only once to the Tyne, and show him how the waggons, without the aid of men or animals, hasten along the iron rail-roads, from the greatest distance to the coast; how, by a simple mechanism, by the aid of two workmen, they are let down in a few seconds to the ships, and discharge themselves in an equally short time, - rise again, and run back to the mine while the second set of loaded waggons runs down: I say, we need but to see this one, or the whole mechanism, how the rags in the manufactory at Scotswood convert themselves into paper, - to be convinced, for our whole life, of the worthlessness of all partial assertions.

A subsidiary theme running throughout this work has been the relationship between the Northumbrians and their Scottish neighbours, and to a lesser extent the links between the languages spoken north and south of the border. Kohl provides us with a final comment on these related topics:

I spent the evening in an agreeable party composed chiefly of Scotch and Northumbrians. The conversation ran very much on the peculiarities to be observed on the two sides of the Tweed, and it afforded me considerable amusement to trace, in the friendly jests and repartees that passed between the borderers, a faint remnant of the sanguinary and warlike state of things that formerly prevailed here. I made the remark that the Northumbrians appeared to me to be half Scotch, instancing among other things they said *hame* for *home*, that they called the gipsies "fawgang", and that like the borderers on the northern side of the Tweed, the Northumbrians always wore clogs and the plaid. My Northumbrian friends, however, protested zealously against the idea of their having anything Scotch about them. They were genuine Englishmen, they said, and more genuine perhaps than those that dwelt further south, for in Northumberland it was that the Angles settled in the greatest numbers, and thence it was that they extended their influence over the rest of England. The Scotch, on the other hand, had always been the chief enemies of the Northumbrians, and Newcastle, generally, the first object of every border inroad. The Newcastle people, in consequence, had known the borderers beyond the Tweed only as *rievers* (robbers) or as "moss-troopers", on account of their always pouring down from the mossy hills into the valleys in front of the town. The Highland drovers

194

too, were formerly never allowed by the magistrates to enter Newcastle except on market days, and even then they were obliged to confine themselves within certain limits, they being at all times suspected of treachery and violent designs.

My Scotch friends admitted all about the frequent robberies of their ancestors; but then the Scotch, they said, were freebooters only in a barbarous age, when strife and violence passed for virtues, whereas the Northumbrians of Newcastle made their commercial dealings subservient to their plundering designs, levying contributions upon their friends in a time of profound peace, not by open violence, but by cunning stratagem.

I diligently led the conversation back to the subject of the colliers, and learned many interesting facts respecting them. They have even dishes and cakes of their own; and among these I was particularly told of their "singing hinnies", a kind of cake that owes its epithet "singing", to the peculiar hissing noise it makes when put into the pan, and to the custom of serving it hissing hot upon the table. These singing hinnies are great favourites. They are very buttery, and must never be absent on a holiday from the table of a genuine pitman.

So it is perhaps appropriate that when von Raumer left Northumberland in August 1835 he took the coach north to Scotland, being reminded on his unseasonably wintry way north of his native Lüneburg heath in northern Germany:

At eight o'clock I left Newcastle, and reached Edinburgh at nine in the evening. Except at some points, for instance at Jedburgh and Melrose, the road is uniform and uninteresting. Even the Cheviot hills are neither beautiful nor sublime in their forms, but wild, cold, and sterile. A very violent north wind discomposed the whole company, and the pain in my eyes and face increased. Among the short grass there are some higher tufts, which are proofs rather of sterility and unfitness for food, than of fertility and of the good quality of the pasture. Scattered sheep wandered on the wide waste, and I involuntarily thought of the heath of Lunenburg, and of the *peuple des Heidschnucks* (so a French writer calls the ragged sheep on that heath).

The Return of Royalty

On 25th September 1849 the Mayor of Newcastle convoked a Special Meeting of the Council to consider the arrangements for the reception of Queen Victoria and her consort Prince Albert. At very short notice the Queen had announced her intention to travel from Balmoral to London by the Eastern Railway, with a short stop at Newcastle:

The Town Clerk said that he had looked into the records of the Corporation for precedents, and he found that the last Sovereign who visited this town was Charles the First. He came to this town in 1633, on his way to Scotland, with great pomp; on that occasion he was addressed by the Corporation, and the Mayor, Mr Ralph Cole, was knighted, a precedent which he hoped would be followed on the present occasion. (Applause).......
The last visit of King Charles the First to this town was under altered circumstances: he came as a prisoner to the Scottish army in 1639. He was nevertheless treated with proper respect by the Corporation. The Council of that day made an order with respect to the cleanliness of the town, which might with propriety be imitated in these days of sanatory [sic] reform.

The Town Clerk who made this report to the Council was John Clayton, a famous antiquary who had inherited the Chesters Estate in 1843 and was largely responsbile for the preservation and reconstruction of much of the central section of Hadrian's Wall. His historical research into the visits of King Charles is however flawed, the correct sequence being given in the opening paragraph of Chapter 2 above. Charles's arrival as a prisoner of the Scots was in 1646 so that the Council's order with respect to the cleanliness of the town referred to his earlier visit in 1639 at the head of an army prepared to invade Scotland. As a result Clayton's point that respect was shown to the King even as a prisoner falls rather flat.

The Queen's visit was well timed, in that Robert Stephenson's High Level Bridge over the Tyne had opened for passenger traffic on 11th August 1849, thus completing the continuous railway link between York and Tweedmouth. Those travelling on this route had previously taken the train to Gateshead and then used a coach to cross the Tyne to Newcastle. Similar arrangements were in place for the crossing of the Tweed between Tweedmouth and Berwick.

At their meeting on 25th September the Council went on to approve the text of a short address to the Queen and to argue about the number of tickets to be allocated to the Councillors for the temporary platform to be erected in the centre of the High Level Bridge. No agreement being reached it was left to the Mayor to make the necessary arrangements with the Railway Company. One of his decisions was to declare the day of the Royal Visit a public holiday. A record of the visit, which took place on 28th September, is given in the official record of events for 1849. Although lengthy it is worth quoting in full as evidence of the amount of pageantry and protocol involved in a halt lasting no more than fifteen minutes:

Unfortunately the weather did not, on this occasion, second the wishes of the countless thousands who assembled to greet their sovereign as she passed along the railway. The day broke brightly, but towards seven o'clock the wind veered round to the east, while thick clouds but too surely foretold that the morning would be wet. But this, however annoying to those who had been eagerly anticipating a day of pleasure and display, in no measure damped the loyal enthusiasm of the inhabitants of, and visitors to, the town. Numerous parties, many of them from considerable distances, had arrived the preceding day; and the influx of visitors was so great, that some had great difficulty in procuring accommodation. This morning every succeeding train swelled the number; and, unfavourable as the weather proved, the excitement and anxiety of the multitude to obtain a glimpse of Her Majesty were very animating. The authorities, municipal, military, and railway, all exerted themselves in making extensive preparations, and affording an opportunity for the greatest number to witness the proceedings connected with the reception of Her Majesty. All the places which commanded even the most distant view of the railway were crowded; and the patience with which the public awaited the arrival of the train, amidst the "pelting of the pitiless storm", proved, if anything could prove, the deep interest they took in the proceedings of the day. The Pensioners were on the railway from Heaton upwards, and the soldiers and Newcastle and Northumberland Volunteer Cavalry were stationed on and near the High-level bridge, where, in conjuction with a strong body of police, under the direction of Mr Stephens, they preserved order, and kept the line from obstruction. In front of the Gateshead station the royal artillery and dragoons were drawn up. The artillery firing a salute on Her Majesty's departure. It certainly marred the effect of the scene to see the officers and soldiers who would otherwise have added in no small degree ot its beauty, if the day had been propitious, dripping, weary, and jaded with the incessant rain. Heaton station was profusely decorated with flags and evergreens; and twelve guns were placed, by order of Mr Ald.Potter, so as to fire a salute, in a manner which would have been creditable to a more important position. At Stepney, three orange and blue flags were placed along the railway, between the workshops and the tunnel; and the works of the line from Heaton to the Manors were thronged with thousands of spectators, who were in many instances doomed to wait for hours without having obtained a sight of the royal party, from the quickness with which the train passed this portion of the line. The eastern end of the tunnel under New Bridge Street was profusely decorated with evergreens, interspersed with dahlias. The letters "V.R." were placed one on each side of the arch, and surrounded with ivy and flowers. There were three banners along the line between the tunnel and the bridge. On the east side of Argyle Street bridge was an inscription, "Welcome to Newcastle and Gateshead"; and it was also decorated with evergreens and flowers. Over the bridge floated a blue and white banner. From Argyle Street to the bridge beyond the Manors station, twelve banners were placed, of various colours. Over the Manor Chare three flags were placed. A blue and yellow banner was also displayed from the battlements of All Saints' Church. A handsome union-jack floated over the Guildhall; a large banner from the old Mansion-house. Numerous private flags were displayed from dwelling-houses; and Mr Robinson's warehouse was decorated with four flags. The royal banner was placed on the castle; and from the northern entrance of the High-level bridge to the centre, nine flags of various sizes and colours, including the beautiful banners of the Trinity House, were placed at intervals along both sides. At the centre of the bridge was a lofty triumphal arch, erected by the Mayor of Gateshead, and decorated with flowers and evergreens, as well as with two banners on each side. Under the centre were the initials "V.R." in iron letters. The inscription, "Welcome to both sides of the Tyne". The arch was surmounted by a handsome crown, decorated externally with dahlias of various colours. The whole of the frame work of the triumphal arch was constructed of iron. The roof of the Moot Hall was full of spectators, as well as the space before its river front. Many ladies and gentlemen occupied the battlements of the castle, whence the guns thundered forth their welcome in anything but a quiet way, and must have rendered the situation extremely uncomfortable to persons not accustomed to "stand fire". The roofs of houses, and every place within view of the High-level bridge and its approaches, were crowded with spectators. The old Tyne bridge was filled from end to end with a dense mass, long before the time announced for the arrival of Her Majesty; and from the distance and want of elevation, thousands on this and other situations must have been disappointed of seeing Her Majesty. The railway authorities made excellent preparations on the High-level bridge, by erecting a platform, and barricades at a few yards distance from each other, to keep off the pressure of the crowd. Tickets were issued for parties to go on the bridge, and it was lined with spectators from end to end. About half-past eleven o'clock, intimation was given, by telegraph, to the Mayor and Council, who were waiting in the Guildhall; and the Councillors, with the Mayor, Recorder, and Town Clerk, in their robes of office, and the corporate insignia of mace, &c, walked in procession to the High-level bridge.

Here, again, the rain proved injurious to the effect of the scene; and by the time they entered the northern approach of the bridge, each gentleman seemed more anxious to attain his position than to remain in the order of procession. Indeed, the numberless umbrellas and cloaks which were used, prevented anything like regularity being observed. Shortly after twelve o'clock, the castle guns announced the arrival of the royal train within the boundaries of the town; and immediately all eyes were fixed upon the first portion of the line visible to the several spectators. The pilot engine then arrived, and the expectations of thousands were raised to their utmost pitch. Soon afterwards, the train, with its royal occupants, was discerned on the viaduct leading through the town, and the hum of voices close at hand and distant cheering marked the onward progress of the carriages. As the train advanced, the enthusiasm of those who obtained a view of Her Majesty was intense, and was frequently acknowledged by the royal party. The carriage in which Her Majesty, Prince Albert, and the Royal Family were, was constructed in such a manner that a full view could be obtained through the plate glass windows; and on the bridge the effect was exceedingly grand to witness the expression of the multitiude as the train slowly threaded its way through the assembled numbers. On reaching the north-west extremity of the line, an engine, No.190, was attached to the train, richly ornamented and decorated with banners and evergreens. At the front of the engine was a crown, formed of beautiful dahlias; and lengthwise was an arch, on which was painted "Success to the British Empire". The arch was also decorated with laurels. This engine was preceded by a pilot engine, No.39, which was also tastefully adorned with an arch, the words encircling it being "God save the Queen", and painted crowns on either side of the fire box. Mr T E Harrison, engineer of the York, Newcastle, and Berwick Railway Company, and Mr Fletcher, superintendent of the locomotive establishment, took charge of the engine to which the royal train was attached. On the raised platform, in the centre of the bridge, were stationed the guard of honour, together with the Right Worshipful the Mayor of Newcastle, the Sheriff, the members of the Town Council, the Recorder, the Town Clerk, the Magistrates &c.; there were also the Mayor of Gateshead, the Council of that Borough, the Town Clerk &c., while around them stood a gay and splendid assemblage of ladies and gentlemen, who had long awaited the arrival of the royal train. Immediately beneath, as the eye looked down upon the river, every vessel was gaily decorated, and the masts of some were literally studded with brave tars. On arriving in front of the platform, the royal party were welcomed with loud and enthusiastic cheers, which the Queen and Prince Albert graciously acknowledged. Indeed, the condescending and animated manner of Her Majesty delighted all, while her light, beaming countenance reflected the pleasure she experienced at the warm and joyous reception which was given to her. Prince Albert also appeared highly gratified; and the Prince of Wales and the other royal children attracted general attention. The Mayor (James Dent Weatherley, Esq.) then presented the loyal address of the Corporation which Her Majesty kindly condescended to receive, repeatedly smiling and bowing to his worship. The Mayor of Gateshead next presented a similar address from the Council of that borough, which was also received with similar gracious tokens of approbation. The attention of Her Majesty was then drawn by Prince Albert to the eastern side of the carriage, when they both took a hasty survey of the river, the old Tyne bridge, the countless multitude upon it, and the great height of the High-level bridge from the water. Her Majesty afterwards resumed her position at the other side of the carriage, and casting her eyes westward, observed to the Mayor that "the view here must be very fine", and also that "it was a most beautiful bridge". His worship immediately responded by saying, "I am very sorry that the day is so wet and gloomy; but I trust your gracious Majesty will have leisure on some other occasion to renew your visit, when the day may be brighter and more propitious"; upon which Her Majesty bowed and smiled so graciously to his worship, as to favour the hope that on her return from Scotland, on another occasion, she will again honour the town with her presence. The Prince of Wales here appeared at the carriage window, and was received with loud cheers; and the Mayor of Newcastle, addressing her Majesty, said, "I hope your Majesty will allow me the honour of shaking hands with the Royal Prince of Wales." Her Majesty graciously assented, and the Prince at the same time freely extended his arm, and gave his worship a truly English shake of the hand. Sir John Fife then handed a present for the Queen to Earl Grey. It was a costly and superb paper cutter, from the manufactory of John Brown and Son, cutlers, Grey Street. The cutter was very elegant, being ornamented with a gold crown, beautifully chased and ornamented with diamonds, rubies, emeralds and other precious stones. It was examined with much attention by the Queen and the Prince, and they appeared to be much gratified by the workmanship. A neatly-worked veil, the production of the inmates of the Royal Victoria Asylum for the Blind, in this town, was also intended to have been presented by the Mayor of Newcastle; but the rain, which had incessantly continued, had damaged the covering, and it was afterwards transmitted to Her Majesty, by railway. The train then took its departure, amidst the final and hearty cheers of all around, the firing of cannon, and ringing of bells. The numerous men in the employ of Messrs Hawks, Crawshay and Co, with two beautiful banners, formed a conspicuous part of the scene at the south end of the bridge; and took a prominent part in the farewell greeting.

The tradition of the royal summer holiday at Balmoral being now firmly established Queen Victoria and Prince Albert stopped again at Newcastle on 29th August 1850 en route from Castle Howard to Edinburgh. On this occasion they arrived at 12.50pm for the opening of the Central Railway Station. After the formal welcome they retired briefly to a room where a buffet had been prepared. Their train then left the station at 1.10pm and arrived at Berwick bridge at 3.20pm. Like the High Level Bridge which the Queen had opened on her previous visit to Newcastle this was designed by Robert Stephenson. The *Newcastle Courant* for 30th August reported the brief ceremony:

> Her Majesty, after taking a view of the viaduct and the beautiful and extensive scenery around, expressed her admiration of what she had witnessed, and graciously condescended to name the viaduct 'The Royal Border Bridge'.

After a mere eight minutes the royal train resumed its journey at 3.28pm and arrived at Edinburgh at 5.05pm. In its report of this event the Newcastle Courant noted that a triumphal arch had been erected at the north end of the viaduct and that "immediately underneath the top of the arch were the words, in conspicuous letters – 'The last act of the Union!'.

Whether that Union will endure remains an open question, but there is no doubt that the opening of Robert Stephenson's bridges at Newcastle and Berwick marked the completion of the direct rail route between York and Edinburgh and meant that those travelling between England and Scotland no longer needed to set foot in Northumberland or to explore its roads and inns. For better or worse an era had drawn to a close, so that Queen Victoria's rapid transit from south to north in 1850, so different from the experience of earlier visitors, is an appropriate point at which to bring this survey to a close.

A NOTE ON SOURCES

GENERAL

The two leading authorities on domestic tourism are: Esther Moir, *The Discovery of Britain: The English Tourists 1540-1840* (RKP 1964), and Ian Ousby, *The Englishman's England: Taste, Travel and the Rise of Tourism* (CUP 1990). Moir has the wider scope, but both focus heavily on the traditional early tourist areas: the Peak District, the Lakes, North Wales and the Highlands of Scotland. Apart from Hadrian's Wall, itself mainly visited by determined antiquaries, the county of Northumberland was off this well beaten track. In this study I propose that the reasons for domestic travel and tourism were rather more varied than those discussed by Moir and Ousby.

In the notes below I have used standard abbreviations for publishing houses. Short references are as follows:

AA   *Archaeologia Aeliana*, the annual research journal of the Society of Antiquaries of Newcastle upon Tyne.

Grose   Francis Grose, *The Antiquarian Repertory*, edited by Edward Jeffrey, London 1807-1809

Mavor   William Mavor, *British Tourists*, printed in 5 volumes in 1798 and in 6 volumes in 1812

Richardson   M A Richardson, *Reprints of Rare Tracts and Imprints of Antient Manuscripts*, Newcastle 1844-1849

References to John Byng are to The Torrington Diaries, edited in 4 volumes by C Bruyn Andrews, Methuen 1934.

CHAPTER 1 – A LABORIOUS JOURNEY

A Royal Progress to Scotland
Agness Strickland, *Lives of the Queens of Scotland and English Princesses connected with the regal succession of Great Britain*, Blackwood 1850-1859, Vol 1. I found the extract about the first wheeled carriage to cross the Tyne in J H Hinde, *The Old North Road*, AA Series 2, Vol 3 (1859).
The account of the journey by the bursar of Meron College is taken from Edward Bateson, *Notes of a Journey from Oxford to Embleton and back in 1464*, AA Series 2, Vol 16 (1894).

A Strategic Defence Review

I have taken the account of the review by Bowes and Elleker from John Hodgson, *History of Northumberland*, Edward Walker 1820-1858, Pt 3, Vol 2.

J Crofts, *Packhorse Waggon and Post*. RKP 1967, ch 1.

The Early Antiquaries

John Leland, *The Itinerary of John Leland*, edited in 5 volumes by Lucy Toulmin Smith, George Bell 1907-1910. I have taken the quote about Dr Davell from Richard Welford, *History of Newcastle and Gateshead*, Walter Scott 1885, Vol 2.

William Camden, *Britannia*, translated by Richard Gough, 2nd edition, London 1806. I found the information given by Archbishop Threkeld in Richardson Vol 7. Richardson attributes this anonymous account (Harleian MSS 473) to Sampson Erdeswicke, but this is disputed by A M Whitworth, *Hadrian's Wall: Some Aspects of its Post-Roman Influence on the Landscape*, British Archaeological Reports, British Series 296 (2000), 46.

I have taken the account of Dr Eedes's journey from Rev H Gee, *A Sixteenth Century Journey to Durham*, AA Series 3, Vol 13 (1916).

A Royal Progess to London

Fynes Moryson, *An Itinerary*, 1617, reprinted by J Maclehose, Glasgow 1907.

Stephen Perlin, *A Description of England and Scotland*, reprinted in Grose Vol 4.

Thomas Platter, *Travels in England*, edited by Clare Williams, Jonathan Cape 1937.

Robert Carey, *Memoirs*, edited by G H Powell, Alexander Moring 1905.

Thomas Millington, *The True Narrative of the Entertainment of His Royal Majesty, from the time of his departure from Edinburgh till his receiving at London, 1603*, reprinted in C H Firth, *Stuart Tracts 1603-1693*, Archibald Constable 1902.

CHAPTER 2 – BEFORE AND AFTER THE CIVIL WARS

Walkers and Riders

I owe the information about Ben Jonson's journey to an article by James Loxley in the TLS for 11th September 2009. Jonson's verses were first printed in William Gray 1649 work *Chorographia*.

The 1630 Folio edition of *The Works of John Taylor* was reprinted by the Spenser Society in 1869. Anyone tempted to follow in his footsteps would do well read Peter Mortimer, *Broke through Britain: One Man's Penniless Odyssey*, Mainstream 1999.

There is a useful Wikepedia entry on Comte Frédéric-Guillaume de Schaumborg-Lippe (1724-1777), a patron on both Gottfried Herder and J C F Bach. The wager mentioned in the text is from Richard Lambert, *The Fortunate Traveller*, A Melrose 1950.

The journey of the Norwich Three is recounted in *A Short Survey of 26 Counties, briefly describing the Cities and their Situations, and the Corporate Towns and Castles therein; Observed in a Seven Weeks Journey begun at the City of Norwich; on Monday, August 11th, 1634, and ending at the same place, By a Captain, a Lieutenant, and an Ancient; all three of the military Company in Norwich*, edited by L G Wickham-Legg, F E Robinson 1904. A splendid example of a 17th century book title.

Captain Rugg's Great Bottle Nose

William Brereton, *Notes of a Journey through Durham and Northumberland in the Year 1635*, in Richardson Vol 7. Brereton has a great fondness for 'dainty' as a term of general commendation.

John Aston, *The Journal of John Aston*, edited by J C Hodgson, Surtees Society Vol 188 (1910).

William Harvey – I owe the quotation to Geoffrey Keynes, *The Life of William Harvey*, Oxford 1966, 315.

A Frenchman's View of Northumberland

Jorevin de Rocheford, *Description of England and Ireland in the 17th Century*, in Grose Vol 4.

An Official Visitor and the Earliest Railways

John Stainsby, *Observations in a Northern Journey*, from article by W C Trevelyan, AA Series 1, Vol 3 (1844).

Roger North, *The Life of the Right Hon Francis North, Baron of Guilford*, 1742, in volume 1 of *The Lives of the Norths*, edited by Augustus Jessop, G Bell & Sons 1890.

Huntingdon Beaumont – see the relevant article in the Oxford Dictionary of National Biography. A detailed history of the early waggonways is given by G Bennett, E Clavering & A Rounding in *A Fighting Trade: Rail Transport in Tyne Coal 1600-1800*, Portcullis Press 1990.

CHAPTER 3 – A QUARTET OF PLEASURE TRIPS 1677-1705

Birds and Bottles

Thomas Kirk, *Journeyings through Northumberland and Durham in the Year 1677*, in Richardson Vol 1.

A Lady of Quality
Celia Fiennes, *The Journeys of Celia Fiennes*, edited by Christopher Morris, Cresset Press 1947.
Ralph Thoresby, *Diary*, edited by Joseph Hunter, London 1830.

A Lawyer's Progress
Anonymous, *North of England and Scotland in 1704*, William Blackwood, Edinburgh 1818.
Archdukes John & Louis – W Richardson, *History of the Parish of Wallsend*, The Northumberland Press Ltd 1923, 233.

Another Lawyer (and Friends)
Joseph Taylor, *Journey to Edenborough in Scotland*, edited by William Cowen, Edinburgh 1903.

CHAPTER 4 – THE NARROW ROAD TO THE DEEP NORTH

For writers already mentioned in earlier chapters please refer to the bibliographical information given above.

The Long Road North
Matsuo Basho, *The Narrow Road to the Deep North*, translated by Nobuyuki Yuasa, Penguin Classics 1966. In *On the Narrow Road to the Deep North: Journey into a Lost Japan* (Jonathan Cape 1989) Lesley Downer gives a fascinating account of her solo journey in Basho's footsteps. The statistics quoted are taken from Charles Harper, *The Great North Road: York to Edinburgh*, 2nd edition, Charles Palmer 1922.
John Evelyn's *Diary* is available in various editions. The extracts quoted are dated 12th April 1644 and 7th July 1656.
I owe the quote from John Taylor to Christopher Morris's introduction to *The Journeys of Celia Fiennes*. The original source is Taylor's 1639 work *Part of This Summers Travels*.
Emanuel Bowen, *Britannia Depicta, or, Ogilby Improved*, 1720, reprinted by Frank Graham 1970.
Stage coaches – see J H Hinde, *The Old North Road*, AA Series 2, Vol 3 (1859), 244.

Journey's End
Thomas Tryon, *A Treatise of Cleanliness in Meats and Drinks*, 1682, quoted in Emily Cockayne, *Hubbub: Filth, Stench and Noise in England, 1660-1770*, Yale University Press 2007, 58.
Joan Parkes, *Travels in England in the Seventeenth Century*, Oxford 1925, 36-37.

William Schellink, *The Journal of William Schellink's Travels in England, 1661-1663*, translated and edited by Maurice Exwood and H L Lehmann, Camden Society 1993, 46.

Crossing the Border
James Boswell, *London Journal*, edited by Frederick A Pottle, William Heinemann 1950, 42-43.
Charles Harper, *The Great North Road*, 202-203.

CHAPTER 5 – NORTH ON BUSINESS

On Her Majesty's Secret Service
Daniel Defoe   *The Letters of Daniel Defoe*, edited by G H Healey, Oxford 1955
A Tour Thro' the Whole Island of Great Britain, edited by G D H Cole, 2 volumes, Peter Davies 1927
The History and Remarkable Life of the truly honourable Colonel Jacque, commonly Call'd Col Jack, edited by Samuel Holt Monk, Oxford 1970, 108.
Elizabeth Montagu, *Her Correspondence from 1720 to 1761*, edited by Emily J Climenson, John Murray 1906.
Elizabeth Carter – R Brimley Johnson, *Bluestocking Letters*, Bodley Head 1926, 260-261.

A Man with a Mission
John Wesley, *The Journals of John Wesley*, edited by Nehemiah Curnock, Epworth Press 1938.

An Actor's Life in the Early Nineteenth Century
Roz Southey   *Music-Making in North-East England during the Eighteenth Century*, Ashgate 2006
The Ingenious Mr Avison, Tyne Bridge Publishing 2009
William Macready, *Macready's Reminiscences and Selections from his Diaries and Letters*, edited by Sir Frederick Pollock, Macmillan 1875. The "Acres" mentioned in the extract on page 98 is Bob Acres, a braggart and poltroon in *The Rivals* by Sheridan.
Post Office circular – J Wilson Hyde, *The Royal Mail, Its Curiosities and Romance*, 3rd edition, Simpkin Marshall 1889, 39-40.

CHAPTER 6 – NORTHERN SURVEYS

On His French Majesty's (not so) Secret Service
Sullivan & Plumptre – I owe both quotations to Esther Moir, *The Discovery of Britain: The English Tourists 1540-1840.*

Gabriel Jars, *Voyages Métallurgiques, ou Récherches et Observations sur les Mines et Forges de fer, la fabrication de l'acier, celle du fer blanc, et plusieurs mines de charbon de terre, faites depuis l'année 1769, en Allemagne, Suède, Norwege, Angleterre & Ecosse*, 3 volumes, Gabriel Regnault, Lyons 1774-1781. Translations by the present author.

Pit Ponies – article of 28th July 2011 in Whitley Bay News Guardian.

Faujas St Fond, *Travels through England and Scotland to the Hebrides in the Year 1784*, Mavor 1812 Vol 5. See Bennett & Others, *A Fighting Trade*, for comment on the self-acting inclined plane waggonway.

A Spell Behind Bars
John Howard, *The State of the Prisons*, 4th edition, London 1792.

D L Howard, *John Howard: Prison Reformer*, Christopher Johnson 1958, 109-110, for details of his journeys, taken from an earlier biographer J Brown, *Memoirs of the Public and Private Life of John Howard, the Philanthropist*, London 1818. I owe Howard's appraisal of Wesley to Rev L Tyermann, *The Life and Times of John Wesley*, Hodder & Stoughton 1890, Vol 3, 495.

An Agricultural Missionary
Arthur Young, *Six Months Tour through the North of England*, London 1770. However the initial extract on page 114 is from his *Travels in France during the Years 1787, 1788, 1789*. In August 1789 Young spent 2 days with Monsieur Faujas St Fond at Montélimar, a visit returned by St Fond on later visit to England.

The description of Belford in 1639 comes from Rawdon, *Court and Times of Charles I*, quoted in Edward Bateson, *A History of Northumberland*, Newcastle 1893, Vol 1, 364.

William Cobbett, *English Grammar*, quoted in Richard Ingrams, *The Life and Adventures of William Cobbett*, Harper Collins 2005,153.

Survey on page 120 – J Bailey & G Culley, *A General View of the Agriculture of the Counties of Northumberland, Cumberland and Westmoreland*, Newcastle 1794, quoted in Norman McCord & Richard Thompson, *The Northern Counties from AD 1000*, Longman 1988, 175-176.

The Natural History of Northumberland
Thomas Pennant, *A Tour of Scotland in 1769*, 3rd edition 1774, reprinted by Melven Press 1979.

Passing Cattle

John Clare, *The Shepherd's Calendar*, edited by Eric Robinson & Geoffrey Summerfield, Oxford 1964. I cannot quote the relevant passage, also relating to East Anglia, because of the copyright claimed and defended by the editors. I owe *The Herdiug Rune* to an article by Rob Gibson on "Cowboy Celtic" in *The Living Tradition* magazine for June/July 1998. For other information I have drawn on K J Bonser, *The Drovers*, Macmillan 1970, and Ian Roberts et al., *Drove Roads of Northumberland*, The History Press 2010. A more recent work is Bridget Gubbins, *The Drovers are Coming to Morpeth Town*, Greater Morpeth Development Trust 2012.

I owe the account of the drovers' dogs making their own way north to A R B Haldane, *The Drove Roads of Scotland*, Thomas Nelson 1952, 26-27. Bridget Gubbins casts doubt on this story.

A Political Progress

William Cobbett, *Rural Rides*, edited by G D H & Margaret Cole, 3 volumes, Peter Davies 1930. For a sympathetic modern appraisal see Richard Ingrams, *The Life and Adventures of William Cobbett*, Harper Collins 2005.

The Duke and the Taxing-man is reprinted in Charles Edmonds, *Poetry of the Anti-Jacobin*, 3rd edition, London 1890, 52.

CHAPTER 7 – IN TIME AND SPACE ALONG THE WALL

In the Footsteps of William Camden

William Camden, *Britannia*, edited by Edmund Gibson, 1695. The ODNB article on Gibson quotes *A congratulatory poem on the translation of the right reverend father in God ,Edmund, from the see of Lincoln, to the see of London* (Oxfordshire Archives, Oxf.Dioc.MSS d.106).

Bishop Nicolson – *Letters of Eminent Men addressed to Ralph Thoresby*, 2 volumes, London 1832.

Christopher Hunter – John Rogan, *Christopher Hunter: Antiquary*, AA Series 4, Vol 32 (1954),

Robert Smith – R C Bosanquet, *Robert Smith and the 'Observations upon the Picts Wall' 1708-1709*, edited by Eric Birley in *Transactions of the Cumberland and Westmoreland Antiquarian and Archaeological Society*, Vol 55 (1956), 154-171. The extracts from Robert Smith's *Observations* can be found in Edmund Gibson's 1722 edition of the *Britannia*..

The Lucid Springs of Truth – Antiquarianism and Ideology

John Horsley, *Britannia Romana*, 1733.

Alexander Gordon, *Itinerarium Septentrionale*, 1726. The ODNB contains useful information on both Gordon and Sir John Clerk. Eric Birley's dismissal of Gordon can be found in his *Research on Hadrian's Wall*, Titus

Wilson 1961, 15. Jonathan Oldbuck is the leading character in Walter Scott, *The Antiquary*.

William Stukeley, *Iter Boreale* and *Itinerarium Curiosum*, 1776. For a sympathetic modern assessment see Stuart Piggott, *William Stukeley: An Eighteenth Century Antiquary*, Thames & Hudson, 2nd edition 1985. I owe to Piggott the mention of Stukeley's lobbying of Princess Augusta.

'The glory of the Roman whores' – David Martin in a review of *Culture Counts* by Roger Scruton, in TLS 11th January 2008.

75 Years On – Walking the Wall in 1801

Tobias Smollett, *Letters*, edited by Lewis M Knapp, Oxford 1970, 134.

Oliver Goldsmith, *Complete Works*, edited by William Spalding, James Blackwood (not dated), 25.

William Hutton, *The History of the Roman Wall*, 2nd edition 1815, with a preface by Catherine Hutton.

John Skinner, *Hadrian's Wall in 1801: Observations on the Roman Wall*, edited by Howard and Peter Coombs, Kingsmead Press 1978.

Claire Nesbitt & Divya Tolia-Kelly, *Hadrian's Wall: Embodied Archaeologies of the Linear Monument*, in *Journal of Social Archaeology* 2009.

Karl Philipp Moritz, *Travels through Various Parts of England*, edited by P E Matheson, London 1924, 100. An abridged reprint can be found in Mavor (1798) Vol 4.

Murder in the Ardèche – Graham Robb, *The Discovery of France*, Picador 2007, ch 1.

CHAPTER 8 – HIGHWAYS AND BYWAYS

Scots Coming South

Tobias Smollet, *Roderick Random* and *Humphrey Clinker*, numerous editions available.

Robert Burns, *Robert Burns's Tour of the Borders*, edited by Raymond Lamont Brown, Boydell Press 1972.

Dear Sister

Richard Pococke, *Northern Journeys of Bishop Richard Pococke*, in *North Country Diaries Volume 2*, edited by J C Hodgson, Surtees Society Vol 124 (1914). The supplementary reference to the Whitton Tower at Rothbury comes from an anonymous work, *The Border Tour throughout the most important and interesting places in the Counties of Northumberland, Berwick, Roxburgh and Selkirk*, 2nd edition 1816, 223-224.

D'un château l'autre

William Hutchinson, *A View of Northumberland, with an Excursion to the Abbey of Mailross in Scotland, Anno 1776*, Newcastle 1778.
The missing postboy – J Wilson Hyde, *The Royal Mail, Its Curiosities and Romance*, Simpkin Marshall 1889, 21.

TheTurnpike Age

North Shields Turnpike - *An Act for repairing the Road from North Shields in the County of Northumberland, to the Town of Newcastle upon Tyne*, 1748.
Turnpikes – Eric Pawson, *Transport and Economy, The Turnpike Roads of Eighteenth Century Britain*, Academic Press 1977.

Holidays in the North

Colonel Thomas Thornton, *A Sporting Tour through the Northern Parts of England and Great Part of the Highlands of Scotland*, new edition, Edward Arnold 1896.
Walter Scott, *The Letters of Sir Walter Scott*, edited in 12 volumes by H J C Grierson, Constable 1938. More about Scott's contacts with Northumberland can be found in Frank Whitehead & Philip Yarrow, *Scott and Northumberland*, AA Series 5, Vol 14 (1986), 167-174.

CHAPTER 9 – THE COMING OF THE RAILWAY

Social Calls

Harriet Martineau, *Selected Letters*, edited by Valerie Saunders, OUP 1990. For her life and her stay in Tynemouth see R K Webb, *Harriet Martineau: A Radical Victorian*, Heinemann 1960.

Trains and Boats and Cows

George Head, *A Home Tour through the Manufacturing Districts of England*, John Murray 1836.
Bill Fawcett, *A History of the Newcastle and Carlisle Railway*, North Eastern Railway Association 2008.

Two Visitors from Germany

Frederick von Raumer, *England in 1835: A Series of Letters Written to Friends in Germany*, translated by H E Lloyd, 3 volumes, John Murray 1836.
J G Kohl, *Ireland Scotland and England*, 3 volumes, Chapman & Hall 1844.

The Return of Royalty

Proceedings of Newcastle Town Council for 25th September 1849 and summary record for the same year.

Lightning Source UK Ltd.
Milton Keynes UK
UKOW02f0626140815

256935UK00002B/43/P